The Ward Family History

by

Alvin L. Ward

Published by:

Roger W. Ward
2016

Palmer Lake, Colorado 80133

Printed in the United States of America

ISBN-13: 978-1535331890
ISBN-10: 1535331895

No part of this book (whether mechanically printed or in electronic format) may be reproduced, stored in a retrieval system, or transmitted by any means—electronic, mechanical, photocopying, recording, or otherwise—without written permission or receiving Branding Rights from the author.

Jim's Grandfather

James (Jim)
Henry Ward

Jim's Father

The Ward Family History

Alvin L. Ward, my father, passed away on January 13, 2003. He left me his loose-leaf notebook containing the information he had collected on the genealogy of the Ward Family. I scanned these many pages, consisting of xerographic copies of old photos and other data he gleaned over many years of research, and personal contact with near and distant relatives. I have shared the PDF files to several of my close relatives, but I'm certain that most of them have never looked at them, nor shared them with other family members. So, I decided to publish them in printed form. This book is the result. I hope you enjoy—and share—it.

Roger W. Ward
July 2016

Since many of the photos contained in Alvin's notebook were of poor quality, I have inserted here photos that I have in my collection that are of higher quality, or are not contained in Alvin's original notebook but that are of interest to the Ward Family. Sorry if I didn't include photos from *your* family—I just grabbed some from my collection.

Alvin, Donald, Charles, Roger

Alvin Ward WWII

Roger, Merna, Alvin, Inga Ward

Bernard, Donald, Jim, Charles, Bertrice

iv

BEATRICE ALVIN MERNA:WARD 1949

Bernice Miller

Buck Miller, Roger, Bernice

? Buck, Myrna, Roger

CHARLES MERNA WARD

Donald, James Henry, Bertrice, Alvin, Charles

Donald, Myrna

Thomas Marvin Ward, Father of James Henry Ward

Anna Parker Creasy, Myrna Ward Boulter
Anna is the mother of Bernice Miller

James Henry Ward, Charles, Donald
Bertrice

Bernard, Donald, Jim, Charles
Bertrice

Myrna and Roger

Myrna

Second from left, back, is Thomas Marvin, Jim's dad. Jim is third from left in front row, next to his grandfather James Alexander Lacy Ward

Myrna Jane Ward

Muriel Miller Ward, Roger & Myrna's mother

Roger, Charles, Donald holding Myrna

Alvin, Donald, Charles, Roger

Back: Muriel, Bertrice, Myrna
Front: Charles, Roger, Donald

Roger and Myrna

Roger Wilson Ward

Bertrice Ward

Donald and Molly's 50th Reunion, with their kids

Donald Glen Ward Family

Charles Richard Ward Family

Myrna Jane Ward Boulter and Lloyd Dale Boulter

Five Generations
Myrna, Ethan, Alvin, Jim, Bertrice

CHARLES RAYE MOORE
JUNE 8, 1913
DECEMBER 3, 1982

EMMA JEAN MOORE
TODD
AUG 6 1926
DEC 25 1947

JAMES BURNARD WARD
TEXAS
PFC 19 INF 24 INF DIV
KOREA PH
MARCH 5 1929 JULY 16 1950

ALVIN L WARD
S SGT US ARMY AIR FORCES
WORLD WAR II

MOORE

LULA E.
AUGUST 17, 1882
SEPTEMBER 28, 1980

JOHN B.
FEBRUARY 10, 1872
MARCH 12, 1945

JOHN KENNETH
MOORE
JUNE 3, 1925
JULY 26, 1986

IN HIS WILL IS OUR PEACE

WARD
BERTRICE
NOVEMBER 18, 1905
OCTOBER 26, 2001
J. H. "JIM"
NOVEMBER 10, 1904
JANUARY 23, 1980

FOUR GENERATIONS OF WARDS

OLDEST - seated at right: MARVIN FULLER WARD _B, 26 Feb. 1837

SEATED- at far left: JAMES ALEXANDER LACY WARD, the first born son of MARVIN FULLER.

STANDING- at back: THOMAS MARVIN WARD, first born son of JAMES ALEXANDER LACY'S.

STANDING- at center: JAMES HENRY WARD, first born of THOMAS MARVIN.

The Ward Family History
Page 2

James Henry "Pampa" Ward

The Ward Family History
Page 4

Thomas Marvin Ward - Father of James Henry Ward

Hattie M. Adams - Mother of James Henry Ward

Amanda A. Robbins - Mother of J.B. Moore

Mattie May Holmes Taylor

Grandma Brewster - Mother of James Morrison Thompson

HOLMES FAMILY

Rebecca Jane Baker Ward – Mother of Thomas Marvin Ward

Marriage Record of James WARD and Mariah HALCOMB – Oct. 5, 1825

Book BB
Page 186

> Territory of Arkansas
> County of Hempstead
>
> This certifies that I joined together in the Holy bonds of matrimony on the 5th day of October 1825 James Ward to Mariah Halcomb according to law. Given under my hand this 21st June 1832.
>
> Tilman Patterson
>
> Recorded 21st June 1832.
> Allen M. Oakley
> Clerk

FAMILY GROUP No. ___

Husband's Full Name: JAMES WARD

This Information Obtained From:
- 1850 CENSUS IN THE 2 WARD TOWNSHIP
- 22 NEW ORLEANS LA.

Husband's Data	Day Month Year	City, Town or Place	County or Province, etc.	State or Country	Add. Info.
Birth	12 DEC 1801			TEN	
Chr'nd					
Mar.	05 Oct 1825				
Death	19 Jun 1870		Johnson	Tex.	
Burial					

Places of Residence:
Occupation: | Church Affiliation: | Military Rec.:
His Father: | Mother's Maiden Name:

Wife's Full Maiden Name: MERIA

Wife's Data	Day Month Year	City, Town or Place	County or Province, etc.	State or Country	Add. Info. on Wife
Birth	3 MAY 1806			KY.	
Chr'nd					
Death					
Burial					

Places of Residence:
Occupation if other than Housewife: | Church Affiliation:
Her Father: | Mother's Maiden Name:

Sex	Children's Names in Full	Event	Day Month Year	City, Town or Place	County or Province	State or Country	Add. Info. on Children
M	1. JOHN W.B.	Birth	1826			ARK.	
		Mar.					
		Death					
		Burial					
F	2. ANN B. (Hodges)	Birth	1831			LA.	
		Mar.					
		Death					
		Burial					
M	3. GEORGE W	Birth	1834			LA.	
		Mar.					
		Death					
		Burial					
M	4. MARVIN FULLER — ELIZABETH J. ROSE	Birth	26 FEB 1837			LA.	
		Mar.	27 JUN 1855				
		Death	5 OCT 1918	PARKER	JOHNSON	TEX.	
		Burial	SEP 1918	PARKER	JOHNSON	TEX.	
M	5. MILES J. — ZENNIA 1862	Birth	1839			LA.	
		Mar.					
		Death					
		Burial					
F	6. MARY C. (AIKEN)	Birth	1842			LA.	
		Mar.					
		Death					
		Burial					
F	7. MARTHA J.	Birth	1847			LA.	OK
		Mar.	1881				
		Death					
		Burial					
	8. H.B. — PARMELIA G 1864	Birth	1851				OK
		Mar.					
		Death					
		Burial					
	9.	Birth					
		Mar.					
		Death					
		Burial					
	10.	Birth					
		Mar.					
		Death					
		Burial					

FAMILY GROUP No. ___

This Information Obtained From:

Handwritten note: ALL BURIED IN JOHNSON CO. WITH JAMES WARD

Husband's Full Name: JAMES WARD

Husband's Data	Day Month Year	City, Town or Place	County or Province, etc.	State or Country	Add. Info. on Husband
Birth	12 DEC 1801			TEN.	
Chr'nd					
Mar.	05 OCT 1825		HEMSTEAD	ARK.	
Death	19 JUN 1870		JOHNSON	TEX.	
Burial					

Places of Residence:
Occupation: FARMER   **Church Affiliation:**   **Military Rec.:**
His Father: **Mother's Maiden Name:**

Wife's Full Maiden Name: MARIAH HOLCUMB

Wife's Data	Day Month Year	City, Town or Place	County or Province, etc.	State or Country	Add. Info. on Wife
Birth	03 MAY 1806			KEN.	
Chr'nd					
Death					
Burial					

Places of Residence:
Occupation if other than Housewife: **Church Affiliation:**
Her Father: **Mother's Maiden Name:**

Sex	Children's Names in Full		Day Month Year	City, Town or Place	County or Province, etc.	State or Country
M	1. JOHN W. B. (NT)	Birth	1826			ARK
	Full Name of Spouse	Mar.				
		Death				
		Burial				
F	2. ANN B.	Birth				
	Full Name of Spouse	Mar.	1831			LA.
		Death				
		Burial				
M	3. GEORGE W.	Birth	1834			LA.
	Full Name of Spouse	Mar.				
		Death				
		Burial				
M	4. MARVIN FULLER	Birth	26 FEB 1837		HEMSTEAD	ARK.
	Full Name of Spouse	Mar.	27 JUN 1855			
	ELIZABETH JANE ROSE	Death	05 OCT 1918	PARKER	JOHNSON	TEX.
		Burial		BONO CEMETERY	JOHNSON	TEX.
M	5. MILES J.	Birth	1839			la.
	Full Name of Spouse	Mar.				
	ZENNIA	Death				
		Burial				
F	6. MARY C.	Birth	1842			LA.
	Full Name of Spouse	Mar.				
	AIKEN	Death				
		Burial				
F	7. MARTHA J.	Birth	1847			LA.
	Full Name of Spouse	Mar.				
		Death				
		Burial				
M	8. HENRY B	Birth	DEC 1850			LA.
	Full Name of Spouse	Mar.	1880			LA.
	PAMELIA G	Death				
		Burial				
	9.	Birth				
	Full Name of Spouse	Mar.				
		Death				
		Burial				
	10.	Birth				
	Full Name of Spouse	Mar.				
		Death				
		Burial				

1860 CENSUS — UNITED STATES

State: Louisiana **County:** Claiborne Parish **Town/Township:** Haynesville **P.O.:** 27 day of July **Call No.** 102

Family Number	Names	Age	Sex	Color	Occupation, etc.	Value - Real Estate	Birthplace	Married within year	School within year	Cannot read or write	Enumeration Date	Remarks
678	Jas. WARD	59	M		Farmer	2000	Tenn.					H.B. was born after last census in 1850. Turns out to be Henry B. Note how all or most all the names are carried down
	M. J.	55	F				Ky					
	M. C.	18	F				La		✓			
	M. J.	12	F				La		✓			
	H. B.	9	M				La		✓			

1850 CENSUS — UNITED STATES

State: Louisiana **County:** Claiborne Parish **Township:** 23rd Ward twn **Call No.** 108

Family Number	Names	Age	Sex	Color	Occupation, etc.	Value - Real Estate	Birthplace	Married within year	School within year	Cannot read or write
196	James WARD	49	M		Planter	1,000	Tenn.			
	Mena Ward	44	F				Ky.			
	John W. B	24	M		Teacher		Ark.		/	
	Ann	19	F				La.		/	
	George W.	16	M				La.		/	
*	Marvin Fuller	14	M				La.		/	
	Miles J.	11	M				La.		/	
	Mary C.	8	F.				La.			
	Martha	3	F				La			
	H.B.									

215

1830-1840 CENSUS — UNITED STATES

State: Louisiana
County: Claiborne Parish
City: ___
Call No.: 107

Head of Family	No. Employed in Agriculture	Free White Males Under 5	5–10	10–15	15–20	20–30	30–40	40–50	50–60	60–70	70–80	80–90	90–100	Over 100	Free White Females Under 5	5–10	10–15	15–20	20–30	30–40	40–50	50–60	60–70	70–80	80–90	90–100	Over 100	Slaves	Free Colored	Foreigners not naturalized
James WARD	3	2	1	1	1		1									1					1										

1830-1840 CENSUS — UNITED STATES

State: ARKANSAS **County:** Hempstead **City:** _____ **Call No.:** _____

Head of Family	Free White Males Under 5	5-10	10-15	15-20	20-30	30-40	40-50	50-60	60-70	70-80	80-90	90-100	Over 100	Free White Females Under 5	5-10	10-15	15-20	20-30	30-40	40-50	50-60	60-70	70-80	80-90	90-100	Over 100	Slaves	Free Colored	Foreigners not naturalized
James WARD	2				1													1											

1870 CENSUS—UNITED STATES

State: Texas **County:** Titus **Town/Township:** — **P.O.:** Mount Pleasant **5th day of August** **Call No. 088**

Dwelling No.	Family No.	Names	Age	Sex	Color	Occupation, etc.	Value - Real Estate	Value - Personal property	Birthplace	Father Foreign born	Mother Foreign born	Month born in year	Month married in year	School in Year	Can't Read or Write	Eligible to vote	Date of
	1062	Ward, Miles J.	35	M	W	Farmer		500	Louisiana								
		Zennia	28	F	W												
		Sila	1	F	W				Texas								
		Ward, Mary J.	18	F	W				Louisiana								
		John	15	M	W				"					/			
		Ward, Martha	22	F	W				"								
		Henry	19	M	W				"								

1870 CENSUS - UNITED STATES

State: Texas County: Johnson Town/Township: Alvarado P.O. Call No. 611

Family No.	Names	Age	Sex	Color	Occupation, etc.	Value - Real Estate	Value - Personal property	Birthplace
481	G. W. G. WARD	34	M	W	Farmer		150	Ark. (should be La.)
	Nancy	33	M	W				Ark.
	A. W.	15	M	W				La.
	J. W.	14	M	W				La.
	W. G	9	M	W				Ark.
	Martha	4	F	W				Ark
	Mariah	2	F	W				Texas

1870 CENSUS - UNITED STATES

County: Titus **Township:** Mt. Pleasant **P.O.:** 5th of August **Call No.:** 088

Family No.	Names	Age	Sex	Color	Occupation, etc.	Value - Real Estate	Value - Personal property	Birthplace
1069	Atkins, James	29	M	W	Farmer		1500-400	Ala.
	Mary C.	28	F	W				La.
	Walter	3						Tx.
	Lula	1						Tx.

1880 CENSUS — UNITED STATES

State: Texas **County:** Franklin **Town/Township:** Pre. 3 **Date:** June 23

Family No.	Names	Color	Sex	Age prior to June 1st	Relationship to head of house	Single	Widowed	Occupation	Miscellaneous Information	Place of birth	Place of birth of father	Place of birth of mother
267	Aikin, Mary C.	W	F	37			1	Keeping house		Ia	Tenn	Ill
	Theodore W.	W	M	13	Son	1		Laborer		Texas	Ala.	Ia
	Lula B.	W	F	11	Daughter	1				Texas	Ala.	Ia

Note: I am sure the maiden name is Mary C. Ward decendent of James Ward, sister to H. B. Ward-family

#268, Also sister to Marvin Fuller Ward.

1880 CENSUS — UNITED STATES

State: Texas County: Franklin Township/Princt. 3 June 23

Family No.	Names	Color	Sex	Age prior to June 1st	Month of birth if born in census yr.	Relationship to head of house	Single	Married	Widowed	Divorced	Married in census year	Occupation	Miscellaneous Information	Cannot read or write	Place of birth	Place of birth of father	Place of birth of mother
268	Ward, Henry B	W	M	28				1							La	Tenn	Ill.
	Pamelia G	W	F	20		Wife		/							Miss		
	Forrester, Mattie C	W	F	7		Neice									Ark		La
	Holmes, Andrew	W	M	23		Boarder									La	Tx	La

The Ward Family History
Page 23

		Surname	Given name	Relation	Color	Sex	Month	Year	Age	Marital	Yrs married	Children born	Living	Birthplace	Father's birthplace
		"	Mary A	Daught	W	F	Feb	18[illegible]	6	S				Texas	Texas
	520	"	Pattie N	Daught	W	F	Nov	1897	2	S				Texas	Texas
920		Allue	Morgan	Head	W	M	Feb	1844	56	M				Mississippi	Virginia
	519		Mary	Wife	W	F	Oct	1844	55	M	36	8	8	Mississippi	[illegible]
		"	Will A.	Son	W	M	Apr	1873	27	S				Mississippi	Mississippi
		"	Tom F	Son	W	M	Apr	1879	21	S				Mississippi	Mississippi
		"	Donnie L	Daught	W	F	Sep	1886	13	S				Mississippi	Mississippi
		Hardin	Maggie	Daught	W	F	July	1870				2	2	Mississippi	Mississippi
		"	John R	Grand son	W	M	Feb	1889	11	S				Mississippi	Mississippi
	521	"	Roy	Grand son	W	M	June	1891	8	S				Mississippi	Mississippi
924		Willhite	Chris	Head	W	M	Apr	1872	28	M	4			Texas	Indiana
	520	"	Lou	Wife	W	F	Apr	1872	28	M	8	6	6	Texas	Texas
		"	Edie	Daught	W	F	Mch	1893	7	S				Texas	Texas
		"	Bessie L	Daught	W	F	Feb	1895	5	S				Texas	Texas
		"	Loha M	Daught	W	F	Jan	1897	3	S				Texas	"
		"	John H	Son	W	M	Aug	1898	1	S				Texas	Texas
	521	"	Olive P.	Son	W	M	Dec	19[illegible]	4/12	S				Texas	Texas
		"	Oskar	Boarder	W	M	Nov	1881	18	S				Texas	Indiana
922		Scott	Kirk	Head	W	M	[illegible]	1874	25	M				Mississippi	Mississippi
		"	Annie B	Wife	W	F	Nov	1880	19	M	3	2	2	Texas	Georgia
		"	Aubrey R	Son	W	M	Dec	1897	2	S				Texas	Mississippi
	523	"	Ben F	Son	W	M	July	1899	10/12	S				Texas	Mississippi
923		White	Robt B	Head	W	M	May	1856	44	M				Texas	Alabama
	522	"	Willie B.	Wife	W	F	July	187[illegible]			7	4	3	Texas	Georgia
		"	Marvin E	Son	W	M	Apr	1890	10	S				Texas	Texas
		"	Robt L.	Son	W	M	Oct	1894	5	S				Texas	Texas
	524	"	Walter W	Son	W	M	Mch	189[illegible]		S				Texas	Texas
924		Gillespie	Russ	Head	W	M	Jan	1868	32	M	9			Texas	Tennessee
	523	"	Ovedia	Wife	W	F	Oct	1872	27	M	9	3	2	Tennessee	Tennessee
		"	Robt D.	Son	W	M	Dec	1891	8	S				Texas	Texas
		"	Aubrey B.	Son	W	M	Apr	1896	4	S				Texas	"
926		Harris	Moc	Head	W	M	Dec	1828	71	M	42			Georgia	Georgia
	525	"	Mary	Wife	W	F	Mch	1842	58	M	42	0	0	Alabama	Virginia
926		Woddell	Joe	Head	W	M	Apr	1880	20	S				Texas	Mississippi
	527	"	Cristine E.	Mother	W	F	Jan	1848	52	Wd		4	1	Mississippi	Georgia
927		Ward	Henry B	Head	W	M	Dec	1850	49	M	20			Louisiana	Kentucky
	526	"	Penelia	Wife	W	F	Mch	1860	40	M	20	6	6	Mississippi	Alabama
		"	Lou D.	Daught	W	F	Apr	1881	19	S				Texas	Louisiana
		"	Myra J	Daught	W	F	Jan	1884	16	S				Texas	Louisiana
		"	Claud F	Son	W	M	June	1886	13	S				Texas	Louisiana
		"	Henry G.	Son	W	M	Aug	1890	9	S				Texas	Louisiana
		"	Willie M	Daught	W	M	Dec	1894	3	S				Texas	Louisiana
		"	Minnie P.	Daught	W	F	Sep	189[illegible]		S				Texas	Louisiana
928	528	Combs	A[illegible]	Head	W	M	Mch	1866	34	M	10			Alabama	Georgia
		"	Jane	Wife	W	F	Jan	1869	31	M	10	5	5	Alabama	Georgia

s	Texas	Texas							
	Texas	[illegible]					Yes		
ippi	Virginia	Virginia	Farmer		Yes	Yes	Yes	R	F 247
ppi	Tennessee	Tennessee			Yes	Yes	Yes		
ppi	Mississippi	Mississippi	[illegible]		Yes	Yes	Yes		
ppi	Mississippi	Mississippi	Farm laborer		Yes	Yes	Yes		
ippi	Mississippi	Mississippi		2	Yes				
ippi	Mississippi	Mississippi			Yes	Yes	Yes		
sippi	Mississippi	Mississippi		3	Yes	No	Yes		
	Mississippi	Mississippi					Yes		
	Indiana	Texas	[illegible]		Yes	Yes	Yes	O	F F 245
	Texas	Texas					Yes		
	Texas	Texas		2	Yes	Yes	Yes		
	Texas	Texas					Yes		
	[illegible]	Texas					Yes		
	Texas	Texas					Yes		
	Texas	Texas					Yes		
	Indiana	Texas	Farmer		Yes	Yes	Yes	R	F 2[illegible]
ppi	Mississippi	Mississippi	Farmer		Yes	Yes	Yes	R	F 250
	Georgia	Alabama			Yes	Yes	Yes		
	Mississippi	Texas					Yes		
	Mississippi	Texas							
	Alabama	Alabama	Farmer				Yes	R	F 251
	Georgia	Georgia					Yes		
	Texas	Texas					Yes		
	Texas	Texas					Yes		
	Texas	Texas					Yes		
	Tennessee	N. Carolina	Farmer		Yes	Yes	Yes	O	F F 252
ee	Tennessee	Tennessee			Yes	Yes	Yes		
	Texas	Tennessee					Yes		
	[illegible]	Tennessee					Yes		
	Georgia	Delaware	Farmer		Yes	Yes	Yes	O	[illegible] 5[illegible]
ia	Virginia	Virginia			Yes	Yes	Yes		
	Mississippi	Mississippi	Farmer		Yes	Yes	Yes		[illegible] 2[illegible]
ippi	Georgia	Georgia					Yes		
ia	Kentucky	Illinois	Farmer		Yes	Yes	Yes	R	F 255
ippi	Alabama	Alabama			Yes	Yes	Yes		
	Louisiana	Mississippi			Yes	Yes	Yes		
	Louisiana	Mississippi			Yes	Yes	Yes		
	Louisiana	Mississippi			Yes	No	Yes		
	Louisiana	Mississippi					Yes		
	Louisiana	Mississippi					Yes		
	Louisiana	Mississippi					Y.		
ia	Georgia	Georgia	Farmer		Yes	Yes	Yes	O	F F 256
ia	Georgia	Alabama			Yes	Yes	Yes		

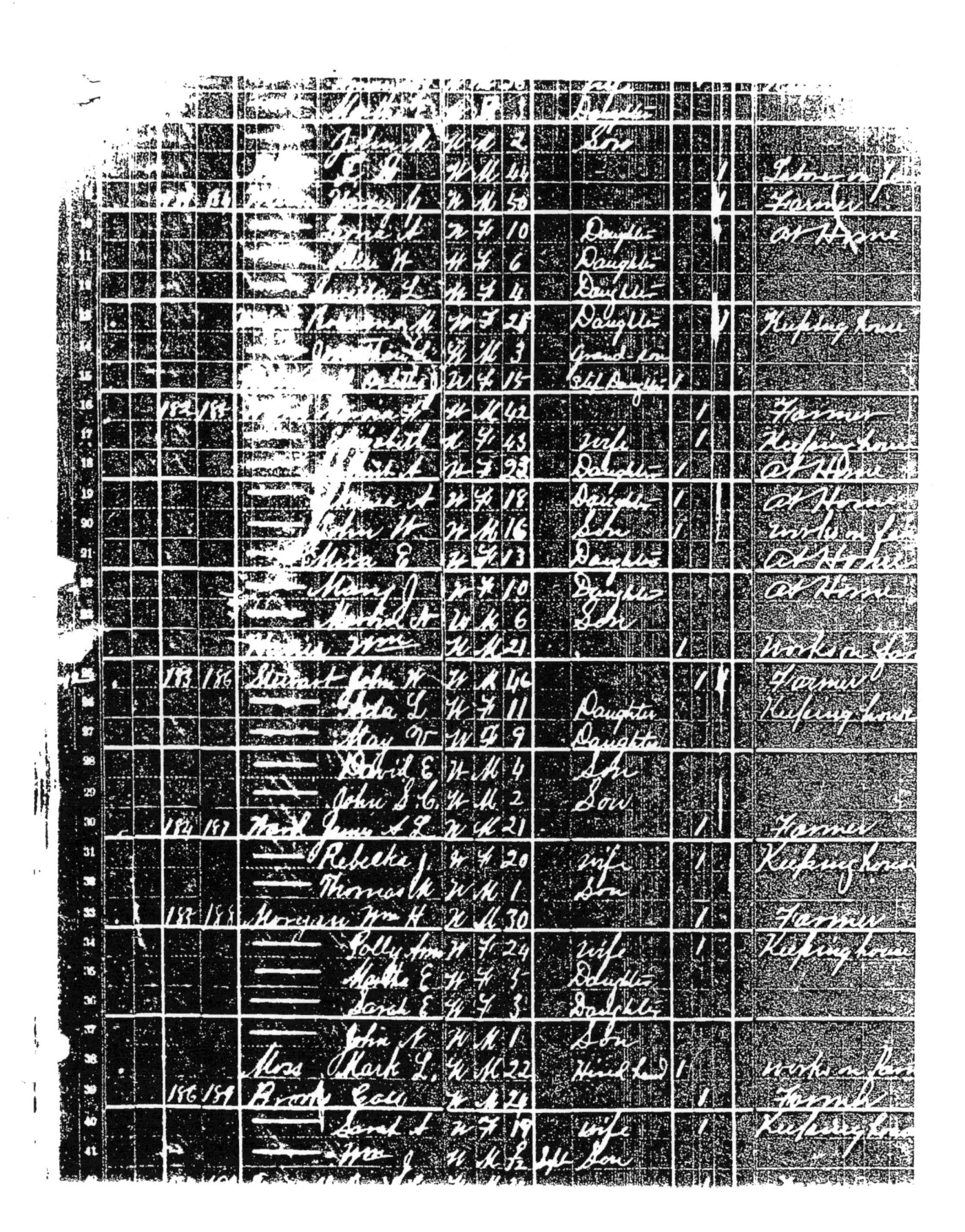

			Joseph	W	M	2	Son		
			E. J.	W	M	44		1	Labor on F
			Sarah L	W	F	50			Farmer
			Sarah L	W	F	10	Daughter		At Home
			Ida H	W	F	6	Daughter		
			Martha L	W	F	4	Daughter		
			Norma M	W	F	25	Daughter	1	Keeping house
			Jonathan L	W	M	3	Grand Son		
			Orbella	W	F	15	Gd Daught		
16	183	184	___ J	W	M	42		1	Farmer
17			Judith	W	F	43	wife	1	Keeping house
18			___ L	W	F	23	Daughter	1	At Home
19			James A	W	F	18	Daughter	1	At Home
20			John W	W	M	16	Son	1	Works on f
21			Miss E	W	F	13	Daughter		At Home
22			Mary J	W	F	10	Daughter		At Home
23			David A	W	M	6	Son		
24			Wm	W	M	21		1	Works on f
25	183	186	Stewart John H	W	M	46		1	Farmer
26			Ada L	W	F	11	Daughter		Keeping house
27			May V	W	F	9	Daughter		
28			David E	W	M	4	Son		
29			John S.C.	W	M	2	Son		
30	184	187	Ward James A L	W	M	21		1	Farmer
31			Rebecka J	W	F	20	wife	1	Keeping house
32			Thomas K	W	M	1	Son		
33	185	188	Morgan Wm H	W	M	30		1	Farmer
34			Polly Ann	W	F	24	wife	1	Keeping house
35			Martha E	W	F	5	Daughter		
36			Sarah E	W	F	3	Daughter		
37			John H	W	M	1	Son		
38			Moss Mark L	W	M	22	Hired hand	1	works on farm
39	186	189	Brooks Eli	W	M	24		1	Farmer
40			Sarah L	W	F	19	wife	1	Keeping house
41			Wm J	W	M		Son		

This letter was written by Marvin Fuller Ward to his granddaughter, Nappie Bell (Ward) Almonrode & her husband Sherrod.

Pickton, Tex.
Oct. Nov. 18, 1914.

Mr. and Mrs. S. W. Almonrode
Murchey, Texas

Dears Sherod Children will
will you a few lines this morning
in answer to your letter

I am come to here in our selling
Wanted to hear from you want to
hear that you was all well this
leaves us as well as usual. Hope
I will reach you all fined, you
all well the convictions are all
well as fair as I know yours truly
Meserve and Bryson was here
this the going to their houses
to hill. Will and Ransom are around
made everything where he lived
in Tex Co. it was of be clip
here but The most of the folks

Will make a week to do their
lodges and sell perfectly good
corn and will water ___
Lots of cotton yes Fannie I am
sorry but Much the medicine we
sent does good I do so wish that
has of beet bog of I think class
good but I get cleaning taken
of which clones us the past go
for many thanks for buddy &
will a cardly think he will get
if you had the ___ for children to have
yours there but it seems that
the little have never left of
the lots as community that I
seems to hope you are peril
come with him so we dear
get any little shaving am just

we got one about 2 weeks a
go ... ...
... my ... ... will
well I reckon Annie has told you a
bout all the news so I will
close love to one and all write
soon as you can your pa

M. H. Ward.

Rioneta Texs.
                Feb. the 7, 1919
Mr. and Mrs. J. W. Ward.
            Gomez Texs

dear sone and famley I will write you a few lines in answer to your kind letter that come to hand a few days sens. was glad to hear from you and to hear that you was all well this leaves us boath as well as common I hope it will find you all well so me of the connection are not well Will Harris is pretty puny and Pearl and her four children are sick with measles the oldest boy has pneumonia with his but is gettin a long very well tho have a nes kind of

2

measles here tha call
german measles if you ha
ve had the measles you
take them all the same there
is lots of sickness in this
contry and lots of deaths.
it has been the coldest win
ter I ever seen we have had
two big snows and lots of
cold windy weather I am
sory to hear that it has been
so bad out there and that
your cow froy to death no
cattle froy here but some
of our chickens froy to deat
h on this rust Marvin is
moving to Oklahoma he
staid nearly a month with
us during the worst

3

weather wee have had he sent Lyddie and the fans young
ist children on the team him and the two oldest are
going through with the wagon tha was sill at Cle
burn last saturday so old man Stuart told us yester
day and tha felis was sic to I am a fired tha are
makin a bad move do you hear from the boyes
wee have not heard from Oshey sens he went off
Ira has not answered our last letter write soon as eve yo
us pa love to all

M. J. Ward.

her heirs legal representatives and assigns against the claim or claims of any and all persons whomsoever lawfully claiming the same or any part thereoff
Witness my hand and Seal use Scroll for Seal
This Dec 30th 1876

        M. F. Ward
        E. P. Ward

The State of Texas }
For Johnson County } Before me J. G. Hix Exofficio Notary M. F. Ward and E. P. Ward his wife parties to the foregoing attached deed bearing date 30th day of December 1876 both of whom are to me known to me who acknowledged severally that they had Signed Sealed and delivered the same for the purposes and consideration therein Stated and the Said E. P. Ward having been examined by me privily and apart from her husband and having had the Same fully explained to her She the Said E. P. Ward acknowledged the same to be her act and deed and declared to me that She had willingly Signed Sealed and delivered the same of her own free will and accord without fear or compulsion on the part of her Said husband and that She wished not to retract it
Witness my Official Seal and Signature at my Office in the Town of Cleburne This 30th day of Dec 1876

        J. G. Hix Exofficio
        Notary Public

Filed for Record Oct 18th 1879 at 5½ Oclock P. M.
And recorded Oct 30th 1879 at 5½ Oclock P. M.
        W. L. Williams
        C. C. C.

The State of Texas }
County of Johnson } Know all men by these presents that we M. A. Hart and A. E. Hart his wife of the county and State aforesaid for and in consideration of the Sum of Two Thousand Dollars ($2000.00) to us in hand paid by M. F. Ward

The State of Texas
County of Johnson } Know all men by these presents that J. M. F. Ward of the County and State aforesaid for and in the consideration of the Sum of five hundred dollars To me in hand paid two hundred and fifty dollars in Cash and a two hundred and fifty dollar promissory Note bearing date even with this Deed The Reciept of which is hereby acknowledged have this day bargained Sold and delivered and by these presents do bargain Sell and Convey unto M. M. Rogers of the County and State aforesaid fifty acres of land Situated in Johnson county it being a part of the Sam Marshal Headright which is Situated in Joh. & Hill counties Said Survey was deed by Sam Marsh. To Joseph Robinson and by Joseph Robinson To M. F. W. Begining at the N E corner of John Griffins Survey fr. which a post Oak brs S 25 W 14½ vrs thence N 60 E 1055 To a Stake from which a post Oak 10 in dia brs S 61 6½ vrs Thence a black jack 6 in dia brs S 11½ W 12 vrs Thence S 30 E 267½ vrs To a Stake from which a post. bears N 59 W 8 vrs another post Oak 10 in dia brs N 11 11 vrs Thence S 60 W 1055½ To a Stake from which a black jack 4 in dia brs S 85 E 6½ vrs another black j. brs N 88 W 2½ thence N 30 W 267½ vrs to the place of begining Containing in all fifty acres mor or le To have and to hold the Said tract or parcel of land together with all the rights privelges appurtinences To the Same belonging To her The Said M. M. Rogers her heirs and assigns forever and the Said M. F. Ward. hereby bind Myself My heirs executors and administ To warrant and forever defend all and Singular th premises aforesaid unto her The Said M. M. Rogers

MR. & MRS. MARVIN FULLER WARD

Elizabeth Jane (Rose) Ward
Born: 14 January, 1836
Died: 28 November, 1899

Marvin Fuller Ward
Born: 26 February, 1837
Died: 05 October, 1918

Date of marriage: 27 June, 1855

The Ward Family History
Page 36

FAMILY GROUP NO. _____ **Husband's Full Name** _____

This Information Obtained From:

Husband's Data	Day Month Year	City, Town or Place	County or Province, etc.	State or Country	Add. Info. on Husband
Birth	26 Feb. 1837	Hayneville,	Claiborne Par.	La.	
Chr'nd					
Mar.	27 June 1855				
Death	05 Oct. 1918			Tex.	
Burial					
Places of Residence	Louisiana, Arkansas and Texas
Occupation	Farmer Church Affiliation Military Rec.
His Father: James Ward	Mother's Maiden Name: Mariah Halcomb

Wife's Full Maiden Name Elizabeth Jane Rose

Wife's Data	Day Month Year	City, Town or Place	County or Province, etc.	State or Country	Add. Info. on Wife
Birth	14 Jan. 1836			Arkansas	
Chr'nd					
Death	28 Nov. 1899				
Burial					

Her Father: Alexander Rose   Mother's Maiden Name: Rachael

Sex	Children's Name in Full	Children's Data	Day Month Year	City, Town or Place	County or Province, etc.	State or Country	Add. Info. on Children
F	1 Submit A Spouse: never married	Birth	20 June 1856		Claiborne	Louisiana	
		Mar.					
		Death	17 June 1901				
		Burial					
M	2 James Alexander Lacy Ward Spouse: Rebecca Jane Baker	Birth	11 Feb. 1859		Claiborne	Louisiana	
		Mar.	27 Aug. 1878				
		Death	03 July 1929	Plainview	Hale	Tex.	
		Burial	05 Jul 1929	Plainview	Hale	Tex.	
F	3 Elanea Ann Ward Spouse: William Harris	Birth	24 Aug. 1861				
		Mar.	12 July 1880				
		Death	23 May 1928	Covington	Hill Co.	Tex.	
		Burial					
M	4 John William Ward Spouse: Docia Hewitt	Birth	29 Feb. 1864	near Texarkana		Arkansas	
		Mar.	01 Aug. 1886		Johnson Co.,	Texas	
		Death	30 Mar. 1940	Hatfield	Polk	Arkansas	
		Burial	01 Apr. 1940	Hatfield (Six Mile Cem.)		Arkansas	
F	5 Mariah A Ward Spouse: E. Walter Holmes	Birth	19 Nov. 1867			Texas	
		Mar.	08 July 1886		Johnson Co.,	Texas	
		Death	23 May 1928	Covington	Hill	Tex.	
		Burial					
F	6 Mary Jane (Mollie) Ward Spouse: Fam F. Smith	Birth	01 Sep. 1870			Texas	
		Mar.	14 Feb. 1889		Johnson	Texas	
		Death	Nov. 1934				
		Burial					
M	7 Marvin N. Ward Spouse:	Birth	15 July 1873		Johnson	Texas	March 1940 was living in Crain, Tex.
		Mar.					
		Death					
		Burial					
F	8 Ella Frances Ward Spouse:	Birth	14 Feb. 1876		Johnson	Texas	
		Mar.					
		Death	19 Aug. 1876		Johnson	Texas	
		Burial	Aug. 1876	Grandview	Johnson	Texas	(Grandview Cemetery)
	9	Birth					
		Mar.					
		Death		Note: Oakland Cemetery is 3 miles west of Grandview and 5 miles east of Highway 17.			
		Burial					
	10	Birth					
		Mar.					
		Death					
		Burial					

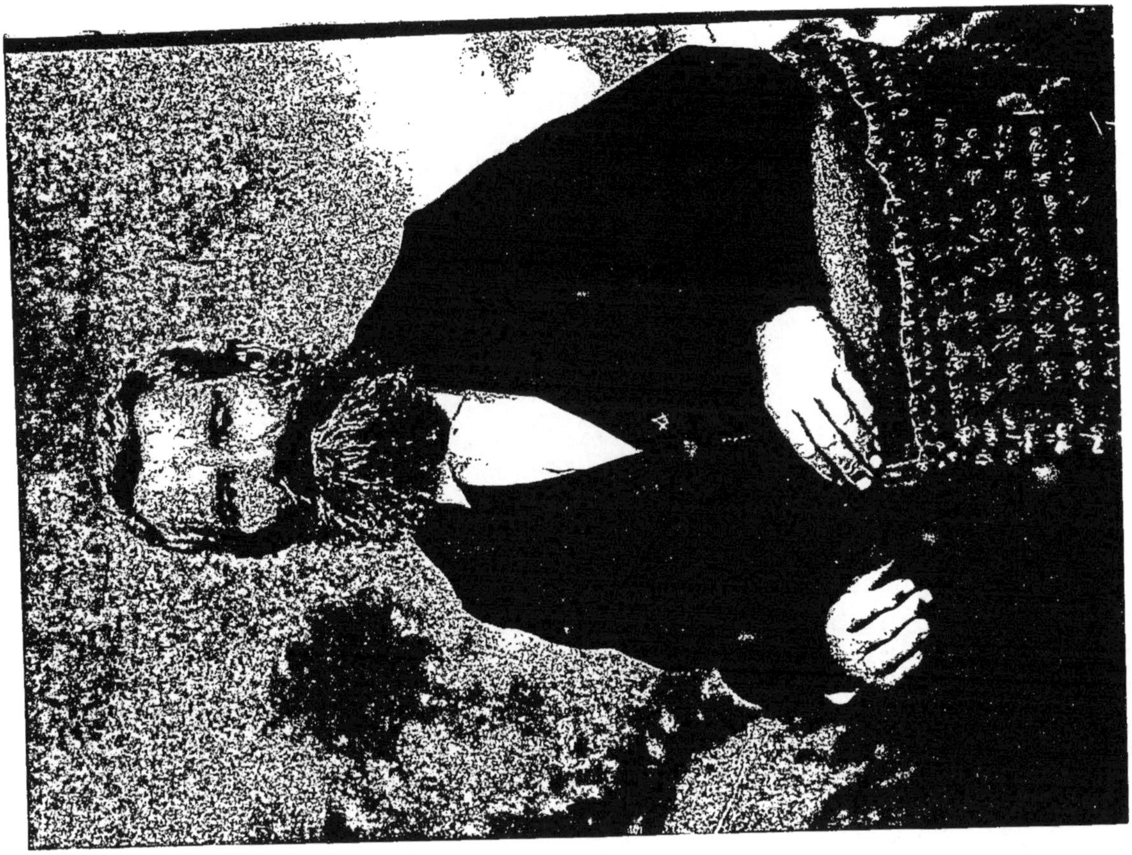

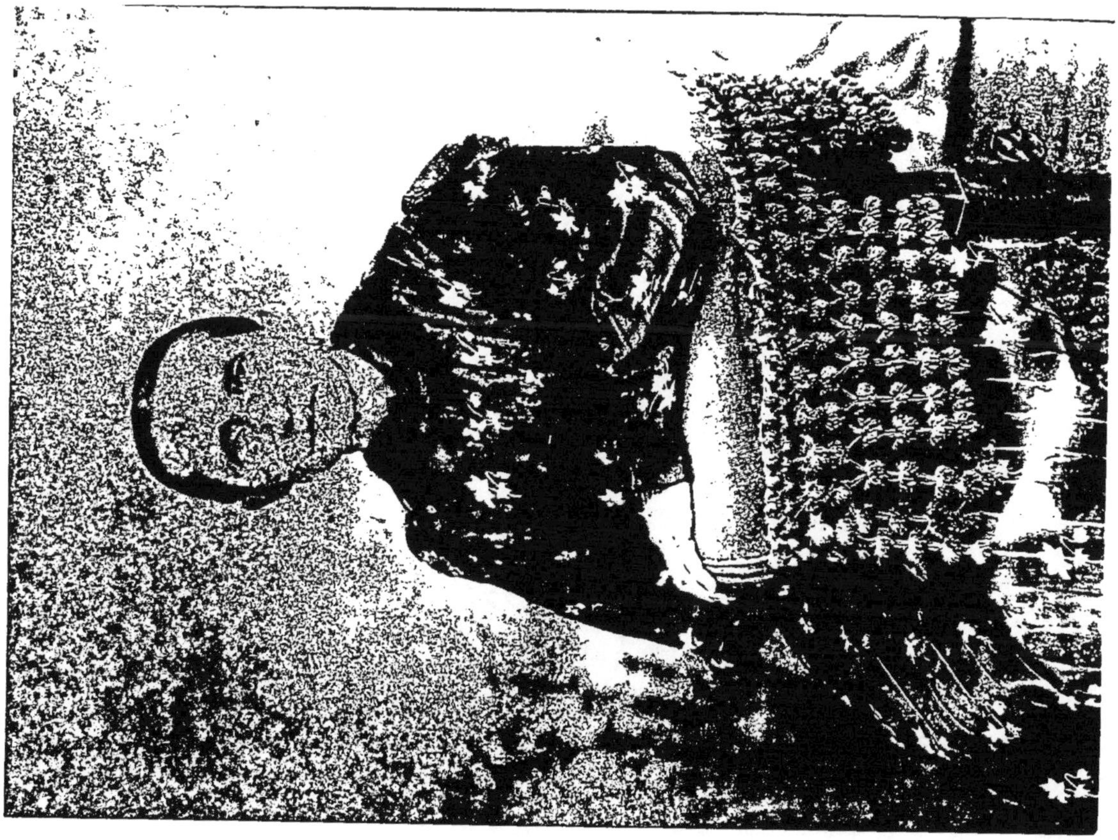

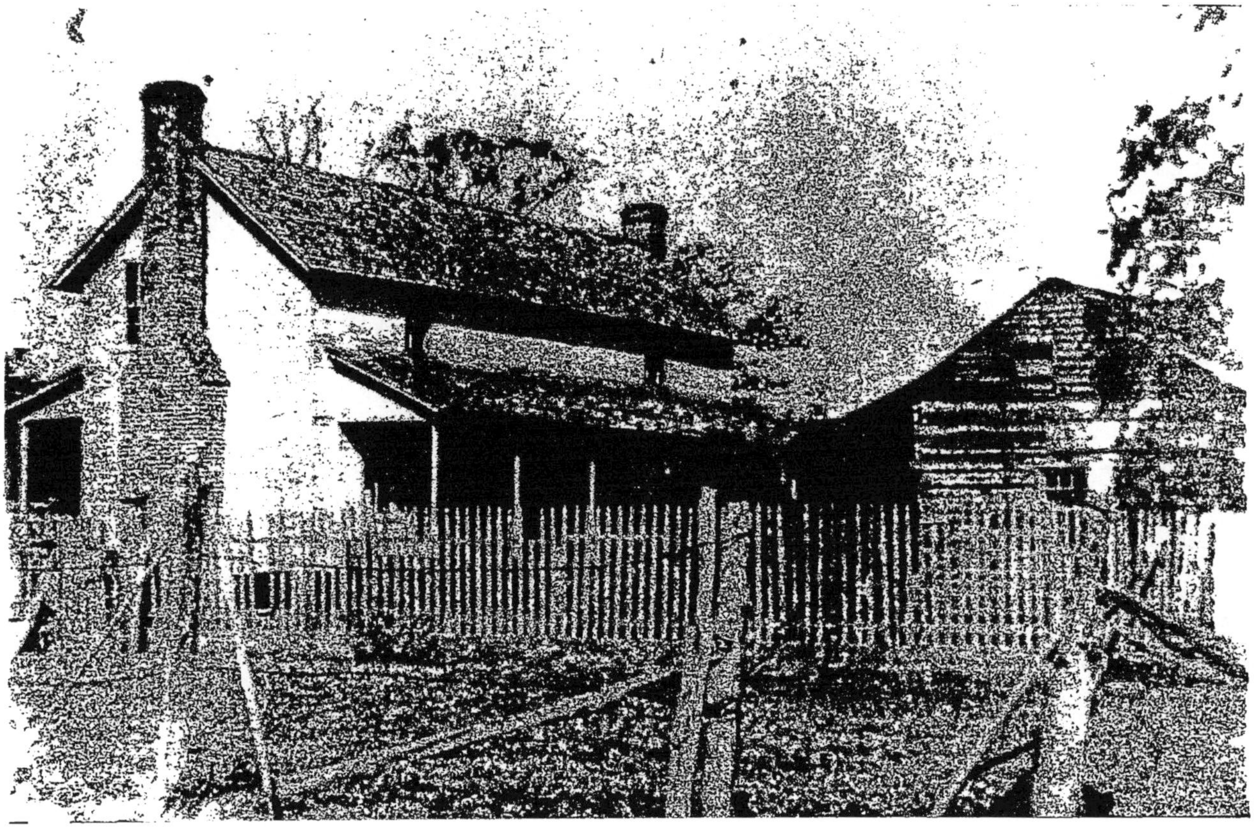

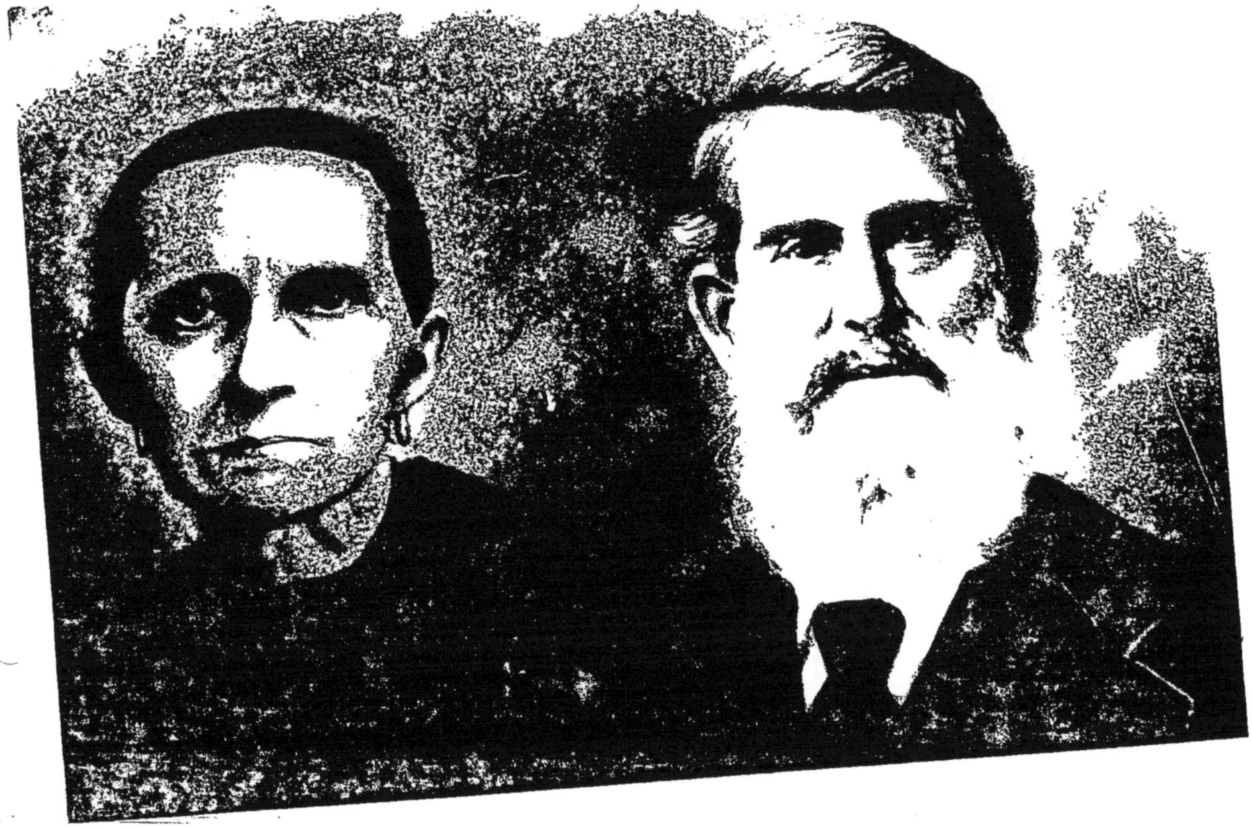

FAMILY GROUP No. ___

Husband's Full Name MARVIN FULLER WARD (BOBBY)

This information Obtained From: 1880 CENCUS OF JOHNSON CO. TEXAS LINE 16-to 23

Husband's Data	Day Month Year	City, Town or Place	County or Province, etc.	State or Country	Add. Info. on Husband
Birth	26 FEB 1837	HAYNEVILLE	CLAIBORN PAR.	LA.	
Chr'nd					
Mar.	27 JUN 1855				
Death	SEP 1918	PARKER	JOHNSON	TEX.	
Burial		PARKER	JOHNSON	TEX.	

Places of Residence
Occupation FARMER   Church Affiliation   Military Rec.
Other wives, if any. No. (1) (2) etc. (2) A. E. ROBERTSON
His Father JAMES WARD   Mother's Maiden Name MARIAH HALCOMB

Wife's Full Maiden Name ELIZABETH JANE ROSE

Wife's Data	Day Month Year	City, Town or Place	County or Province, etc.	State or Country	Add. Info. on Wife
Birth	14 JAN 1836			ARK.	
Chr'nd					
Death	28 NOV 1899	PARKER	JOHNSON	TEX.	
Burial		PARKER	JOHNSON	TEX.	

Compiler Alvin L. Ward   Places of Residence
Address P.O Box 1756   Occupation if other than Housewife   Church Affiliation
City, State Denver City, TX   Other husbands, if any. No. (1) (2) etc.
Date DEC. 1988   Her Father Alexander ROSE   Mother's Maiden Name

Sex	Children's Names in Full (Arrange in order of birth)	Children's Data	Day Month Year	City, Town or Place	County or Province, etc.	State or Country	Add. Info. on Children
1	SUEMITH A. / NEVER MARRIED	Birth	20 JUN 1856	HAYNEVILLE	CLAIBORNE PAR.	LA.	
		Mar.					
		Death	17 JUN 1901				
		Burial					
2	JAMES ALEXANDER LACY / REBECKA JANE BAKER	Birth	11 FEB 1859	HAYNEVILLE	CLAIBORN PAR.	LA.	
		Mar.	27 AUG 1878				
		Death	3 JUL 1929	PLAINVIEW	HALE	TEX.	
		Burial	5 JUL 1929	PLAINVIEW	HALE	TEX.	
3	(KANSA) A. / WILLIAM HARRIS	Birth	24 AUG 1861	HAYNEVILLE	CLAIRBORN PAR.	LA.	
		Mar.	12 JUL 1880		JOHNSON	TEX.	
		Death	23 MAY 1928	PARKER	JOHNSON	TEX.	
		Burial	MAY 1928	PARKER	JOHNSON	TEX.	
4	JOHN WILLIAM / DOCIA HEWITT	Birth	29 FEB 1864	TEXARKANA	MILLER	ARK	
		Mar.	30 JUL 1886	RIO VISTA	JOHNSON	TEX.	
		Death	30 MAR 1940	HATFIELD	POLK	ARK	
		Burial	6 MILE CEMETERY	HATFIELD	POLK	ARK.	
5	MARIAH ALMETTIE / Emmy Walton HOLMES	Birth	19 NOV 1867	RIO VISTA	JOHNSON	TEX	
		Mar.	08 JUL 1880	PARKER	JOHNSON	TEX.	
		Death	08 APR 1891	PARKER	JOHNSON	TEX.	
		Burial		JOHNSON CO. TEX.			
6	MARY JANE (MOLLIE) / SAMUEL FREDRICK SMITH	Birth	1 SEP 1869	RIO VISTA	JOHNSON	TEX.	
		Mar.	14 FEB 1889	RIO VISTA	JOHNSON	TEX.	
		Death	23 Nov 1934	PLAINVIEW	HALE	TEX	
		Burial	25 Nov 1934	PLAINVIEW	HALE	TEX.	
7	MARVIN NEWTON / LIDDIE	Birth	15 JUL 1873		JOHNSON	TEX.	WAS LIVING IN CRAIN, TEX. IN 1940
		Mar.	1896	CLEBURNE	JOHNSON	TEX.	
		Death					
		Burial					
8	ELLA F.	Birth	14 FEB 1876		JOHNSON	TEX.	
		Mar.					
		Death	19 AUG 1876		JOHNSON	TEX	
		Burial					

Marvin Fuller Ward
Born: 26 Feb. 1837 — Died 05 October 1918

M. F. Ward was the son of James Ward
and Mariah Halcomb Ward

Elizabeth Jane (Rose) Ward
Born: 14 January, 1836 -- Died: 28 Nov. 1899

Elizabeth Jane was the daughter of
Alexander and Rachael Rose

Marvin Fuller Ward - Annie M. (Robertson) Ward

Marvin Fuller Ward and his second wife, Annie.

Ranch Home of Marvin Fuller WARD & Eliz. J. ROSE WARD, 500 Acres in Withers Johnson Co., TEXAS. 1867 Note: After the new two story house was built, the family used the old house at the right of the picture to cook and eat their meals 1910

I have copied information from the Johnson Co. Texas 1896 tax roll recorded at the Texas State Library. It gave the patent number and name of the originl land owner, so I was able to locate the farm area of Marvin Fuller Ward and sons. Only part of the land of R. Hope and Batterson as shown was sold to the Wards — some was sold to the Hewitt family, etc. The map was in my Okla. Historical Library.

Tax role information as follows: 1896 Johnson Co. Texas

Name	Original Owner	No Acres	Value	Horses Mules	Cattle
Marvin F Ward	Batterson	153	$1,015		
James A L Ward	R. Hope	75	515	8	7
John W Ward	R. Hope	47	375	5	5
Marvin N. Ward				3	

Map of southern Johnson Co. original land owners attached.

Of course, I have not found the farm except on paper. I would like to if it remains. If you want to try perhaps this will help. Note how close to Hill. My dad, Willy B. Ward, said "Marvin F Ward gave each of the boys some land when they got married" — shown above.

Billie Ward Creech — Aug 9, 1989

By: Billie Ward Creech
Refer to Ward History (wardtax)

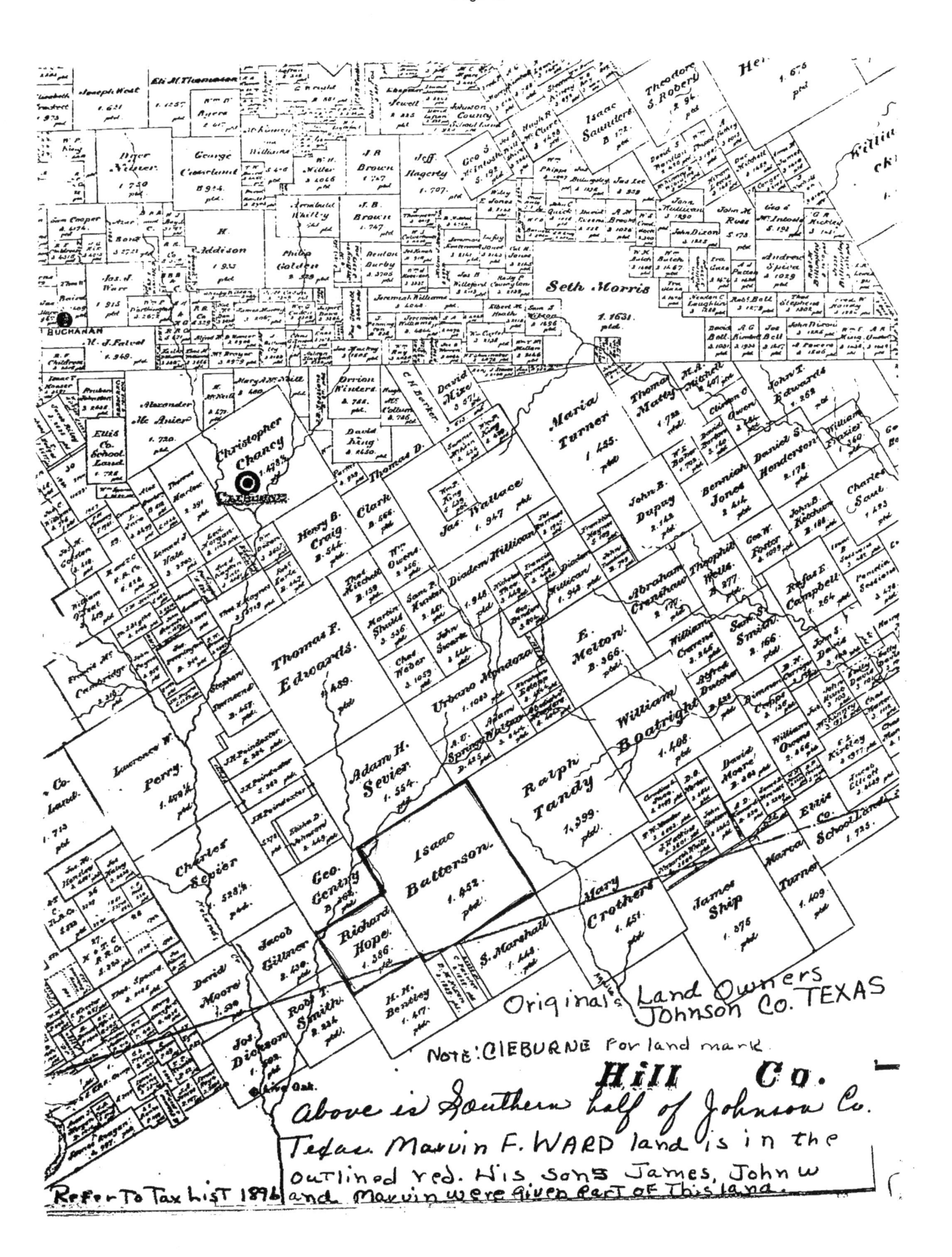

Original Land Owners Johnson Co. TEXAS

NOTE: CLEBURNE for land mark.

Hill Co.

Above is Southern half of Johnson Co. Texas. Marvin F. WARD land is in the outlined red. His sons James, John W and Marvin were given part of this land.

Refer To Tax List 1896

FAMILY GROUP No. ___

This Information Obtained From:

TAKEN OUT OF THE
WARD FAMILY BIBLE
BELONG TO
ADDIS RUCKLE

Husband's Full Name: MARVIN FULLER WARD (BOBBY)

Husband's Data	Day Month Year	City, Town or Place	County or Province, etc.	State or Country	Add. Info. on Husband
Birth	26 FEB 1837			LA.	SCOTCH IRISH
Chr'nd					
Mar.	10 NOV 1993				
Death	SEPT 1918	PARKER	JOHNSON CO.	TEXAS	
Burial					

Places of Residence:
Occupation:
Church Affiliation:
Military Rec.:
Other wives, if any: 1 ELIZABETH JANE ROSE
His Father: JAMES
Mother's Maiden Name: MATA

Wife's Full Maiden Name: A. E. ROBERTSON

Wife's Data	Day Month Year	City, Town or Place	County or Province, etc.	State or Country	Add. Info. on Wife
Birth	25 NOV 1855				
Chr'nd					
Death					
Burial					

Places of Residence:
Occupation if other than Housewife:
Church Affiliation:
Other husbands, if any:
Her Father:
Mother's Maiden Name:

Children:

1. NO ISSUE

J. A. L. Ward Dies Suddenly

J. A. L. Ward, aged 70, and a citizen of Plainview for many years, dropped dead in the kitchen of his home, corner Second and Columbia streets shortly after 5 o'clock this morning. Dr. C. A. Cantrell was called and said that death probably occurred from the bursting of a blood vessel or from apoplexy.

Mr. Ward had just arisen for the day and presumably had gone into the kitchen to light the stove when death came. Justice of the Peace J. P. Siler held the coroner's inquest.

Mr. Ward is survived by his wife and the following children: T. M. O'Donnell; L. O. Palmer; John, Munday; Mrs. Florence Goodman, Milford; Henry, Roscoe; Herman, Snyder; Mrs. Stella Swain, Anaheim, Calif.; Mrs. Cagle, Knox City. His cousin, Bud Ward, lives in Seth Ward addition and he was the first to discover the body, as Mrs. War is ill and confined to her bed. All the children are expected to come here for the funeral, final arrangements for which are not been made.

Funeral Service Held Today for Local Resident

Funeral services were held at the Lindsey Funeral chapel at ten o'clock this morning for J. A. L. Ward, 71, who died at his home in Hillcrest Wednesday morning. The services were conducted by Rev. S. L. Cartwright, pastor of the First Methodist Church of this city. Interment followed in the Plainview cemetery. The funeral was in charge of the local I. O. O. F.

Mrs. Ward, widow of the dead man, was not expected to live yesterday morning but today was reported as being greatly improved.

Mr. Ward had been a resident of Plainview for the past nine years, coming here from Floydada. He was born in Louisiana.

Among the relatives and friends from out-of-the city, who were here for the funeral were T. M. Ward of Tahoka, Mr. and Mrs. L. O. Ward of Palmer, Henry B. Ward of Roscoe, J. W. Ward of Knox City, Mrs. W. H. Goodman of Itasca, Bill Cagle of Knox City, Jack Ward of Snyder, S. F. Smith, E. W. Holmes and Fred Taylor, all of Floydada, and O. C. Cleaveland and family of Idalou.

Texas State Board of Health, Bureau of Vital Statistics, Standard Certificate of Death

Reg. Dis. No. _____
Registered No. 213

1. PLACE OF DEATH
   County: Scurry
   City: Hermleigh
   (No. _____ St., _____ Ward)

2. FULL NAME: Mrs. J. F. Ward
   (a) RESIDENCE. No. _____ St., _____
   (If non-resident give city or town and State)
   Length of residence in city or town where death occurred _____ yrs. _____ mos. _____ ds.
   How long in U.S., if of foreign birth? _____ yrs. _____ mos. _____ ds.

PERSONAL AND STATISTICAL PARTICULARS

3. SEX: Female
4. COLOR OR RACE: White
5. SINGLE, MARRIED, WIDOWED OR DIVORCED: (write the word)
6. DATE OF BIRTH: May 12, 1860
7. AGE: 71 yrs. _____ mos. _____ ds.
   If less than 2 years state if breast fed Yes _____ No _____
   If less than 1 day _____ hrs. _____ mins.
8. OCCUPATION
   (a) Trade, profession or particular kind of work: Housekeeper
   (b) General nature of industry, business or establishment in which employed (or employer): _____
9. BIRTHPLACE (State or country): Texas
10. NAME OF FATHER: Baker
11. BIRTHPLACE OF FATHER (State or country): Do not know
12. MAIDEN NAME OF MOTHER: "
13. BIRTHPLACE OF MOTHER (State or country): "
14. THE ABOVE IS TRUE
    (Informant) J. F. Ward
    (Address) Hermleigh, Texas

15. Filed 2-12, 1931   W. A. Haider? Registrar

MEDICAL PARTICULARS

16. DATE OF DEATH: Feb 11, 1931

17. I HEREBY CERTIFY, That I attended deceased from Feb 3, 1931, to Feb 11, 1931, that I last saw h__ alive on Feb 11, 1931, and that death occurred on the date stated above, at 4 a.m.
    The CAUSE OF DEATH* was as follows: Influenza, senility, & heart
    (duration) _____ yrs. _____ mos. _____ ds.
    Contributory (Secondary) _____
    (duration) _____ yrs. _____ mos. _____ ds.

18. Where was disease contracted if not at place of death? At home
    Did an operation precede death? No   Date of _____
    Was there an autopsy? No
    What test confirmed diagnosis? None

    (Signed) W. J. Ward, M.D.
    2-12, 1931, (Address) Hermleigh, Tex.

*State the Disease Causing Death, or in deaths from Violent Causes, state (1) Means and Nature of Injury, and (2) whether Accidental, Suicidal or Homicidal.

19. PLACE OF BURIAL OR REMOVAL: Fairview, Tex
    DATE OF BURIAL: 2-12, 1931

20. UNDERTAKER: O. N. Odom
    ADDRESS: Snyder

TEXAS STATE BOARD OF HEALTH
BUREAU OF VITAL STATISTICS
STANDARD CERTIFICATE OF DEATH

Registered No. 179

1. PLACE OF DEATH
County: Tdah
City: Glenmier Texas (No. 201 Columbia St.)
Reg. Dis. No. 179

2. FULL NAME: J. A. L. Ward
(a) Residence: No. 301 Street Columbia Ward
(If non-resident give city or town and state.)
Length of residence in city or town where death occurred ___ yrs. ___ mos. ___ ds. How long in U.S., if of foreign birth? ___ yrs. ___ mos. ___ ds.

PERSONAL AND STATISTICAL PARTICULARS

3. SEX: Male
4. COLOR OR RACE: White
5. SINGLE, MARRIED, WIDOWED OR DIVORCED: Married
6. DATE OF BIRTH: July 11, 1858 (Month) (Day) (Year)
7. AGE: 70 yrs. 4 mos. 23 ds.
   If less than 2 years state if breast fed ___ If less than 1 day ___ hrs. ___ mins.
8. OCCUPATION
   (a) Trade, profession or particular kind of work: Farmer
   (b) General nature of industry, business or establishment in which employed (or employer): ___
9. BIRTHPLACE (State or country): Louisiana

PARENTS

10. NAME OF FATHER: M. T. Ward
11. BIRTHPLACE OF FATHER (State or country): Louisiana
12. MAIDEN NAME OF MOTHER: Elizabeth Rose
13. BIRTHPLACE OF MOTHER (State or country): Louisiana

14. THE ABOVE IS TRUE
(Informant) J. B. Ward
(Address) Pearse, Texas

15. Filed July 8, 1929. Mrs. C. Hunt, Registrar.

MEDICAL PARTICULARS

16. DATE OF DEATH: July 3, 1929 (Month) (Day) (Year)

17. I HEREBY CERTIFY, That I attended deceased from July 3, 1929 to July 3, 1929 that I last saw h__ alive on July 3, 1929, and that death occurred on the date stated above, at 7 a.m.

THE CAUSE OF DEATH* was as follows:
Apoplexy (duration) ___ yrs. ___ mos. ___ ds.
Contributory: age (duration) ___ yrs. ___ mos. ___ ds.
(Secondary)

18. Where was disease contracted if not at place of death? ___
Did an operation precede death? ___ Date of ___
Was there an autopsy? ___
What test confirmed diagnosis? ___

(Signed) C. A. Cantell M.D.
July 4, 1929 (Address) Glenmier Texas

19. PLACE OF BURIAL OR REMOVAL: Glenmier Texas
DATE OF BURIAL: July 4, 1929
20. UNDERTAKER: W. D. Lindsay ADDRESS: Glenmier Texas

Recorded the 10 day of July A.D. 1929

Statement of Claim
Genealogical Proof

My Present Address is Plainview, Texas.

Know all men by these presents that I **Rebecca Ward**, was born in **Pulaskey**, County of **Giles**, State of **Tenn.**, and am a lineal or blood descendant of **Lewis Baker**.

I was married to **J.A.L. Ward Aug. 27th. 1873/** in the year of **1873**, my **maiden** name was **Rebecca Baker** born **5-12-1854**

to our union we have **eight** children:

Names and births: T.M. was born May 25th. 1879
Florence April 12th. 1881
Henry November 8th. 1882
John November 14th. 1884
Ucia November 11th. 1886
Beulah February 8th. 1889
Stella April 7th. 1894
Norman August 8th. 1896

My father **Lewis Baker** was the son of **Robert J. Baker** who was born in **Feb. 19, 1810**. County of ___ State of ___ died **May 1881**

My mother **Rebecca O Baker** was the daughter of ___ who was born in **Dec. 4, 1813** County of ___ State of ___ and were married in ___ and died ___

To their union were born the following children **William J Baker Nov. 25, 1840**
Sara Ann Baker Born Nov. 10 1847
Samuel B. Baker " May 3 1850
Lucenda J Baker " Aug. 17 1851
Thomas W Baker " Oct 31, 1855
Seth B. Baker " May 12, 1857
Rebecca J

My grandfather **Robert J Baker** was born **1750** and died **1855**

My grandmother ___ was born ___ and died ___ Date of their marriage ___

To their union were born the following children **Lewis Baker Born Feb. 19 1810**

My great grandfather was **Peter Baker Jr.** born **1656** and died ___

My great grandmother was _Sour Barb_ born _1656_
died _unkn_
To their union were born the following children
Thomas + Jacob + Daniel + Frederick +
Henry + Joel + Isaac + Elizabeth

My great great grandfather was _Gary Pet. Buts_ born _1680_ died ___
My great great grandmother was _Christina Dellen_ born ___ died ___
To their union were born the following children _Was Born_
Harrisburg, given
+ their children: Henry + Joan +
Williams + Rachel + Jokah + peter +
Garge + Bertie + Dustin

My great great great grandfather was _Jacob Baker_ born _1656_ died
His unknown to this union
Was Born gary peter Baker
My great great great grandmother was ___ born _1656_ died ___

The following statement by my _____ before his or her death:

State when your ancestors emigrated to America
and the names of those who came:

Have you any old Family Bible, records or papers showing your parents, grand parents, great grand parents or great great grand parents? _____

I hereby certify, to the best of my knowledge and belief, that the above statement is true and correct from family records of history and stated and told me by my parents and relatives.

WITNESS my hand and seal this ___ day of ___ A. D. 192_

Witness: _____ (Seal)
_____ (Seal) _____ (Seal)

State of _____ County of _____

Be it known that on this ___ day of ___ A. D. 192_
before me, a Notary Public, in and for said County and said State, personally came _____
_____, to know and known to me to be the individual person who made the above statement, and make affidavit that the foregoing above statement made by _____
_____ is true and correct according to the best of _____
knowledge and belief.

_____
Notary, Justice of the Peace or Alderman.

The Ward Family History
Page 52

(1) HATTIE (ADAMS) WARD
(2) THOMAS "TAPPIE" WARD
(3) FLORENCE ELIZABETH BELL WARD
(4) BEULAH WARD
(5) NELLIE (JOHN WARD'S WIFE)
(6) MILBURN WARD
(7) JOHN W WARD
(8) STELLA WARD
(9) LACEY OCIA WARD
(10) GERTRUDE WARD
(11) STELLA (FOWLER) WARD
(12) ALLIE (SMITH) WARD
(13) HENRY B. WARD
(14) INEZ WARD
(15) GLADYS
(16) REBECCA JANE (BAKER) WARD
(17) HERMAN (JACK) WARD
(18) J. A. L. WARD
(19) KATIE BELL
(20) GOLDIE WARD
(21) ILA
(22) JAMES H. WARD

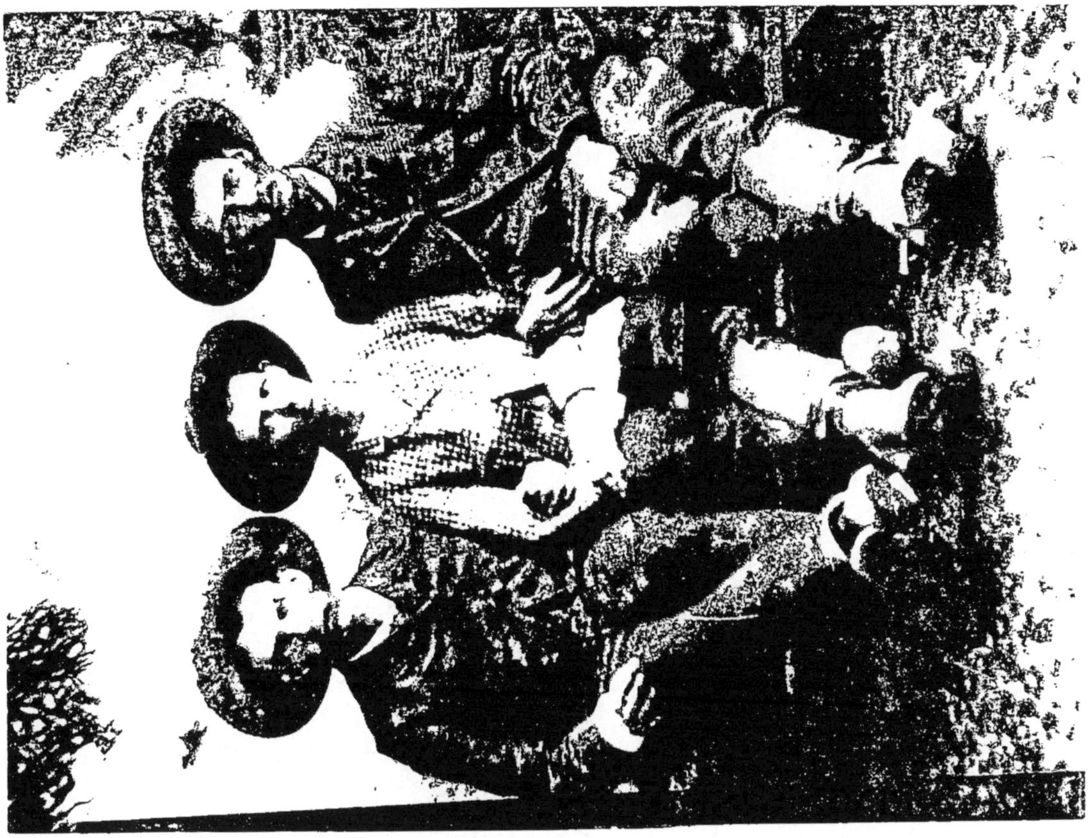

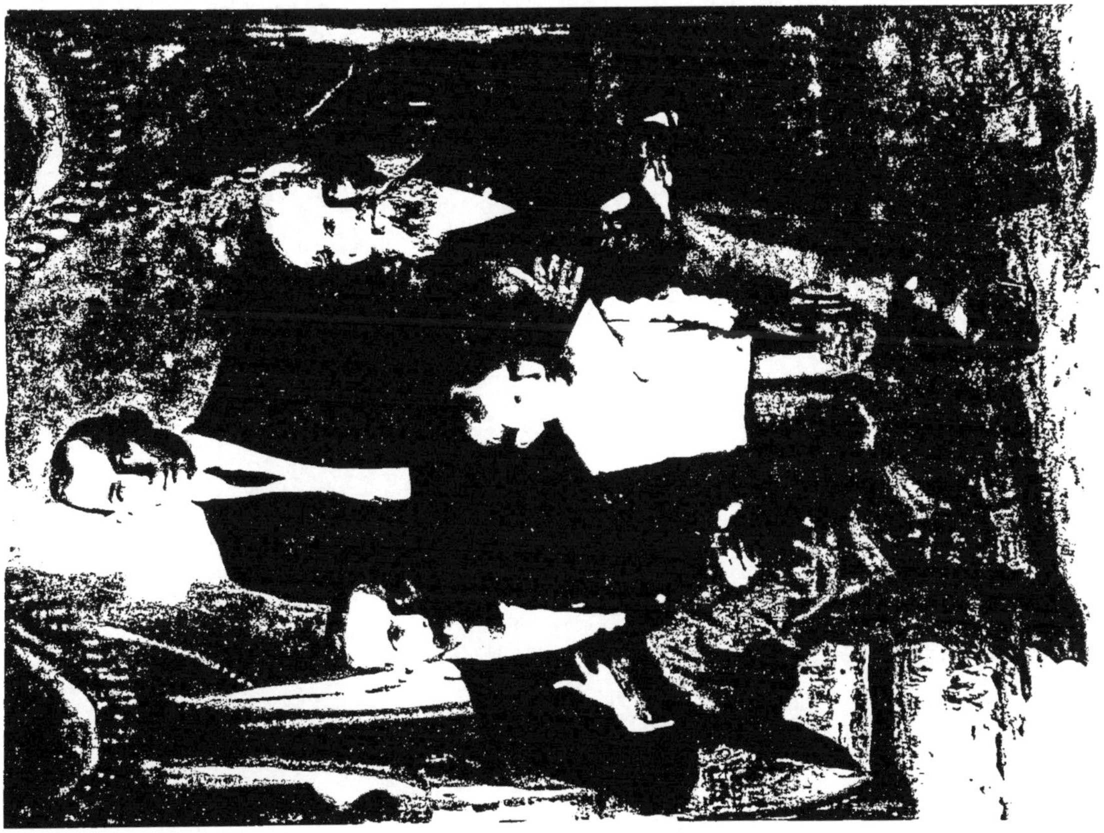

The family of James Alexander Lacy WARD and Rebecca Jane (Baker) WARD

L. to R. - James Alexander Lacy Ward, holding Herman - Rebecca - Stella - Henry - Florence - Marvin - Beulah - John Walter and Ocie.

The Ward Family History
Page 55

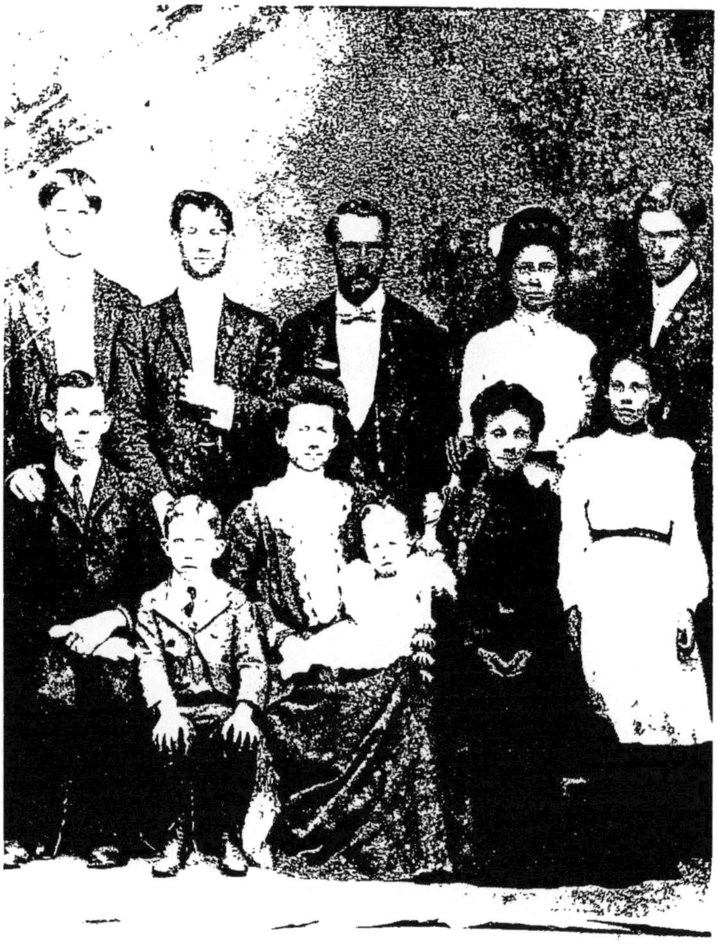

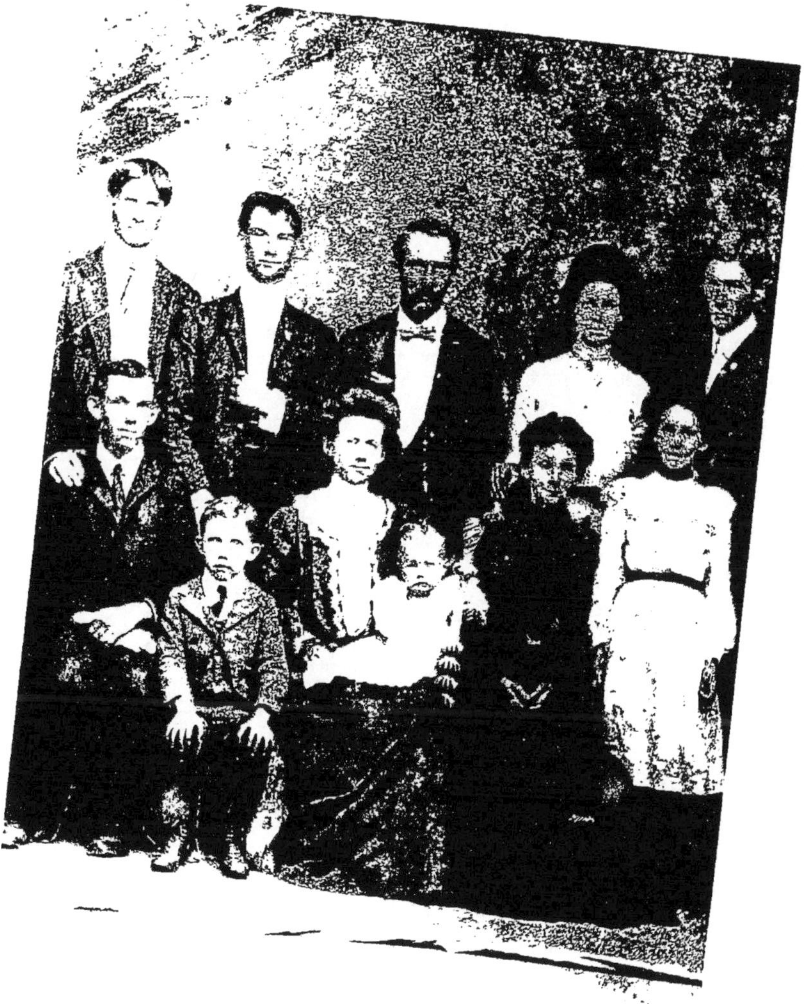

1900 CENSUS

State: TEXAS **County:** JOHNSON

Name	Relation	Color	Sex	Month of Birth	Year of Birth	Age	Marital Status	Years Married	Mother # ch	# living	Place of Birth	Father's Birthplace	Mother's Birthplace	Occupation	Mo. not employed	Attended school	Can read	Can write	Can speak English	Home owned/rented	Owned free/mortgaged	Farm or house
WARD, JAMES A. L.	H	W	M	FEB	59	41	M	21			ARK.	LOU.	ARK.	FARMER	0	0	Y	Y	Y		M	F
REBECA	W	W	F	MAY	60	40	M	21	10	8	TENN	TENN.	TENN				Y	Y	Y			
MARVIN T.	S	W	M	MAY	79	21	S				TEX	ARK,	TENN	FARMER	0		Y	Y	Y			
FLORENCE	D	W	F	APR	81	19	S				TEX.	ARK.	TENN				Y	Y	Y			
HENRY	S	W	M	NOV	82	17	S				TEX.	ARK.	TENN	FARM LABORER	2	2	Y	Y	Y			
JNONIE	S	W	M	NOV	84	15	S				TEX.	ARK.	TENN.	FARM LABORER	1½	1½	Y	Y	Y			
OCIE	S	W	M	NOV	86	13	S				TEX	ARK.	TEN.	FARM LABORER	3½	3½	Y	Y	Y			
BULAH	D	W	F	FEB	89	11	S				TEX.	ARK.	TEN.				Y	Y	Y			
ESTELLAH F.	D	W	F	APR	94	6	S				TEX.	ARK	ARK.		2	3½	N	N	N			
HERMAN	S	W	M	AUG	96	3	S				TEX	ARK	TEN				N	N	N			
MARVIN FULLER	F	W	M	FEB	37	63	WD				LOU.	LOU	ARK.				Y	Y	Y			
SUBMIT A.	SIS	W	F	JUN	56	43	S				ARK	LOU.	ARK.				N	N	N			

Family Group Record

Husband's Full Name: JAMES ALEXANDER LACEY WARD

This Information Obtained From: THERE WERE 10 CHILDREN BORN OF THIS MARRIAGE ONLY 8 OF THEM LIVED TO BE GROWN. THIS CAME FROM THE 1900 CENSUS. WHEN THE CENSUS WAS TAKEN MARVIN FULLER, AND SUBMITA A. WARD WAS LIVING WITH J.A.L. AND FAMILY.

Husband's Data	Day Month Year	City, Town or Place	County or Province, etc.	State or Country
Birth	11 FEB 1857	CLAIBORN		LA.
Chr'nd				
Mar.	27 AUG 1878			
Death	3 JUL 1929	PLAINVIEW	HALE	TEX.
Burial	5 JUL 1929	PLAINVIEW	HALE	TEX.

Places of Residence: Parker, Knox City, Plainview, Floydada
Occupation: FARMER Church Affiliation: Methodist Military Rec.
His Father: MARVIN FULLER WARD Mother's Maiden Name: ELIZABETH JANE ROSE

Wife's Full Maiden Name: REBECKA JANE BAKER

Wife's Data	Day Month Year	City, Town or Place	County or Province, etc.	State or Country
Birth	12 MAY 1857	PULASKEY	GILES	TEN.
Chr'nd				
Death	11 FEB 1931	HERMLEIGH	SCURRY	TEX.
Burial	13 FEB 1931	PLAINVIEW	HALE	TEX.

Compiler: Alvin Ward
Address: P.O. Box 1756
City, State: Denver City, Tx.
Date: Dec 1988

Places of Residence
Occupation if other than Housewife Church Affiliation: Methodist
Her Father: LEWIS BAKER Mother's Maiden Name: REBECKA O.

Children

#	Name / Spouse	Event	Day Month Year	City, Town or Place	County	State
1	THOMAS MARVIN / HATTIE ADAMS	Birth	25 MAY 1879	PARKER	JOHNSON	TEX.
		Mar.	2 JUL 1902	ABILENE	TAYLOR	TEX.
		Death	27 NOV 1936	LUBBOCK	LUBOCK	TEX.
		Burial	29 NOV 1936	TAHOKA	LYNN	TEX.
2	FLORENCE ELIZABETH BE / WILLIAM HARRISON GOODM	Birth	4 DEC 1881	PARKER	JOHNSON	TEX.
		Mar.	25 APR 1901	ABILENE	TAYLOR	TEX
		Death	30 AUG 1945	MILFORD	ELLIS	TEX.
		Burial	1 SEP 1945	MILFORD	ELLIS	TEX.
3	HENRY BASCUM / ALLIE J. SMITH	Birth	2 NOV 1882	PARKER	JOHNSON	TEX.
		Mar.		TRENT	NOLAN	TEX.
		Death	13 AUG 1971	HAMLIN	JONES	TEX.
		Burial	15 AUG 1971	SYLVESTER	FISHER	TEX.
4	JOHN WALTER / NELLIE A. DOUGLASS	Birth	14 NOV 1884	PARKER	JOHNSON	TEX.
		Mar.	08 AUG 1905	MERKEL	TAYLOR	TEX.
		Death	25 FEB 1971	KNOX CITY	KNOX	TEX.
		Burial	27 FEB 1971	MUNDAY	KNOX	TEX.
5	LACEY OCIA / STELLA LEE FOWLER	Birth	11 NOV 1886	PARKER	JOHNSON	TEX.
		Mar.	1906	CLEBURN	JOHNSON	
		Death	22 MAY 1971			
		Burial				
6	BEULAH / EDWIN MASHBURN	Birth	8 FEB 1889	PARKER	JOHNSON	TEX.
		Mar.				TEX.
		Death				TEX.
		Burial		KNOX CITY	KNOX	TEX.
7	ESTELLAH F. / JOHN WILLIAM SWAIN	Birth	07 APR 1894	PARKER	JOHNSON	TEX.
		Mar.				
		Death	15 MAY 1971			CAL.
		Burial				CAL.
8	JAMES HERMAN (JACK) / ILA KAY REYNOLDS	Birth	8 AUG 1896	PARKER	JOHNSON	TEX.
		Mar.				
		Death	13 JAN 1939	PLAINVIEW	HALE	TEX.
		Burial	15 JAN 1939	PLAINVIEW	HALE	TEX.

J. A. L. Ward & Rebecca Baker were married 27th August 1878 to their union ten children were born & lived to be grown.

Thomas Marvin born May 25 - 1879
Florence   " April 12 - 1881
Henry   " Nov. 3 - 1882
John   " Nov - 14 - 1884
Ocia   " Nov - 11 - 1886
Beulah   " Feb - 8 - 1889
Stella   " April 7 - 1894
Herman   " Aug - 8 - 1896

Rebecca Baker Ward was the daughter of Lewis & Rebecca O Baker.

Rebecca O Baker was born Dec 4. 18.
Lewis Baker, son of Robert J. Baker was born Feb - 19 - 1810 and died in May 1881

Other children of the Lewis Baker were William F. Baker Nov - 25 18 4
Sara Ann   Nov - 10 - 1847
Samuel B.   May 3 - 1850
Lucendy F.   Aug - 17 - 1851
Thomas W.   Oct 31 - 1855
and Rebecca   May 12 - 1857

1929 – 1930 City Dir

J. L. NISBET HARDWARE
BUILDERS HARDWARE—STOVES AND RANGES—GUNS AND AMMUNITION —FARM MACHINERY — WINDMILLS — CHINAWARE—CUTLERY—HARNESS
"IF IT'S FROM NISBET'S, IT'S GOOD"
712 BROADWAY   PHONE 244

DIRECTORY OF PLAINVIEW

Watson D B (Lillie) prop domino hall r 804 Austin
Watson G A (Willie) emp W Texas Gas Co r 411 W 5th
Watson J E pres Plainview Business College r 608 Columbia
Watson Marsh (Lola O) abstracter Hale Co Abstract r 513 Nassau
Watson Morris student r 411 W 5th
Watson Mrs Tillie wid C M) housekeeper r 500 E 6th
Watson William (Pearl) stockman rms Knoohuizen Boyd Apt
Ward B (Molly) lab r 301 E 13th
Ward C C (Nell) emp Continental Oil Co r 314 E 4th
Ward Herbert E (Beverly) meat cutter Hokus-Pokus r 213 W 9th
Ward J A L (Rebecca) farmer r 201 Columbia
Ward J F (Vira) carpr r 327 Ash
Ward Jim (Beatrice) mech Swan Motor Co r 901 El Paso
Ward Johnnie lab r 327 Ash
Ward Nell emp Model Laundry r 327 Ash

SOUTH PLAINS DRUG COMPANY, Inc.
PLAINVIEW'S FINEST DRUG STORE
521 Broadway   Phones 856 OFFICE / 857 PUBLIC

Ward Thomas A (Jeannette) emp Broadway Furniture r 703 E 3rd
Wardlaw Herman Jack (Faye Tom) bkpr Mistletoe Creameries r 604 W 10th
Warner Alvah clk Acorn Store r 900 W 12th
Warren Beverly student r 1507 W 7th
Warren B H (Ollie) tchr r 1507 W 7th
Warren Edith student r 1507 W 7th
Warren E E (Katherine) trav slsmn r 1001 W 10th
Warren Louise tchr r 1507 W 7th
Warren W E (Maggie) emp B & B Sign Shop r S Columbia
Watkins Marcellus (Jessie) Baptist minister r 1211 W 10th
Wayland Constance student r 714 Denver
Wayland Jo W (Frances) county clerk r 711 Denver
Wayland, L. C. (Connie) Physician, Office Suite 1, Donohoo Bldg., Phone 197; res. 714 Denver, Phone 20.

Knoohuizen, Boyd & Davenport
City Loans **General Insurance** Farm Loans
GROUND FLOOR SKAGGS BLDG.   TELEPHONE 341

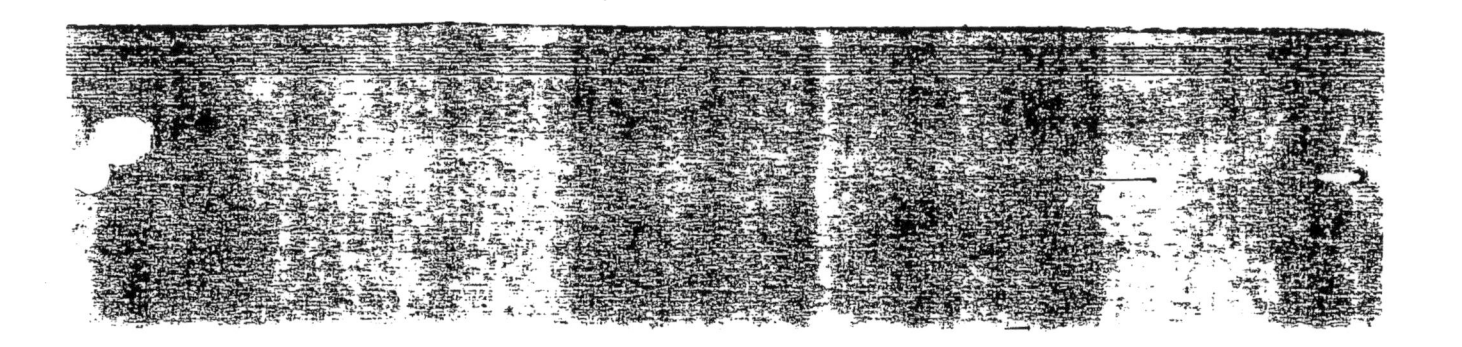

FOUR GENERATIONS OF WARDS

Oldest – seated at right: Marvin Fuller Ward – B. 26 Feb. 1837
Seated at far left: James Alexander Lacy Ward, the first born son of Marvin Fuller.
Standing at back: Thomas Marvin Ward, J.A. Lacy's first born son.
Standing at center: James Henry (Jimmie) Ward, Marvin's son.

C. N. Dome,   Prescott, Ark.

Vol 3 Page 206

THE STATE OF TEXAS,
County of Taylor

To any Regularly Licensed or Ordained Minister of the Gospel, Jewish Rabbi, Judge of the District or County Court, or any Justice of the Peace, in and for Taylor County—GREETING:

YOU ARE HEREBY AUTHORIZED TO SOLEMNIZE THE RITES OF MATRIMONY BETWEEN Mr. T M Ward and Miss Hattie Adams and make due return to the Clerk of the County Court of said County within sixty days thereafter, certifying your action under this License.

Witness my official signature and seal of office, at office in Abilene the 28 day of June 1902

Seal

S K Garrison, Clerk of County Court, Taylor County,
By J F Garrison, Deputy.

I, A J Leach, hereby certify that on the 2 day of July 1902 I united in Marriage Mr T M Ward and Miss Hattie Adams the parties above named.

Witness my hand this 2 day of July 1902

A J Leach Ordained Minister of the Gospel

Returned and filed for record the 4 day of July 1902, and recorded the 4 day of July 1902

S K Garrison, County Clerk,
By Deputy.

FAMILY GROUP No. ___

Husband's Full Name: THOMAS MARVIN WARD

This information Obtained From:

Husband's Data	Day Month Year	City, Town or Place	County or Province, etc.	State or Country	Add. Info. on Husband
Birth	25 MAY 1879		JOHNSON	TEX.	
Chr'nd					
Mar.	2 JUL 1902	ABILENE	TAYLOR	TEX.	
Death	27 NOV 1936	LUBBOCK	LUBBOCK	TEX.	
Burial	29 NOV 1936	TAHOKA	LYNN	TEX.	

Places of Residence:
Occupation: FARMER   Church Affiliation: Military Rec.:

His Father: JAMES ALEXANDER LACEY WARD   Mother's Maiden Name: REBECKA JANE BAKER

Wife's Full Maiden Name: HATTIE ADAMS

Wife's Data	Day Month Year	City, Town or Place	County or Province, etc.	State or Country	Add. Info. on Wife
Birth	1884			ARK.	
Chr'nd					
Death					
Burial					

Places of Residence:
Occupation if other than Housewife: Church Affiliation:

Her Father: W. H. ADAMS   Mother's Maiden Name:

Children

1. JAMES HENRY
Spouse: OLPHA BERTRICE MOORE

	Day Month Year	City, Town or Place	County or Province, etc.	State or Country
Birth	10 NOV 1904	MEADS	IND. TER.	OKLA.
Mar.	7 DEC 1924	O'DONELL	LYNN	TEX.
Death	28 JAN 1980	LUBBOCK	LUBBOCK	TEX.
Burial	30 JAN 1980	TAHOKA	LYNN	TEX.

OLPHA BERTRICE MOORE 1st BORN OF JOHN BELL MOORE

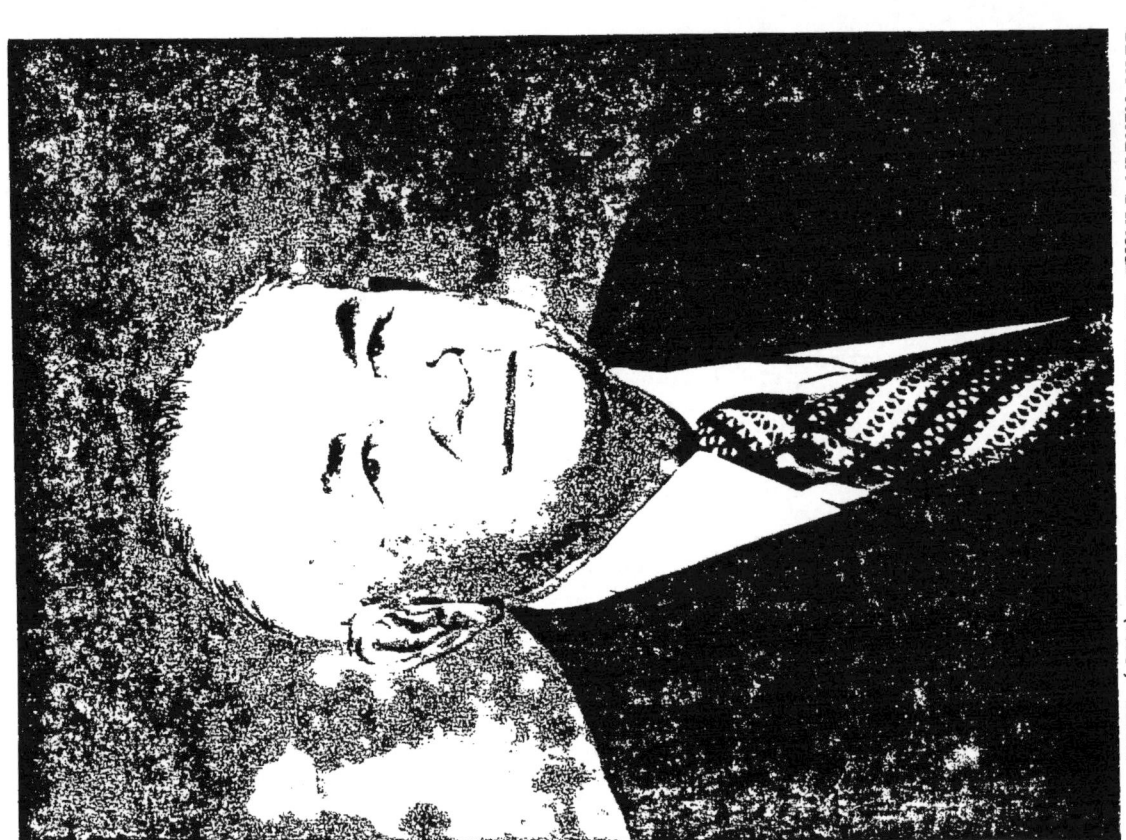

JAMES (JIM) HENRY WARD 1st BORN OF THOMAS MARVIN WARD

The State of Texas — Marriage License
County of LYNN
No. 171

To any Regularly Licensed or Ordained Minister of the Gospel, Jewish Rabbi, Judge, District or County Court, or any Justice of Peace, in the State of Texas — Greeting:

You are hereby authorized to solemnize the Rites of Matrimony

Between Mr. Jim Ward and Miss Burtrice Moore and make due return to the Clerk of the County Court of said County within sixty days thereafter, certifying your action under this License.

Witness my official signature and seal of office at TAHOKA, Texas, the 6 day of Dec. 1924.

W. E. Smith, Clerk of County Court
By Inez Weatherford, Deputy
LYNN County, Texas

I, W. B. Hicks, hereby certify that on the 7 day of Dec. 1924, I united in Marriage Mr. Jim Ward and Miss Burtrice Moore the parties above named.

Witness my hand, this 15 day of December 1924
W. B. Hicks
(Minister of Gospel)

I, W. E. Smith, Clerk County Court, LYNN County, Texas, hereby certify that the above is the original marriage license, issued to the above named parties, and with the return thereon, was duly recorded in my office in book 1, page 371, Marriage License Record of LYNN County on the 17 day of Dec. 1924.

Witness my hand and seal of office, this the 17 day of Dec. 1924.
W. E. Smith, County Clerk
Inez Weatherford, Deputy
LYNN County, Texas

JAMES HENRY WARD (JIM) OLPHA BERTRICE MOORE (BERT) JAMES BERNARD, AND DONALD GLYNN ARE STANDING. ALVIN LAVELL, AND HIS FIRST WIFE ANNA MURIEL MILLER. CHARLES RICHARD IS IN HIS FATHERS LAP.

WORSHIP SERVICE
IN MEMORY OF JAMES HENERY WARD

JANUARY 24, 1980
1:00 p.m.

CALL TO WORSHIP	CONGREGATION
*THE HYMN "HOW GREAT THOU ART"......NO.17	
WORDS OF PRAYER	REV. DANIEL
ANTHEM "I SAW A MAN"	CHOIR
SCRIPTURE READING	REV. WARD
*GLORIA PATRI	CONGREGATION

Glory be to the Father, and to the Son,
and to the Holy Ghost, As it was in the
beginning, is now, and ever shall be,
world without end. AMEN

ANTHEM "HE TOUCHED ME"	CAROL BOYD
*CONGREGATIONAL READING	PSALMS 23

The Lord is my shepherd; I shall not want.
He maketh me to lie down in green pastures;
he leadeth me beside the still waters. He
restoreth my soul; he leadeth me in the
paths of righteousness for his name's sake.
Yea, though I walk through the valley of the
shadow of death, I will fear no evil; for
thou art with me; thy rod and thy staff they
comfort me. Thou preparest a table before
me in the presence of mine enemies: thou
anointest my head with oil; my cup runneth
over. Surely goodness and mercy shall follow me all the days of my life; and I will
dwell in the house of the LORD for ever.

READING OF OBITUARY	REV. DANIEL

James Henry Ward was born November 10,1904
in Mead,Oklahoma. He passed away January 2
23,1980 at the age of 75. He was married to
Bertrice Moore December 7,1924 in O'Donnell,
Texas. He was a retired farmer. He moved to
Seagraves from Tahoka in 1949. He is survived by his wife,Bertrice; 3 sons; Don of
Seagraves, Alvin of Denver City, Charles of
Las Cruses, N.M.; 3 brothers; T.M. of Houston, E.C. of Uvalde, Eugene of Fort Worth;
1 step-sister; Mrs. Willie Eaker of LaPryor,
Texas; 11 grandchildren; and 5 great-grandchildren.

SPECIAL MUSIC HE TOUCHED ME	CAROL BOYD
THE MESSAGE	REV. KLAVERWEIDEN
*THE HYMN FARTHER ALONG	CONGREGATION

IN MEMORY OF
JAMES HENRY WARD
WHO DEPARTED THIS LIFE
January 23, 1980
Lubbock, Texas

BORN
November 10, 1904
Mead, Oklahoma

Marriage
Miss Beatrice Moore
December 7, 1924
O'Donnell, Texas

SERVICES HELD
Thursday, January 24, 1980 1 p.m.
First United Methodist Church
Seagraves, Texas

OFFICIATING
Rev. Jerry Klaverweiden
Rev. Jimmy Ward
Rev. Wesley Daniels

PALLBEARERS

Tommy Billings	Alton Billings
Cecil Dorman	Leonard Dorman
Walter Billings	Larry Moore
Kenneth Eaker	Marvin Joe Ward

CONCLUDING SERVICES
Tahoka Cemetery 4 p.m.
Tahoka, Texas

CERTIFICATE OF DEATH

STATE OF TEXAS

1. Name of Deceased	James Henry Ward
2. Sex	Male
3. Date of Death	1-23-1980
4. Race	White
5. Date of Birth	11-10-1904
7. Age	75
8a. Name of Hospital	Methodist Hospital
8d. Inside City Limits	Yes
3a. Place of Death — County	Lubbock
10. Birthplace	Oklahoma
11. Citizen of What Country	USA
12. Was Decedent Ever in U.S. Armed Forces?	No
13. Surviving Spouse	Bertrice Moore
9. Married / Never Married / Widowed / Divorced	Widowed
14. Social Security No.	462-01-7106
15a. Usual Occupation	Farmer
15b. Kind of Business or Industry	Agriculture
16. Residence — State	Texas
16b. County	Gaines
16c. City or Town	Seagraves
16d. Inside City Limits	Yes
16e. Street Address	605 Avenue G
17. Father's Name	Marvin Ward
18. Mother's Maiden Name	Hattie Adams
19. Signature of Informant	Alvin L. Ward

Cause of Death
- (a) Immediate cause: cardio-respiratory arrest — immediate
- (b) Due to: Quadriplegia — 4 days
- (c) Due to: fractured cervical spine — cervical 6 level — 4 days

21. Autopsy? No

22a. Accident, Suicide, Hom., Undet. or Pending Invest.: —
22b. Date of Injury: 1-18-80
22c. Hour of Injury: M
22d. Injury at Work: no
22e. Place of Injury: home
22f. Describe How Injury Occurred: fell and struck head on couch
22g. Location — City or Town: Seagraves, Texas

23a. Certifying Physician Signature
23b. Date Signed: February 1, 1980
23c. Hour of Death: 2:04 A.M.
23d. Name of Attending Physician: Lloyd Garland, M.D.

25. Name of Cemetery or Crematory: Tahoka Cemetery
25a. Burial, Cremation, Removal: Removal
25b. Location: Tahoka, Texas
25c. Date: 1-23-1980

26. Signature of Funeral Director: Sanders Funeral Home by: Linda J. Thomas

Date Received by Local Registrar: FEB 12 1980
Registrar's File No.: 183

VS-112, REV. 1/80 — Texas Department of Health — BUREAU OF VITAL STATISTICS

THE STATE OF TEXAS
CITY OF LUBBOCK

I hereby certify this to be a true photocopy of the record of death of **JAMES HENRY WARD**, Filed in my office and recorded in Volume 63, Page 183, Issued this February 25, 1980.

Jaxie M. Norwood
Deputy Jaxie M. Norwood   Local Registrar Linda Thomas

FAMILY GROUP No. ___

Husband's Full Name: JAMES HENRY WARD (JIM)

This Information Obtained From:

Husband's Data	Day Month Year	City, Town or Place	County or Province, etc.	State or Country	Add. Info. on Husband
Birth	10 NOV 1904	MEADS	INDIAN TERITORY	OKL.	
Chr'nd					
Mar.	7 DEC 1924	O'DONNELL	LYNN	TEX.	
Death	23 JAN 1980	LUBBOCK	LUBBOCK	TEX.	
Burial	25 JAN 1980	TAHOKA	LYNN	TEX.	

Places of Residence: O'DONNELL, TAHOKA, LUBBOCK, BROWNFIELD, ABILENE
Occupation: MECH. FARMER Church Affiliation: METHODIST Military Rec.

His Father: THOMAS MARVIN WARD Mother's Maiden Name: HATTIE ADAMS

Wife's Full Maiden Name: OLPHA BERTRICE MOORE

Wife's Data	Day Month Year	City, Town or Place	County or Province, etc.	State or Country	Add. Info. on Wife
Birth	18 NOV 1905	DENNIS	PARKER	TEX.	
Chr'nd					
Death					
Burial					

Places of Residence: BROCK, SEAGRAVES, PLAINVIEW, LAMESA
Occupation if other than Housewife Church Affiliation: METHODIST

Her Father: JOHN BELL MOORE Mother's Maiden Name: LULA ESTELL THOMAS

Sex	Children's Names in Full	Children's Data	Day Month Year	City, Town or Place	County or Province	State or Country
1	ALVIN LAVELL Spouse: ANNA MURIEL MILLER	Birth	19 APR 1926	T-BAR	LYNN	TEXAS
		Mar.	1 SEP 1943	BROWNFIELD	TERRY	TEX.
		Death				
		Burial				
2	JAMES BERNARD Spouse:	Birth	5 MAR 1929	O'DONNELL	LYNN	TEX.
		Mar.				
		Death	25 JUL 1950	PUSON		KOREA
		Burial	22 FEB 1952	TAHOKA	LYNN	TEX.
3	DONALD GLYNN Spouse: MOLLY RUTH BRASHER	Birth	13 JUL 1933	O'DONNELL	LYNN	TEX.
		Mar.	15 JUN 1956	SEAGRAVES	GAINS	TEX.
		Death				
		Burial				
4	CHARLES RICHARD Spouse: NORMA FAY MARTIN	Birth	25 MAR 1940	TAHOKA	LYNN	TEX.
		Mar.	27 AUG 1961	SEAGRAVES	GAINS	TEX.
		Death				
		Burial				

FAMILY GROUP No. _____

Husband's Full Name: ALVIN LAVELL WARD

Husband's Data	Day Month Year	City, Town or Place	County or Province, etc.	State or Country	Add. Info. on Husband
Birth	19 APR 1926	T-BAR	LYNN	TEX.	
Chr'nd					
Mar.	1 SEP 1943	BROWNFIELD	TERRY	TEX.	
Death					
Burial					

Places of Residence: O'DONNELL, TAHOKA, PLAINVIEW, LUBBOCK, FORT WORTH
Occupation: **Church Affiliation:** METHODIST **Military Rec.:** AIR FORCE
Other wives, if any: (2) P. B. THEDFORD (3) I. BEYER (4) ELHEYEN (5) M. WILSON
His Father: JAMES HENRY WARD **Mother's Maiden Name:** OLPHA BERTRICE MOOR

Wife's Full Maiden Name: ANNA MURIEL MILLER

Wife's Data	Day Month Year	City, Town or Place	County or Province, etc.	State or Country	Add. Info. on Wife
Birth	12 AUG 1926				
Chr'nd					
Death					
Burial					

Her Father: DALTON WILSON MILLER **Mother's Maiden Name:** ANNA BERNICE PARKER

Children

Sex	Children's Names in Full		Day Month Year	City, Town or Place	County or Province, etc.	State or Country
1	ROGER WILSON	Birth	2 DEC 1944	PARIS	LAMAR	TEX.
	Spouse: PATRICIA ELAINE (Ann) LAMBRIGHT	Mar.	18 Aug 1967	PAMPA	GRAY CO	TEX.
		Death				
		Burial				
2	MYRNA JANE	Birth	16 AUG 1949	FORT WORTH	TARRENT	TEX.
	Spouse: LLOYD DALE BOULTER	Mar.	16 SEP 1967	DENVER CITY	YOAKUM	TEX.
		Death				
		Burial				

FAMILY GROUP No. ___

Husband's Full Name ALVIN LAVELL WARD

This Information Obtained From:

Husband's Data	Day Month Year	City, Town or Place	County or Province, etc.	State or Country	Add. Info. on Husband
Birth	19 APR 1926	T-BAR	LYNN	TEX.	
Chr'nd					
Mar.		SEAGRAVES	GAINS	TEX.	
Death					
Burial					

Places of Residence
Occupation — Church Affiliation — Military Rec.
Other wives, if any. No. (1) (2) etc. (1) M. MILLER (2) P. THEDFORD (3) I.M. BEYER (5) M.E. WILSON
His Father JAMES HENRY WARD — Mother's Maiden Name OLPHA BERTRICE MOORE

Wife's Full Maiden Name EIDTH LORINE HEYEN HAGGLEBURGER

Wife's Data	Day Month Year	City, Town or Place	County or Province, etc.	State or Country	Add. Info. on Wife
Birth		ALBANY		N.Y.	
Chr'nd					
Death					
Burial					

Places of Residence
Occupation if other than Housewife — Church Affiliation
Other husbands, if any. No. (1) (2) etc.
Her Father — Mother's Maiden Name

Sex	Children's Names in Full		Day Month Year	City, Town or Place	County or Province, etc.	State or Country
1	(ADOPTED) DAVID LESLEY (HEYEN)	Birth	5 MAR			
		Mar.				
		Death				
		Burial				
2	(ADOPTED) BOBBIE ANN (HEYEN) Spouse: JACK PRICE	Birth	27 DEC			
		Mar.	1988	HONDO	MEDINA	TEX.
		Death				
		Burial				

ALVIN LAVELL WARD AND HIS WIFE MARY ELIZABETH (DULIN) WARD

FAMILY GROUP No. ___

Husband's Full Name ALVIN LAVELL WARD

This Information Obtained From:

Husband's Data	Day Month Year	City, Town or Place	County or Province, etc.	State or Country	Add. Info. on Husband
Birth	19 APR 1926	T-BAR	LYNN	TEX.	
Chr'nd					
Mar.	27 MAR 1976	LAS VEGAS	CLARK	NEV.	
Death					
Burial					

Places of Residence
Occupation   Church Affiliation   Military Rec.
Other wives, if any. No. (1) (2) etc.

His Father JAMES HENRY WARD   Mother's Maiden Name OLPHA BERTRICE MOORE

Wife's Full Maiden Name MARY ELIZABETH DULIN

Wife's Data	Day Month Year	City, Town or Place	County or Province, etc.	State or Country	Add. Info. on Wife
Birth	9 APR 1945	EL PASO	EL PASO	TEX.	
Chr'nd					
Death					
Burial					

Places of Residence
Occupation if other than Housewife   Church Affiliation BAPTIST
Other husbands, if any. No. (1)(2) etc.   (1) FRANKIE JOE WILSON

Her Father WALTER BRYANT DULIN SR   Mother's Maiden Name BLANCHE MAPLE CURREY

Sex	Children's Names in Full		Day Month Year	City, Town or Place	County or Province, etc.	State or Country
1	MARY KAY WILSON Spouse: LESLIE JACK RAGAN	Birth Mar. Death Burial	11 FEB 1966 18 APR 1986	ODESSA DENVER CITY	ECTOR YOAKUM	TEX. TEX.
2	STACEY RENEE WILSON Spouse: BRETT ALAN JACKSON	Birth Mar. Death Burial	6 AUG 1967 21 DEC 1985	ODESSA DENVER CITY	ECTOR YOAKUM	TEX. TEX.
3	TOMMY JOE WILSON	Birth Mar. Death Burial	8 OCT 1971	HOBBS	LEA	N.M.

THE MAN MENTIONED IN THIS ARTICLE IS MY SON ROGER WILSON WARD OF SALT LAKE CITY.

Retired McMurry professor's work led to your quartz watch

By JIM CONLEY
Senior Staff Writer

Anyone who tunes a modern radio or operates fancy military electronics gear such as radar is using something developed partly by Abilene's Dr. Virgil Bottom.

In fact, anyone who owns a quartz watch or clock is using something the retired McMurry College professor of physics helped develop.

That's because Bottom, who taught at McMurry from 1958 to 1973, is one of the world's pioneers and foremost authorities on quartz crystal design.

Those are the little crystals which are vibrated mechanically from thousands of times to 100 million times a second or more to determine the frequencies of modern radios and such.

The crystals' replacement of the old bulky copper wires and related radio devices has allowed modern communications gear to be as small as it is.

Bottom's honors in his field are extensive and enduring enough to have earned him the "Man of the Year" award this year from the Quartz Devices Section of the Electronic Industries Association.

That's the association of the nation's electronics manufacturers who produce the radios, TVs, radar and other diverse items.

Bottom virtually "wrote the book" on quartz crystals. His text, "Introduction to Quartz Crystal Design," published in 1982 as an outgrowth of many other publications he has written, is used as a standard reference in the field.

His contributions to the development of the quartz crystal over the past 45 years have led to him still being in demand to explain many facets of quartz technology not only to students but also to professional engineers and technicians around the world.

Since "retiring," he has traveled to such places as Hong Kong and Singapore to give in-house training seminars on the manufacture and design of quartz crystal units.

Bottom, of 3441 High Meadows, said his seminars are usually for electrical engineers who go into their field without having much training in the quartz crystal field.

Although Bottom is even credited with six individual patents, he doesn't take credit for any fantastic discoveries, saying he's only "part of the chain" of technological development in his field.

"I think if I made contributions to the field, it's been my students," he said. "Up to half the people in the field have been my students, either in college or in seminars. And in many cases, they are now the leaders in their field."

He mentioned, for example, that former student Roger Ward has done a lot of important work on the tiny quartz crystals that have revolutionized the wrist watch industry.

These little crystals, so small that one or two dozen might be needed to cover someone's little fingernail, are

Gerald Ewing/Reporter-News

Crystal gazing: Dr. Virgil Bottom examines the type of man-made crystals which have revolutionized electronic communications.

actually tiny tuning forks, said Bottom.

The quartz crystal tuning forks are vibrated 32,768 times per minute to make a watch run, said Bottom.

That compares to the crystals in broadcast stations, which are vibrated at much higher rates. Bottom said that a radio station which holds 750 on the AM dial would have crystals vibrated at 750,000 times per second. Station 101 FM, however, has crystals vibrated mechanically at 101 million times per second.

Since retiring from McMurry, Bottom estimates he has given intensive training about quartz crystals to about 750 people.

He said most of the people were graduate electrical engineers because Northern Illinois University is the nation's only college that even has a course in the specialty — even though the subject is one that hundreds of engineers eventually need much more information on.

FAMILY GROUP No. _____

This Information Obtained From:

Husband's Full Name ROGER WILSON WARD

Husband's Data	Day	Month	Year	City, Town or Place	County or Province, etc.	State or Country	Add. Info. on Husband
Birth	02	DEC	1944	PARIS	LAMAR	TEX.	
Chr'nd							
Mar.	18	Aug	1967	PAMPA	GRAY	TEX.	
Death							
Burial							

Places of Residence
Occupation PHYSICIST   Church Affiliation METHODIST   Military Rec.
Other wives, if any. No. (1) (2) etc. (2) KIMBERLEY ELAINE LOHMAN
His Father ALVIN LAVELL WARD   Mother's Maiden Name ANNA MURIEL MILLER

Wife's Full Maiden Name PATRICIA ELAINE (Ann) LAMBRIGHT

Wife's Data	Day	Month	Year	City, Town or Place	County or Province, etc.	State or Country	Add. Info. on Wife
Birth	20	MAY	1947	PAMPA	GRAY	TEX.	DIVORCED IN 1979
Chr'nd							
Death							
Burial							

Compiler
Address
City, State
Date

Places of Residence
Occupation if other than Housewife BARRY   Church Affiliation METHODIST
Other husbands, if any. No. (1) (2) etc. (2) ~~BART~~ BOLLN
Her Father B. J. LAMBRIGHT   Mother's Maiden Name FRANCIS COTTON

Sex	Children's Names in Full (Arrange in order of birth)	Children's Data	Day	Month	Year	City, Town or Place	County or Province, etc.	State or Country	Add. Info. on Children
1	NO ISSUE / Full Name of Spouse	Birth / Mar. / Death / Burial		Billy Jack					
2	Full Name of Spouse	Birth / Mar. / Death / Burial							
3	Full Name of Spouse	Birth / Mar. / Death / Burial							
4	Full Name of Spouse	Birth / Mar. / Death / Burial							
5	Full Name of Spouse	Birth / Mar. / Death / Burial							
6	Full Name of Spouse	Birth / Mar. / Death / Burial							
7	Full Name of Spouse	Birth / Mar. / Death / Burial							
8	Full Name of Spouse	Birth / Mar. / Death / Burial							
9	Full Name of Spouse	Birth / Mar. / Death / Burial							
10	Full Name of Spouse	Birth / Mar. / Death / Burial							

*If married more than once No. each mar. (1) (2) etc. and list in "Add. info. on children" column. Use reverse side for additional children, other notes, references or information.

The Ward Family History
Page 78

FAMILY GROUP NO. _____ **Husband's Full Name** ROGER WILSON WARD

Husband's Data	Day Month Year	City, Town or Place	County or Province, etc.	State or Country	Add. Info.
Birth	02 Dec 1944	PARIS	LAMAR	TEX.	
Chr'nd					
Mar.	04 May 1979	ORANGE	ORANGE	CAL.	
Death					
Burial					

Places of Residence: TEXAS, IND., CAL., COL., FLORIDA, UTAH, COLO
Occupation: PHYSICIST   Church Affiliation: METHODIST   Military Rec.:
Other wives: (1) PATRICIA ANN LAMBERT
His Father: ALVIN L. WARD   Mother's Maiden Name: ANNA MURIEL MILLER

Wife's Full Maiden Name KIMBERLEY ELAINE LOHMAN

Wife's Data	Day Month Year	City, Town or Place	County or Province, etc.	State or Country	Add. Info. on Wife
Birth	08 Apr 1957	COMPTON	LOS ANGELOS	CAL.	ADOPTED AT BIRTH
Chr'nd					
Death					
Burial					

Places of Residence: CALIF., COL., FLORIDA, UTAH
Occupation if other than Housewife: Church Affiliation:
Other husbands: (1) LAWRENCE EDWARD RYERSON
Her Father: MYRON WILTON LOHMAN   Mother's Maiden Name: CHARLAINE SUE LEWIS

Sex	#	Children's Names in Full	Children's Data	Day Month Year	City, Town or Place	County or Province, etc.	State or Country	Add. Info. on Children
F	1	ADOPTED TARA DEANNE	Birth	12 FEB 1975	ORANGE	ORANGE	CAL.	ADOPTED
m	2	ERIC NEWTON DALTON	Birth	20 SEP 1979	LOVELAND	LARIMER	COL.	

FAMILY GROUP No.		Husband's Full Name LLOYD DALE BOULTER				
This Information Obtained From:	Husband's Data	Day Month Year	City, Town or Place	County or Province, etc.	State or Country	Add. Info. on Husband
	Birth	26 SEP 1946	BROWNFIELD	TERRY	TEX.	
	Chr'nd					
	Mar.	16 SEP 1967	DENVER CITY	YOAKUM	TEX.	
	Death					
	Burial					
	Places of Residence					
	Occupation ABSTRACT		Church Affiliation CHURCH OF CHRIST Military Rec.			
	Other wives, if any. No. (1) (2) etc. Make separate sheet for each mar.					
	His Father LLOYD LEROY BOULTER		Mother's Maiden Name EDITH MERL DONLEY			

Wife's Full Maiden Name MYRNA JANE WARD

	Wife's Data	Day Month Year	City, Town or Place	County or Province, etc.	State or Country	Add. Info. on Wife
	Birth	16 AUG 1949	FORT WORTH	TARRANT	TEX.	
	Chr'nd					
	Death					
	Burial					
Compiler	Places of Residence					
Address	Occupation if other than Housewife		Church Affiliation CHURCH OF CHRIST			
City, State	Other husbands, if any. No. (1) (2) etc. Make separate sheet for each mar.					
Date	Her Father ALVIN LAVELL WARD		Mother's Maiden Name ANNA MURIEL MILLER			

Sex	Children's Names in Full (Arrange in order of birth)	Children's Data	Day Month Year	City, Town or Place	County or Province, etc.	State or Country	Add. Info. on Children
1	LLOYD JAMES	Birth	21 APR 1968	DENVER CITY	YOAKUM	TEX.	
	Full Name of Spouse	Mar.					
		Death					
		Burial					
2	EMILY DIANNA	Birth	29 SEP 1976	DENVER CITY	YOAKUM	TEX.	
	Full Name of Spouse	Mar.					
		Death					
		Burial					

Eagle Scout honor........

JIM BOULTER [left] with John Madden, Denver City's Scoutmaster for Troop #777, holds the medals and patches to be presented to him during the Court of Honor to be held in February. Jim says it has taken him about two years to finish the 21 merits he needed to earn the Eagle Scout Honor. He is a freshman at Denver City High School. PRESSfoto

Jim Boulter attains rank of Eagle Scout

By Linda Jones
Staff Writer

Jim Boulter has become the 25th Eagle Scout of Denver City's Boy Scout Troop #777. He is the son of Mr. and Mrs. Dale Boulter. He was born and raised mostly in the Denver City area except for about five years. He is an active member of the Denver City Church of Christ.

The highest rank obtainable while a Boy Scout is to become an Eagle Scout. Only one out of 100 boys who become Boy Scouts in America reach the rank. Jim was the 4th in 1982 to become an Eagle Scout from the Denver City Troop.

There are 21 required merit badges a Scout has to complete on the Eagle trail. He completed approximately 22 or 23 in all. Some of the badges he received were: First Aid, Safety, Citizenship in the Community, Nation and World; Emergency Preparedness, Camping, Personal Management, Wilderness survival and life Saving. Jim says the Life Saving badge was the hardest for him to complete.

On the trail, Scouts select an Eagle Scout Project and the one Jim completed was the "Bicycle Safety Rodeo" held last September in Denver City.

Jim attended the National Boy Scout Jamboree held at Fort A.P. Hill Virginia in 1981 with the South Plains Council in Lubbock. About 96 boys with the council attended from this area of which DC had the most attending from one single troop. He was albe to work on his merit badges at the Jamboree and placed first in piano solo and first in vocal solo there.

He says it took about 2½ years to complete all the things for his badges in becoming on Eagle Scout.

He is a Freshman at Denver City High School and has been All-Region Band and Choir for two years in a row. He's on the Student Council, in the Stage Band and an Honor Student. He is involved in Persuasive Speaking, UIL, also in Sole UIL in four categories.

Leaders of Denver City's Boy Scout Troop are John Madden, Scoutmaster, Dale Boulter, Terry Maynard and C.G. Hulse, Assistant Scoutmasters and Randy Gooch, Troop chairman.

DC Girl Scouts begin cookie sale

The Annual Girl Scout Cookie Sale by Denver City troops began Friday and will continue through Sunday, Feb. 13, announce local Girl Scout

FAMILY GROUP No. ___

This Information Obtained From:

Husband's Full Name: MICHAEL DANE FUNDERBURK

Husband's Data	Day Month Year	City, Town or Place	County or Province, etc.	State or Country	Add. Info. on Husband
Birth	17 MAR 1960	ALEXANDERIA	RAPIDES	LA.	
Chr'nd					
Mar.					
Death					
Burial					

Places of Residence:
Occupation: | Church Affiliation: | Military Rec.:
Other wives, if any.

His Father: TROY WINFORD FUNDERBURK **Mother's Maiden Name:** JOYCE LILLIAN PETERS

Wife's Full Maiden Name: MARY KAY WILSON (WARD)

Wife's Data	Day Month Year	City, Town or Place	County or Province, etc.	State or Country	Add. Info. on Wife
Birth	11 FEB 1966	ODESSA	ECTOR	TEX.	
Chr'nd					
Death					
Burial					

Places of Residence:
Occupation if other than Housewife: | Church Affiliation:

Her Father: FRANKIE JOE WILSON **Mother's Maiden Name:** MARY ELIZABETH DULIN

Sex	Children's Names in Full (Arrange in order of birth)	Children's Data	Day Month Year	City, Town or Place	County or Province, etc.	State or Country	Add. Info. on Children
1	KEIGAN DANIELLE	Birth	3 AUG 1984	DENVER CITY	YOAKUM	TEX.	
		Mar. / Death / Burial					
2		Birth / Mar. / Death / Burial					
3		Birth / Mar. / Death / Burial					
4		Birth / Mar. / Death / Burial					
5		Birth / Mar. / Death / Burial					
6		Birth / Mar. / Death / Burial					
7		Birth / Mar. / Death / Burial					
8		Birth / Mar. / Death / Burial					
9		Birth / Mar. / Death / Burial					
10		Birth / Mar. / Death					

The Ward Family History

FAMILY GROUP No. ___ **Husband's Full Name** LESLIE JACK RAGAN JR

This Information Obtained From:

Husband's Data	Day Month Year	City, Town or Place	County or Province, etc.	State or Country	Add. Info. on Husband
Birth	31 JUL 1964	ALBUQUERQUE	BERNALILLO	N.M.	
Chr'nd					
Mar.					
Death					
Burial					

Places of Residence

Occupation Church Affiliation Military Rec.

His Father LESLIE JACK RAGAN SR. Mother's Maiden Name CATHREN WEST ARNOLD

Wife's Full Maiden Name MARY KAY WILSON (WARD)

Wife's Data	Day Month Year	City, Town or Place	County or Province, etc.	State or Country	Add. Info. on Wife
Birth	11 FEB 1966	ODESSA	ECTOR	TEX.	
Chr'nd					
Death					
Burial					

Places of Residence

Occupation if other than Housewife Church Affiliation

Her Father FRANKIE JOE WILSON Mother's Maiden Name MARY ELIZABETH DULIN

Children

#	Child's Name	Event	Day Month Year	City, Town or Place	County or Province	State or Country
1	JORDON KAHL	Birth	19 OCT 1987	LUBBOCK	LUBOCK	TEX.

FAMILY GROUP No. _____

Husband's Full Name BRETT ALAN JACKSON

This Information Obtained From:

Husband's Data	Day Month Year	City, Town or Place	County or Province, etc.	State or Country	Add. Info. on Husband
Birth	10 NOV 1965	EASTLAND	EASTLAND	TEX.	
Chr'nd					
Mar.	21 Dec. 1985	DENVER CITY	YOAKUM	TEX.	
Death					
Burial					

Places of Residence

Occupation   Church Affiliation METHODIST   Military Rec.

Other wives, if any. No. (1) (2) etc. Make separate sheet for each mar.

His Father JAMES MARLYN JACKSON   Mother's Maiden Name TIA WANNA ALFORD

Wife's Full Maiden Name STACEY RENEE WILSON (WARD)

Wife's Data	Day Month Year	City, Town or Place	County or Province, etc.	State or Country	Add. Info. on Wife
Birth	6 AUG 1967	ODESSA	ECTOR	TEX.	
Chr'nd					
Death					
Burial					

Compiler   Places of Residence
Address   Occupation if other than Housewife   Church Affiliation BAPTIST
City, State
Date   Her Father FRANKIE JOE WILSON   Mother's Maiden Name MARY ELIZABETH DULIN

Sex	Children's Names in Full (Arrange in order of birth)	Children's Data	Day Month Year	City, Town or Place	County or Province, etc.	State or Country	Add. Info. on Children
M	1 CHRISTOPHER BRETT	Birth	31 Dec. 1988	LUBBOCK	LUBBOCK	TEXAS	
	Full Name of Spouse	Mar.					
		Death					
		Burial					
	2	Birth					
	Full Name of Spouse	Mar.					
		Death					
		Burial					
	3	Birth					
	Full Name of Spouse	Mar.					
		Death					
		Burial					
	4	Birth					
	Full Name of Spouse	Mar.					
		Death					
		Burial					
	5	Birth					
	Full Name of Spouse	Mar.					
		Death					
		Burial					
	6	Birth					
	Full Name of Spouse	Mar.					
		Death					
		Burial					
	7	Birth					
	Full Name of Spouse	Mar.					
		Death					
		Burial					
	8	Birth					
	Full Name of Spouse	Mar.					
		Death					
		Burial					

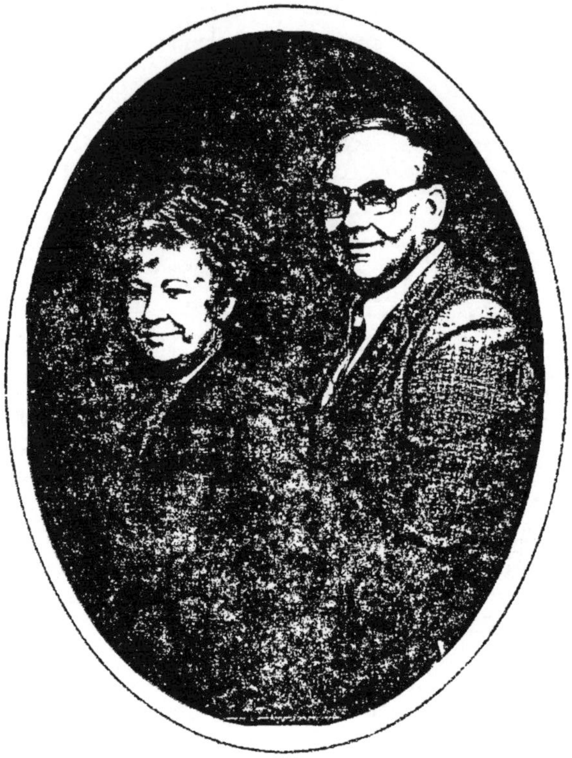

DONALD GLENN WARD AND HIS WIFE MOLLY RUTH BRASHER

Family Group No. ___

Husband's Full Name: DONALD GLYNN WARD

Husband's Data	Day Month Year	City, Town or Place	County or Province, etc.	State or Country	Add. Info. on Husband
Birth	13 JUL 1933	O'DONNELL	LYNN	TEX.	
Chr'nd					
Mar.	15 JUN 1956	SEAGRAVES	GAINS	TEX.	
Death					
Burial					

Places of Residence
Occupation: FARMER   Church Affiliation: METHODIST   Military Rec.

His Father: JAMES HENRY WARD   Mother's Maiden Name: OLPHA BERTRICE MOORE

Wife's Full Maiden Name: MOLLY RUTH BRASHER

Wife's Data	Day Month Year	City, Town or Place	County or Province, etc.	State or Country	Add. Info. on Wife
Birth	28 SEP 1941				
Chr'nd					
Death					
Burial					

Places of Residence
Occupation if other than Housewife   Church Affiliation: METHODIST

Her Father: MARVIN E. BRASHER   Mother's Maiden Name: ERMA ESTELL GREEN

Sex	Children's Names in Full (Arrange in order of birth)	Children's Data	Day Month Year	City, Town or Place	County or Province, etc.	State or Country
1	JIMMY DON Spouse: JAN KAY WALKER	Birth Mar. Death Burial	14 MAR 1957 12 FEB 1977	Seminole SEAGRAVES	GAINS GAINS	TEX. TEX.
2	AARON MAX Spouse: DONNA JANE BELKNAP	Birth Mar. Death Burial	3 MAR 1959	SEMINOLE SEAGRAVES	GAINS GAINS	TEX. TEX.
3	JERRY TED Spouse: DONA ELINE BAILEY	Birth Mar. Death Burial	25 NOV 1961 02 AUG 1980	SEMINOLE BROWNFIELD	GAINS TERRY	TEX. TEX.
4	PAMALA DAWN Spouse: CECIL ORBIA CALLOWAY	Birth Mar. Death Burial	3 SEP 1963 16 AUG 1988	SEMINOLE SEAGRAVES	GAINS GAINS	TEX. TEX.

FAMILY GROUP No. ___

Husband's Full Name: JIMMY DON WARD

Husband's Data	Day Month Year	City, Town or Place	County or Province, etc.	State or Country	Add. Info. on Hu
Birth	14 MAR 1957	SEMINOLE	GAINS	TEX.	
Chr'nd					
Mar.	12 FEB 1977	SEAGRAVES	GAINS	TEX.	
Death					
Burial					

Places of Residence
Occupation: TEACHER Church Affiliation: METHODIST Military Rec.

His Father: DONALD GLYNN WARD Mother's Maiden Name: MOLLY RUTH BRASHER

Wife's Full Maiden Name: JAN KAY WALKER

Wife's Data	Day Month Year	City, Town or Place	County or Province, etc.	State or Country	Add. Info. on Wife
Birth	18 JUN 1959	HOBBS	LEE	N.M.	
Chr'nd					
Death					
Burial					

Places of Residence
Occupation if other than Housewife: NURSE Church Affiliation: METHODIST

Her Father: J. R. WALKER JR. Mother's Maiden Name: DORATHY MAE DONAGHY

Sex	Children's Names in Full	Children's Data	Day Month Year	City, Town or Place	County or Province, etc.	State or Country	Add. Info. on Children
F	1. JULA KAY	Birth	21 MAR 1979	BROWNFIELD	TERRY	TEX.	
F	2. JENNIFER JANAE	Birth	29 MAY 1981	PLAINVIEW	HALE	TEXAS	

FAMILY GROUP No. ___

Husband's Full Name: AARON MAX WARD

This Information Obtained From:

Husband's Data	Day Month Year	City, Town or Place	County or Province, etc.	State or Country	Add. Info. on Husband
Birth	3 MAR 1959	SEMINOLE	GAINS	TEX.	
Chr'nd					
Mar.					
Death					
Burial					

Places of Residence
Occupation: ELECTRICAN Church Affiliation: BAPTEST Military Rec.
Other wives, if any. No. (1) (2) etc. Make separate sheet for each mar.

His Father: DONALD GLYNN WARD Mother's Maiden Name: MOLLY RUTH BRASHER

Wife's Full Maiden Name: DONNA JOANE BELKNAP

Wife's Data	Day Month Year	City, Town or Place	County or Province, etc.	State or Country	Add. Info. on Wife
Birth					
Chr'nd					
Death					
Burial					

Places of Residence
Occupation if other than Housewife Church Affiliation: BAPTIST
Other husbands, if any. No. (1) (2) etc.

Her Father: ALONZO MARION BELKNAP Mother's Maiden Name: DORIS LAURA

Sex	Children's Names in Full (Arrange in order of birth)	Children's Data	Day Month Year	City, Town or Place	County or Province, etc.	State or Country	Add. Info. on Children
M	1 AARON MICHAEL	Birth	30 OCT 1987	LUBBOCK	LUBBOCK	TEX.	
		Mar.					
		Death					
		Burial					
	2	Birth					
		Mar.					
		Death					
		Burial					
	3	Birth					
		Mar.					
		Death					
		Burial					
	4	Birth					
		Mar.					
		Death					
		Burial					
	5	Birth					
		Mar.					
		Death					
		Burial					
	6	Birth					
		Mar.					
		Death					
		Burial					
	7	Birth					
		Mar.					
		Death					
		Burial					
	8	Birth					
		Mar.					
		Death					
		Burial					
	9	Birth					
		Mar.					
		Death					
		Burial					
	10	Birth					
		Mar.					
		Death					
		Burial					

*If married more than once No. each mar. (1) (2) etc. and list in "Add. info. on children" column. Use reverse side for additional children, other notes, references or information.

FAMILY GROUP NO.

Husband's Full Name: JERRY TED WARD

Husband's Data	Day Month Year	City, Town or Place	County or Province, etc.	State or Country
Birth	25 NOV 1961	SEMINOLE	GAINS	TEX.
Chr'nd				
Mar.		BROWNFIELD	TERRY	TEX.
Death				
Burial				

Places of Residence:
Occupation: C.P.A.   **Church Affiliation:** METHODIST   **Military Rec.:**

His Father: DONALD GLYNN WARD   **Mother's Maiden Name:** MOLLY RUTH BRASHER

Wife's Full Maiden Name: DONA ELINE BAILEY

Wife's Data	Day Month Year	City, Town or Place	County or Province, etc.	State or Country
Birth	10 JAN 1961	BROWNFIELD	TERRY	TEX.
Chr'nd				
Death				
Burial				

Places of Residence:
Occupation if other than Housewife: **Church Affiliation:** METHODIST

Her Father: LARRY RIVERS BAILEY   **Mother's Maiden Name:** JACQULINE FULGHAM

Children

Sex	Children's Names in Full	Event	Day Month Year	City, Town or Place	County or Province, etc.	State or Country
F	1. AMANDA RANEE	Birth	9 MAR 1982	SAN ANGELO	TOM GREEN	TEX.
F	2. MEAGAN MICHELLE	Birth	16 AUG 1984	DENVER CITY	YOAKUM	TEX.
	3. STEPHANI LeANN	Birth	1 MAY 1987	ANDREWS	ANDREWS	TEX.

The Ward Family History

FAMILY GROUP No. _____

Husband's Full Name CECIL ORBIA CALLOWAY

Husband's Data	Day Month Year	City, Town or Place	County or Province, etc.	State or Country	Add. Info. on Husb.
Birth	18 AUG 1954	LUBBOCK	LUBBOCK	TEX.	
Chr'nd					
Mar.	16 AUG 1988	SEAGRAVES	GAINS	TEX.	
Death					
Burial					

Places of Residence
Occupation   Church Affiliation   Military Rec.
Other wives, if any. No. (1) (2) etc. Make separate sheet for each mar.

His Father CECIL WAYNE CALLOWAY   Mother's Maiden Name LAFAYNE MOORE

Wife's Full Maiden Name PAMALA DAWN WARD

Wife's Data	Day Month Year	City, Town or Place	County or Province, etc.	State or Country	Add. Info. on Wife
Birth	3 SEP 1963	SEMINOLE	GAINS	TEX.	
Chr'nd					
Death					
Burial					

Places of Residence
Occupation if other than Housewife NURSE   Church Affiliation METHODIST
Other husbands, if any. No. (1) (2) etc. Make separate sheet for each mar.

Her Father DONALD GLYNN WARD   Mother's Maiden Name MOLLY RUTH BRASHER

Sex	Children's Names in Full (Arrange in order of birth)		Day Month Year	City, Town or Place	County or Province, etc.	State or Country	Add. Info. on Children
1	DAREL BRINT	Birth	29 NOV 1988	SAN ANGELO	TOM GREEN	TEX.	
	Full Name of Spouse	Mar.					
		Death					
		Burial					

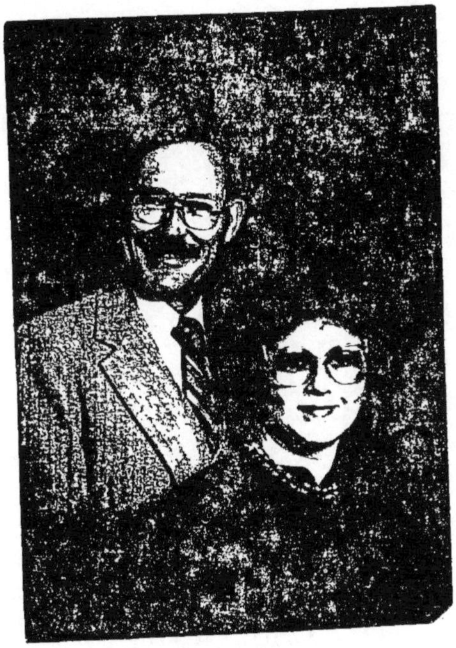

DR. CHARLES RICHARD WARD, and HIS WIFE NORMA FAY (MARTIN) WARD.

Family Group Record

Husband's Full Name: CHARLES RICHARD WARD (DR)

Husband's Data	Day Month Year	City, Town or Place	County or Province, etc.	State or Country	Add. Info. on Husband
Birth	25 MAR 1940	TAHOKA	LYNN	TEX.	
Chr'nd					
Mar.	27 AUG 1961	SEAGRAVES	GAINS	TEX.	
Death					
Burial					

Places of Residence:
Occupation: TEACHER Church Affiliation: METHODIST Military Rec.:

His Father: JAMES HENRY WARD Mother's Maiden Name: OLPHA BERTRICE MOORE

Wife's Full Maiden Name: NORMA FAYE MARTIN

Wife's Data	Day Month Year	City, Town or Place	County or Province, etc.	State or Country	Add. Info. on Wife
Birth	2 JUL 1943	BROWNFIELD	TERRY	TEXAS	
Chr'nd					
Death					
Burial					

Places of Residence:
Occupation if other than Housewife: Church Affiliation: NAZARENE

Her Father: ANDREW BERT MARTIN Mother's Maiden Name: EULA MAY STEPHENSON

Children

Sex	Children's Names in Full	Data	Day Month Year	City, Town or Place	County or Province, etc.	State or Country
F	1. BEVERLY JAN — Spouse: BRUCE EDWARD CAMPBELL	Birth	27 MAR 1962	LUBBOCK	LUBBOCK	TEX.
		Mar.	3 JUN 1983	ARTESIA	EDDY	N.M.
M	2. CHARLES EDWARD — Spouse: MICHELLE LYNN McHAM	Birth	3 SEP 1965	LUBBOCK	LUBBOCK	TEX.
		Mar.	19 SEP 1987	LAS CRUCES	DONA ANA	N.M.

FAMILY GROUP No. ___

Husband's Full Name: BRUCE EDWARD CAMPBELL

Husband's Data	Day Month Year	City, Town or Place	County or Province	State or Country	Add. Info. on Hus
Birth	27 DEC 1959	ARTESIA	EDDY	N.M.	
Chr'nd					
Mar.	3 JUL 1983	ARTESIA	EDDY	N.M.	
Death					
Burial					

Places of Residence:
Occupation: CHEM. APPL. Church Affiliation: NAZARENE Military Rec.
Other wives: (1) LESLIEE PATERSON
His Father: BILL DEAN CAMPBELL Mother's Maiden Name: MARELENE JOYCE MILLER

Wife's Full Maiden Name: BEVERLY JAN WARD

Wife's Data	Day Month Year	City, Town or Place	County or Province	State or Country	Add. Info. on Wife
Birth	27 MAR 1962	LUBBOCK	LUBBOCK	TEX.	
Chr'nd					
Death					
Burial					

Places of Residence:
Occupation if other than Housewife: Church Affiliation: NAZARENE
Other husbands:
Her Father: CHARLES RICHARD WARD Mother's Maiden Name: NORMA FAYE MARTIN

Sex	#	Children's Names in Full	Event	Day Month Year	City, Town or Place	County or Province	State or Country
M	1	JEREMY SCOTT	Birth	2 AUG 1982	ROSWELL	CHAVES	N.M.
M	2	BRUCE EDWARD JR.	Birth	30 SEP 1983	ROSWELL	CHAVES	N.M.
M	3	NICHOLAS ALLAN	Birth	20 APR 1985	ROSWELL	CHAVES	N.M.
F	4	AMBER NICHOLE	Birth	15 JUL 1987	CARLSBAD	EDDY	N.M.

Family Group Record

Husband's Full Name: BRUCE EDWARD CAMPBELL

Husband's Data	Day Month Year	City, Town or Place	County or Province	State or Country
Birth	27 DEC 1959	ARTESIA	EDDY	N.M.
Chr'nd				
Mar.				
Death				
Burial				

Places of Residence:
Occupation: Church Affiliation: Military Rec.:
Other wives: (2) BEVERLY JAN WARD
His Father: BILL DEAN CAMPBELL Mother's Maiden Name: MARELENE JOYCE MILLER

Wife's Full Maiden Name: JAN LESLEY PATERSON

Wife's Data	Day Month Year	City, Town or Place	County or Province	State or Country
Birth				
Chr'nd				
Death				
Burial				

Children

Sex	Name	Event	Day Month Year	City, Town or Place	County	State
F	1. CHARLA CHERYCE	Birth	26 AUG 1978	TWIN FALLS	TWIN FALLS	IDA.

FAMILY GROUP No.

Husband's Full Name: CHARLES EDWARD WARD

Husband's Data	Day Month Year	City, Town or Place	County or Province, etc.	State or Country
Birth	03 SEP 1965	LUBBOCK	LUBBOCK	TEX.
Chr'nd				
Mar.	19 sep 1987	LAS CRUCES	DONA ANA	N.M.
Death				
Burial				

Church Affiliation: NAZARENE

His Father: CHARLES RICHARD WARD **Mother's Maiden Name:** NORMA FAYE MARTIN

Wife's Full Maiden Name: MICHELLE LYNN McHAM

Wife's Data	Day Month Year	City, Town or Place	County or Province, etc.	State or Country
Birth	15 OCT 1965	NORRISTOWN	MONTGOMERY	PA.
Chr'nd				
Death				
Burial				

Church Affiliation: NAZARENE

Her Father: JOE ANTOM McHAM **Mother's Maiden Name:** JOAN NANCY BREWER

Children

1. M — JARON EDWARD

	Day Month Year	City, Town or Place	County or Province, etc.	State or Country
Birth	25 JUL 1988	LAS CRUCES	DONA ANA	N.M.

The State of Texas,
County of Young

To any Regularly Licensed or Ordained Minister of the Gospel, Jewish Rabbi, Judge of the District or County Court, or any Justice of the Peace in and for _____ County, Texas—GREETING:

YOU ARE HEREBY AUTHORIZED TO CELEBRATE THE RITES OF MATRIMONY Between Mr. G. M. Ward and Mrs. Viola Lazenby and make due return to the Clerk of the County Court of said County within sixty days thereafter, certifying your action under this License.

WITNESS MY OFFICIAL SIGNATURE AND SEAL OF OFFICE, At office in _____ the 3rd day of Jany. A. D. 1911.

[SEAL]

J. A. Martin, Clerk County Court Young County, Texas,
By R. W. King, Deputy.

I, N. C. Wright, certify that on the third day of Jan. A. D. 1911, I united in Marriage Mr. G. M. Ward and Mrs. Viola Lazenby the parties above named.

WITNESS MY HAND This fourth day of Jany. A. D. 1911.

N. C. Wright
Young City, Texas

RETURNED AND FILED FOR RECORD The 5th day of Jany. A. D. 1911, and recorded the 18th day of Dec. A. D. 1911.

J. A. Martin, County Clerk
By R. A. King, Deputy

1910 CENSUS INDEX FAMILY

TEXAS

HEAD OF FAMILY	Ward Marvin	E.D. 154	SHEET 167
COLOR W	AGE 30	BIRTHPLACE	VOL 89
COUNTY Knox		CITY	

OTHER MEMBERS OF FAMILY

NAME	RELATION	AGE	BIRTHPLACE
Nancy	D	5	Okla
Laura Mae	Li	29	
Gladys	Ni	6	

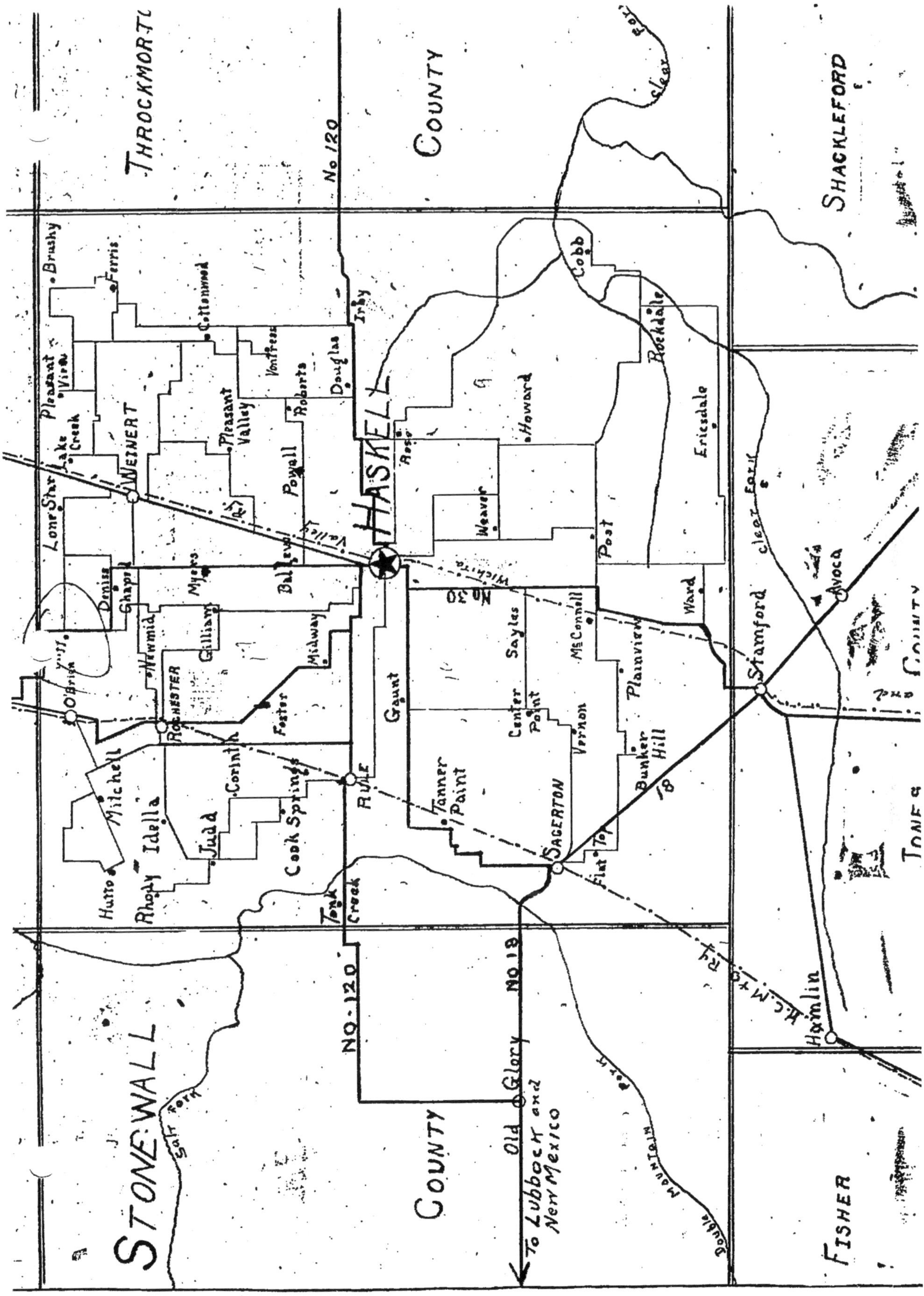
THROCKMORTON
COUNTY
SHACKLEFORD
No 120
Brushy
Ferris
Cottonwood
Pleasant View
Lake Creek
Vontress
Roberts
Douglas
Irby
Cobb
Rockdale
Howard
Ericsdale
Pleasant Valley
Powell
WEINERT
Lone Star
HASKELL
Rose
Weaver
Post
Ward
Stamford
Avoca
Clear Fork
Denis
Chapel
Myers
Ballew
Newmid
Gilliam
Midway
O'Brien
ROCHESTER
Foster
Gaunt
No 30
Sayles
McConnell
Plainview
Center Point
Vernon
Bunker Hill
Mitchell
Idella
Corinth
Judd
Cook Springs
RULE
Tanner Point
SAGERTON
Flat Top
Hutto
Rhody
Tonk Creek
NO. 120
NO 18
18
Hamlin
Old Glory
To Lubbock and New Mexico
STONEWALL
COUNTY
Salt Fork
FISHER
JONES
COUNTY
Double Mountain Fork
Wichita Valley
K.C.M.&O. Ry

22

T. M. Ward et ux To C. C. Cargill

The State of Texas,
County of Tray

Know all Men by these Presents:

That we, T. M. Ward and wife Hattie Ward, of the County of ___ State of Texas, for and in consideration of the sum of One Thousand Dollars, to us paid and secured to be paid by C. C. Cargill as follows: Five Hundred Dollars ($506.00) cash in hand, the receipt of which is hereby acknowledged, and Two Vendor's Lien notes of even date, Note No. 1 for $193 Lawford Dollars payable on January 15th 1910 Note No. 2 for Three Hundred Dollars payable November 1st 1910. The above notes bearing interest at the rate of 8 per centum from date do grant, sell and convey unto the said C. C. Cargill of the county of Tray state of Texas all that certain Lot tract or parcel of land lying and being situated in the county of Tray and State of Texas described as follows to-wit: Beginning at the South East corner of Section No. 1, D. & P. Ry Co. land, thence west 1678 feet to stake, thence North 308 feet thence North 308 feet, thence west 150 feet, thence 33 feet to stake, thence East 150 feet, place of beginning. Being which 300 feet, thence East 150 feet, place of beginning. Being East ½ of Block No. 3 in the Chapman addition to Troy City Tex.

TO HAVE AND TO HOLD the above described premises, together with all and singular the rights and appurtenances thereto in anywise belonging unto the said C. C. Cargill his heirs, executors and administrators, to Warrant and Forever Defend all and singular the said premises unto the said C. C. Cargill his heirs and assigns, against every person whomsoever lawfully claiming or to claim the same or any part thereof.

But it is expressly agreed and stipulated that the Vendor's Lien is retained against the above described property, premises and improvements until the above described note ___, and all interest thereon, are fully paid according to their face and tenor, effect and reading when this deed shall become absolute.

WITNESS our hands at Troy City Texas this 9 day of Sept A. D. 1909

Witnesses at request of Grantor:

T. M. Ward
Hattie Ward

THE STATE OF TEXAS,
County of Tray

BEFORE ME, W. J. Tompkins, Notary Public
T. M. Ward

The Ward Family History

FAMILY GROUP No. ___

Husband's Full Name THOMAS MARVIN WARD

Husband's Data	Day Month Year	City, Town or Place	County or Province, etc.	State or Country	Add. Info. on Husband
Birth	25 may 1879		JOHNSON	TEX.	
Chr'nd					
Mar.	3 JAN 1911	KNOX CITY	KNOX	TEX.	
Death	27 NOV 1936	LUBBOCK	LUBBOCK	TEX.	
Burial	29 NOV 1936	TAHOKA	LYNN	TEX.	

Places of Residence:
Occupation: FARMER   Church Affiliation: Military Rec.:
Other wives, if any: (1) HATTIE ADAMS
His Father: JAMES A. L. WARD   Mother's Maiden Name: REBECKA JANE BAKER

Wife's Full Maiden Name MINNIE VIOLA ALTON

Wife's Data	Day Month Year	City, Town or Place	County or Province, etc.	State or Country	Add. Info. on Wife
Birth	1880	ATKINS	POPE	ARK.	
Chr'nd					
Death	16 AUG 1961	LA PRYOR	ZAVALA	TEX.	
Burial		LA PRYOR	ZAVALA	TEX.	

Places of Residence:
Occupation if other than Housewife: Church Affiliation:
Other husbands, if any:
Her Father: Mother's Maiden Name:

Children

Sex	Children's Names in Full	Data	Day Month Year	City, Town or Place	County or Province	State or Country	Add. Info.
1	ORVILLE LEE LAZENBY	Birth	1902	BONHAM	FANNIN	TEX.	
	Full Name of Spouse	Mar.					
		Death	1963	FORT WORTH	TARENT	TEX.	
		Burial	1963	FORT WORTH	TARENT	TEX.	
2	Willie	Birth	05 JUL 1907	KNOX CITY	KNOX	TEX.	
		Mar.					
		Death					
		Burial					
3	RAYMOND	Birth	1914	KNOX CITY	KNOX	TEX.	
	THOMAS MARVIN	Mar.	18 JAN 1914				
		Death	1931	O'DONNELL	LYNN	TEX.	
		Burial	1931	O'DONNELL		TEX.	
4	E.C.	Birth	22 JAN 1920	KNOX CITY	KNOX	TEX.	
	Velda Rea Drummond	Mar.					
		Death					
		Burial					
5	HERBERT EUGENE	Birth	20 OCT 1922	KNOX CITY	KNOX	TEX.	
	CLORITA E. SHOLDERS	Mar.	30 MAR 1947	O'DONNELL	LYN	TEX.	
		Death					
		Burial					
6	JUANITA	Birth	15 Sep 1925	O'DONNELL	LYN	TEX.	
		Mar.					
		Death	3 AUG 1979	GREELY	WELD	COL.	
		Burial	5 AUG 1979	GREELY	WELD	COL.	

FAMILY GROUP No. ___

Husband's Full Name: THOMAS MARVIN WARD

This Information Obtained From:

Husband's Data	Day Month Year	City, Town or Place	County or Province, etc.	State or Country	Add. Info. on Husband
Birth	25 MAY 1879	PARKER	JOHNSON	TEX.	
Chr'nd					
Mar.	03 JAN 1911	KNOX CITY	KNOX	TEX.	
Death	27 NOV 1936	LUBBOCK	LUBBOCK	TEX.	
Burial	29 NOV 1936	TAHOKA	LYNN	TEX.	

Places of Residence: PARKER, KNOX CITY & O'DONNELL
Occupation: FARMER **Church Affiliation:** **Military Rec.:**
Other wives: (1) HATTIE ADAMS
His Father: JAMES A. L. WARD **Mother's Maiden Name:** REBECKA JANE BAKER

Wife's Full Maiden Name: MINNIE VIOLA ALTON

Wife's Data	Day Month Year	City, Town or Place	County or Province, etc.	State or Country	Add. Info. on Wife
Birth	1880	ATKINS	POPE	ARK.	
Chr'nd					
Death	16 AUG 1961	LA PRYOR	ZAVALA	TEX.	
Burial		LA PRYOR	ZAVALA	TEX.	

Places of Residence: BONHAM, KNOX CITY, O'DONNELL, & LA PRYOR, TEX.
Occupation if other than Housewife: **Church Affiliation:**
Other husbands: (1) CHARLES LAZENBY
Her Father: **Mother's Maiden Name:**

Sex	Children's Names in Full (Arrange in order of birth)	Children's Data	Day Month Year	City, Town or Place	County or Province, etc.	State or Country	Add. Info. on Children
M	1. ORVILLE LEE LAZENBY	Birth	1902	BONHAM	FANNIN	TEX.	THE FIRST 2
	Full Name of Spouse	Mar.					CHILDREN A[RE]
		Death	1963	FORT WORTH	TARRENT	TEX.	MINNIE VIO[LA'S]
		Burial		FORT WORTH		TEX.	FROM HER FI[RST]
F	2. WILLIE LAZENBY	Birth	05 JUL 1907	KNOX CITY	KNOX	TEX.	MARRAGE.
	Full Name of Spouse	Mar.	09 OCT 1930	LOVINGTON	LEE	N.M.	
	MELVIN EAKER	Death					
		Burial					
M	3. RAYMOND WARD	Birth	1914	KNOX CITY	KNOX	TEX.	
	Full Name of Spouse	Mar.					
		Death	1931	O'DONNELL	LYNN	TEX.	
		Burial	1931	TAHOKA	LYNN	TEX.	
M	4. (T. M.) THOMAS MARVIN WARD	Birth	18 JAN 1916	KNOX CITY	KNOX	TEX.	
	Full Name of Spouse	Mar.					
		Death					
		Burial					
M	5. E. C. WARD	Birth	23 JAN 1920	KNOX CITY	KNOX	TEX.	
	Full Name of Spouse	Mar.	01 APR 1939	O'DONNELL	LYNN	TEX.	
	VELDA REE DRUMMOND	Death					
		Burial					
M	6. HERBERT EUGENE WARD	Birth	20 OCT 1922	KNOX CITY	KNOX	TEX.	
	Full Name of Spouse	Mar.	30 MAR 1947	O'DONNELL	LYNN	TEX.	
	CLORITA E. SHOLDERS	Death					
		Burial					
F	7. JUANITA LEE WARD	Birth	15 SEP 1925	O'DONNELL	LYNN	TEX.	
	Full Name of Spouse	Mar.	06 AUG 1945	DENVER	ARAPAHOE	COL.	
	EARNEST RODRIQUES	Death	03 AUG 1979	GREELY	WELD	COL.	
		Burial		GREELY	WELD	COL.	

Family Group Record

Husband's Full Name: ORVILLE LEE LAZENBY

Husband's Data	Day	Month	Year	City, Town or Place	County or Province, etc.	State or Country	Add. Info. on Husband
Birth			1909	KNOX CITY	KNOX	TEX	
Chr'nd							
Mar.							THIS IS A STEP BROTHER TO JIM WARD
Death			1963	FORT WORTH	TARRENT	TEX	
Burial							

Places of Residence:
Occupation: Church Affiliation: Military Rec.:
Other wives, if any.

His Father: LAZENBY   Mother's Maiden Name: MINNIE VIOLA ALTON

Wife's Full Maiden Name:

Wife's Data	Day	Month	Year	City, Town or Place	County or Province, etc.	State or Country	Add. Info. on Wife
Birth							
Chr'nd							
Death							
Burial							

Places of Residence:
Occupation if other than Housewife: Church Affiliation:
Other husbands, if any.

Her Father: Mother's Maiden Name:

FAMILY GROUP No. ___

Husband's Full Name: MELVIN EAKER

Husband's Data	Day Month Year	City, Town or Place	County or Province, etc.	State or Country	Add. Info. on Husband
Birth	03 OCT 1909	BRADY	McCULLOCH	TEX	
Chr'nd					
Mar.	09 OCT 1930	LOVINGTON	LEE	N.M	
Death					
Burial					

Places of Residence:
Occupation: FARMER   Church Affiliation: BAPTIST   Military Rec.

His Father: WILLIAM A. EAKER   Mother's Maiden Name: ANNIE REBECCA DOYLE

Wife's Full Maiden Name: WILLIE LASENBY

Wife's Data	Day Month Year	City, Town or Place	County or Province, etc.	State or Country	Add. Info. on Wife
Birth	05 JUL 1907	KNOX CITY	KNOX	TEX.	
Chr'nd					
Death					
Burial					

Places of Residence:
Occupation if other than Housewife: Church Affiliation: BAPTIST

Her Father: CHARLES LASENBY   Mother's Maiden Name: MINNIE VIOLA ALTOM

Sex	Children's Names in Full	Children's Data	Day Month Year	City, Town or Place	County or Province, etc.	State or Country
M	1. MELVIN EDGAR — Spouse: FRANCES ROSE	Birth / Mar.	01 AUG 1931 / 15 SEP 1951	PLAINS / UVALDE	MEADE / UVALDE	KAN. / TEX.
M	2. KENNETH WAYNE — Spouse: FRANCIS ANN HARTWIG	Birth / Mar.	01 JUL 1937 / 08 SEP 1958	O'DONNELL / WESLACO	LYNN / HIDALGO	TEX. / TEX.
M	3. HAROLD GLYNN — Spouse: KAREN ROCHELLE ROBINSON	Birth / Mar.	15 APR 1941 / 17 JUN 1961	O'DONNELL / LA PRYOR	LYNN / ZAVALA	TEX. / TEX.
M	4. JIMMY LEE — Spouse: JO ANN FOWLER	Birth / Mar.	27 NOV 1964	O'DONNELL / UVALDE	LYNN / UVALDE	TEX. / TEX.

FAMILY GROUP No. ____

Husband's Full Name: MELVIN EDGAR EAKER

This Information Obtained From:

Husband's Data	Day Month Year	City, Town or Place	County or Province, etc.	State or Country	Add. Info. on Husband
Birth	01 AUG 1931	PLAINS	MEAD	KAN.	
Chr'nd					
Mar.	15 SEP 1951	UVALDE	UVALDE	TEX.	
Death					
Burial					

Places of Residence:
Occupation: FARMER Church Affiliation: BAPTIST Military Rec.
Other wives, if any, No. (1) (2) etc.

His Father: MELVIN EAKER Mother's Maiden Name: WILLIE LASENBY

Wife's Full Maiden Name: FRANCIS ROSE

Wife's Data	Day Month Year	City, Town or Place	County or Province, etc.	State or Country	Add. Info. on Wife
Birth					
Chr'nd					
Death					
Burial					

Compiler
Address
City, State
Date

Places of Residence:
Occupation if other than Housewife Church Affiliation: BAPTIST
Other husbands, if any, No. (1) (2) etc.

Her Father: JIM ROSE Mother's Maiden Name: CERESSA HAKETT

Sex	Children's Names in Full	Children's Data	Day Month Year	City, Town or Place	County or Province, etc.	State or Country	Add. Info. on Children
1		Birth / Mar. / Death / Burial					
2		Birth / Mar. / Death / Burial					
3		Birth / Mar. / Death / Burial					
4		Birth / Mar. / Death / Burial					
5		Birth / Mar. / Death / Burial					
6		Birth / Mar. / Death / Burial					
7		Birth / Mar. / Death / Burial					
8		Birth / Mar. / Death / Burial					
9		Birth / Mar. / Death / Burial					
10		Birth / Mar. / Death / Burial					

*If married more than once No. each mar. (1) (2) etc. and list in "Add. info. on children" column. Use reverse side for additional children, other notes, references or information.

FAMILY GROUP No. ___

Husband's Full Name KENNETH WAYNE AKERS

This Information Obtained From:

Husband's Data	Day Month Year	City, Town or Place	County or Province, etc.	State or Country	Add. Info. on Husband
Birth	01 JUL 1937	O'DONNELL	LYNN	TEX	
Chr'nd					
Mar.	08 SEP 1937	WESLACO	HIDALGO	TEX.	
Death					
Burial					

Places of Residence
Occupation FARMER   Church Affiliation BAPTIST   Military Rec.
Other wives, if any. No. (1) (2) etc. Make separate sheet for each mar.

His Father MELVIN EAKER   Mother's Maiden Name WILLIE LASENBY

Wife's Full Maiden Name FRANCIS ANN HARTWIG

Wife's Data	Day Month Year	City, Town or Place	County or Province, etc.	State or Country	Add. Info. on Wife
Birth					
Chr'nd					
Death					
Burial					

Compiler
Address
City, State
Date

Places of Residence
Occupation if other than Housewife   Church Affiliation BAPTIST
Other husbands, if any. No. (1) (2) etc.

Her Father LEWIS HARTWIG   Mother's Maiden Name FRANKIE GOODWIN

Sex	Children's Names in Full (Arrange in order of birth)	Children's Data	Day Month Year	City, Town or Place	County or Province, etc.	State or Country	Add. Info. on Children
1		Birth/Mar./Death/Burial					
2		Birth/Mar./Death/Burial					
3		Birth/Mar./Death/Burial					
4		Birth/Mar./Death/Burial					
5		Birth/Mar./Death/Burial					
6		Birth/Mar./Death/Burial					
7		Birth/Mar./Death/Burial					
8		Birth/Mar./Death/Burial					
9		Birth/Mar./Death/Burial					
10		Birth/Mar./Death/Burial					

FAMILY GROUP No. ____

Husband's Full Name HAROLD GLYNN AKERS

Husband's Data	Day Month Year	City, Town or Place	County or Province, etc.	State or Country	Add. Info. on Husband
Birth	15 APR 1941	O'DONNELL	LYNN	TEX.	
Chr'nd					
Mar.	17 Jun 1961	LA PRYOR	ZAVALA	TEX.	
Death					
Burial					

Places of Residence
Occupation FARMER   Church Affiliation BAPTIST   Military Rec.

His Father MELVIN EAKER   Mother's Maiden Name WILLIE LASENBY

Wife's Full Maiden Name KAREN ROCHELLE ROBINSON

Wife's Data	Day Month Year	City, Town or Place	County or Province, etc.	State or Country	Add. Info. on Wife
Birth					
Chr'nd					
Death					
Burial					

Places of Residence
Occupation if other than Housewife   Church Affiliation BAPRIST

Her Father CECIL CLARENCE ROBINSON   Mother's Maiden Name GLADYS ISABEL GIBBON

FAMILY GROUP No. ___

Husband's Full Name JIMMY LEE EAKER

Husband's Data	Day Month Year	City, Town or Place	County or Province, etc.	State or Country	Add. Info. on Husband
Birth	27 NOV 1964	O'DONNELL	LYNN	TEX.	
Chr'nd					
Mar.		UVALDE	UVALDE	TEX.	
Death					
Burial					

Places of Residence
Occupation FARMER   Church Affiliation BAPTIST   Military Rec.

His Father MELVIN EAKER   Mother's Maiden Name WILLIE LASENBY

Wife's Full Maiden Name JO ANN FOWLER

Her Father LESTER B. FOWLER   Mother's Maiden Name OVID GAY HANKINS

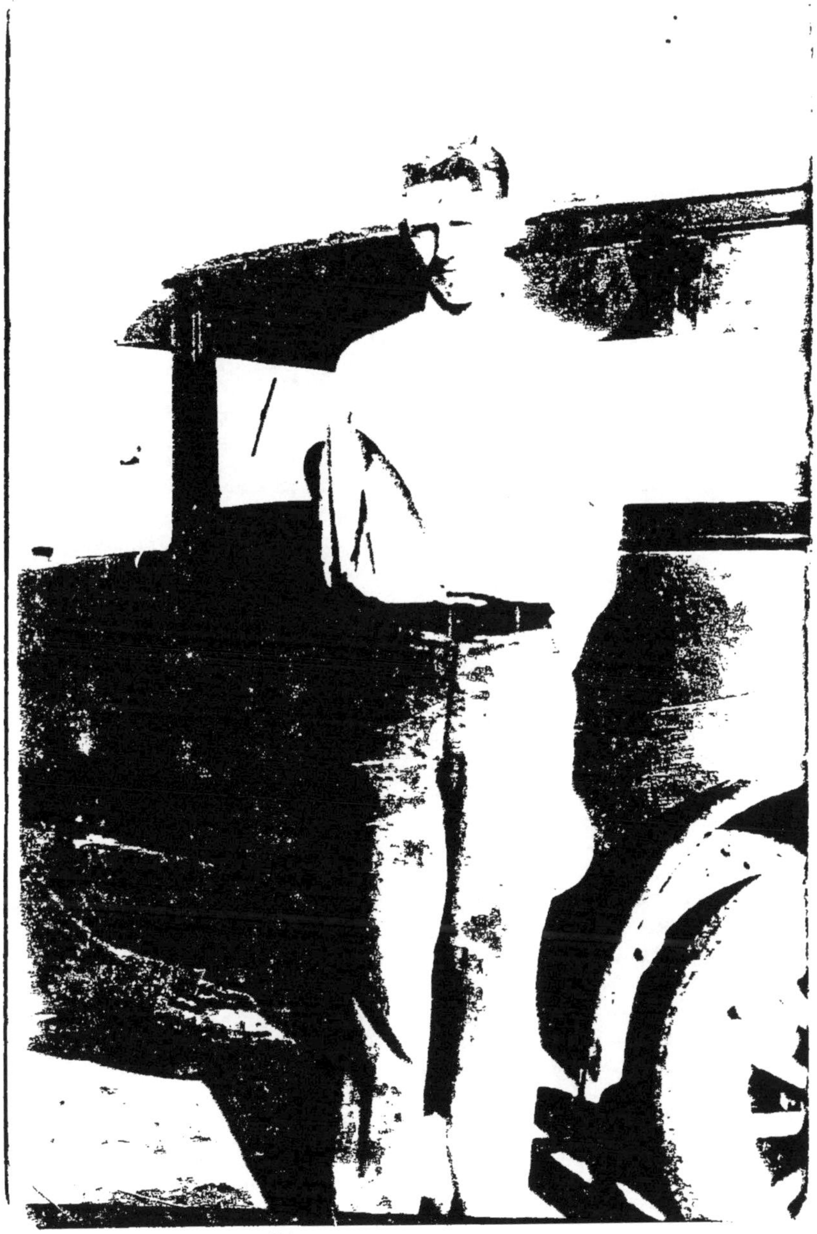

FAMILY GROUP No. _____

Husband's Full Name RAYMOND WARD

This Information Obtained From:

Husband's Data	Day	Month	Year	City, Town or Place	County or Province, etc.	State or Country	Add. Info. on Husband
Birth			1914	KNOX CITY	KNOX	TEX.	
Chr'nd							
Mar.							
Death			1931	ODONNELL	LYNN	TEX.	
Burial			1931	TAHOKA	LYNN	TEX.	

Places of Residence

Occupation _____ Church Affiliation _____ Military Rec. _____

Other wives, if any, No. (1) (2) etc. Make separate sheet for each mar.

His Father THOMAS MARVIN WARD   Mother's Maiden Name MINNIE VIOLA ALTOM

Wife's Full Maiden Name

Wife's Data	Day	Month	Year	City, Town or Place	County or Province, etc.	State or Country	Add. Info. on Wife
Birth							
Chr'nd							
Death							
Burial							

Compiler _____   Places of Residence

Address _____   Occupation if other than Housewife _____ Church Affiliation _____

City, State _____   Other husbands, if any, No. (1) (2) etc.

Date _____   Her Father _____ Mother's Maiden Name _____

FAMILY GROUP No. ___

This Information Obtained From:
E. C. WARD
116 BARRY
UVALDE, TEXAS 78801

Husband's Full Name E. C. WARD

Husband's Data	Day Month Year	City, Town or Place	County or Province, etc.	State or Country	Add. Info. on Husband
Birth	23 JAN 1920	KNOX CITY	KNOX	TEX.	
Chr'nd					
Mar.	01 APR 1939	O'DONNELL	LYNN	TEX.	
Death					
Burial					

Places of Residence
Occupation SALES CLERK Church Affiliation C of CHRIST Military Rec. U.S INF. 44-46

His Father THOMAS MARVIN WARD Mother's Maiden Name MINNIE VIOLA ALTOM

Wife's Full Maiden Name VELDA REE DRUMMOND

Wife's Data	Day Month Year	City, Town or Place	County or Province, etc.	State or Country	Add. Info. on Wife
Birth	26 APR 1918	PALESTINE	ANDERSON	TEX.	
Chr'nd					
Death					
Burial					

Compiler ALVIN L. WARD
Address P.O. BOX 1756
City, State DENVER CITY, TEX. 79323
Date FEB 13, 1989

Places of Residence
Occupation if other than Housewife Church Affiliation CHURCH of CHRIST

Her Father THOMAS F. DRUMMOND Mother's Maiden Name LOU OTIE ROBERTSON

Sex	Children's Names in Full (Arrange in order of birth)		Day Month Year	City, Town or Place	County or Province, etc.	State or Country
M	1. ELDON LLOYD Spouse: JANE DOAK	Birth Mar. Death Burial	19 FEB 1941 14 SEP 1964	O'DONNELL UVALDE	LYNN UVALDE	TEX. TEX.
F	2. CAROLYN D. WARD Spouse: NORMAN F. PARSONS	Birth Mar. Death Burial	27 JUL 1942 02 SEP 1960	O'DONNELL UVALDE	LYNN UVALDE	TEX. TEX.

Family Group Record

FAMILY GROUP No. ___

Husband's Full Name: ELDON LLOYD WARD

Husband's Data	Day Month Year	City, Town or Place	County or Province, etc.	State or Country	Add. Info. on Husband
Birth	19 FEB 1941	O'DONNELL	LYNN	TEX.	
Chr'nd					
Mar.	14 SEP 1964	UVALDE	UVALDE	TEX.	
Death					
Burial					

Places of Residence:
Occupation: **Church Affiliation:** **Military Rec.:**
Other wives, if any, No. (1) (2) etc.: (2) DEANNA HARBOUR LINCECUM
His Father: E. C. WARD **Mother's Maiden Name:** VELDA REE DRUMMOND

Wife's Full Maiden Name: JANE DOKE

Wife's Data	Day Month Year	City, Town or Place	County or Province, etc.	State or Country	Add. Info. on Wife
Birth					
Chr'nd					
Death					
Burial					

Places of Residence:
Occupation if other than Housewife: **Church Affiliation:**
Other husbands, if any, No. (1) (2) etc.:
Her Father: **Mother's Maiden Name:**

Children

Sex	Children's Names in Full	Data	Day Month Year	City, Town or Place	Add. Info. on Children
M	1. BRYAN SCOTT WARD	Birth	07 JUN 1969		
		Mar.			
		Death			
		Burial			

FAMILY GROUP No. _____

Husband's Full Name NORMAN F. PARSONS

This Information Obtained From:

Husband's Data	Day Month Year	City, Town or Place	County or Province, etc.	State or Country	Add. Info. on Husband
Birth					
Chr'nd					
Mar.	02 SEP 1960	UVALDE	UVALDE	TEX.	
Death					
Burial					

Places of Residence
Occupation   Church Affiliation   Military Rec.
Other wives, if any. No. (1) (2) etc. Make separate sheet for each mar.
His Father   Mother's Maiden Name

Wife's Full Maiden Name CARYLON D. WARD

Wife's Data	Day Month Year	City, Town or Place	County or Province, etc.	State or Country	Add. Info. on Wife
Birth	27 JUL 1942	O'DONNELL	LYNN	TEX.	
Chr'nd					
Death					
Burial					

Places of Residence
Occupation if other than Housewife   Church Affiliation
Other husbands, if any. No. (1) (2) etc. Make separate sheet for each mar.
Her Father E. C. WARD   Mother's Maiden Name VELDA REE DRUMMOND

Sex	Children's Names in Full (Arrange in order of birth)	Children's Data	Day Month Year	City, Town or Place	County or Province, etc.	State or Country	Add. Info. on Child
F	1. SANDRA — Spouse: TIMOTHEY HOWELL	Birth	07 JUN 1961				
F	2. DEBRA — Spouse: DAVID EVANS	Birth	09 JAN 1963				
M	3. STEVE	Birth	18 FEB 1965				
F	4. MELANIE	Birth	23 MAY 1972				

FAMILY GROUP RECORD

Husband's Full Name: TIMOTHY HOWELL

Husband's Data	Day	Month	Year	City, Town or Place	County or Province, etc.	State or Country
Birth						
Chr'nd						
Mar.						
Death						
Burial						

Places of Residence:
Occupation: Church Affiliation: Military Rec.:
His Father: Mother's Maiden Name:

Wife's Full Maiden Name: SANDRA PARSONS

Wife's Data	Day	Month	Year	City, Town or Place	County or Province, etc.	State or Country
Birth	07	JUN	1961			
Chr'nd						
Death						
Burial						

Her Father: NORMAN F. PARSONS   Mother's Maiden Name: CAROLYN D. WARD

Children

Sex	Name	Event	Day	Month	Year
M	1. CHARLES DANIEL	Birth	13	Mar	1984
M	2. JEREMY WAYNE	Birth	06	FEB	1987

The Ward Family History — Page 114

FAMILY GROUP No. ___

Husband's Full Name DAVID EVANS

This Information Obtained From:

Husband's Data	Day	Month	Year	City, Town or Place	County or Province, etc.	State or Country	Add. Info. on Husband
Birth							
Chr'nd							
Mar.							
Death							
Burial							

Places of Residence

Occupation   Church Affiliation   Military Rec.

Other wives, if any. No. (1) (2) etc. Make separate sheet for each mar.

His Father   Mother's Maiden Name

Wife's Full Maiden Name DEBRA PARSONS

Wife's Data	Day	Month	Year	City, Town or Place	County or Province, etc.	State or Country	Add. Info. on Wife
Birth	09	JAN	1963				
Chr'nd							
Death							
Burial							

Compiler
Address
City, State
Date

Places of Residence

Occupation if other than Housewife   Church Affiliation

Other husbands, if any. No. (1) (2) etc. Make separate sheet for each mar.

Her Father NORMAN F. PARSONS   Mother's Maiden Name CAROLYN D. WARD

Sex	Children's Names in Full (Arrange in order of birth)	Children's Data	Day	Month	Year	City, Town or Place	County or Province, etc.	State or Country	Add. Info. on Children
M	1. DAVID LEE / Full Name of Spouse	Birth Mar. Death Burial	03	DEC	1983				
	2. / Full Name of Spouse	Birth Mar. Death Burial							
	3. / Full Name of Spouse	Birth Mar. Death Burial							
	4. / Full Name of Spouse	Birth Mar. Death Burial							
	5. / Full Name of Spouse	Birth Mar. Death Burial							
	6. / Full Name of Spouse	Birth Mar. Death Burial							
	7. / Full Name of Spouse	Birth Mar. Death Burial							
	8. / Full Name of Spouse	Birth Mar. Death Burial							
	9. / Full Name of Spouse	Birth Mar. Death Burial							
	10. / Full Name of Spouse	Birth Mar. Death Burial							

*If married more than once No. each mar. (1) (2) etc. and list in "Add. info. on children" column. Use reverse side for additional children, other notes, references or information.

GOLDEN MEMORIES

Ex-classmates, friends and teachers, whichever path of life you took;
Builders, bankers, farmers or preachers, and one who published a book;
A brief recap of my ups and downs, of my happy years on earth;
How we moved to near O'Donnell town, one year after my birth.

"Go west, young man," was the cry back there in nineteen twenty-three;
Talk of success filled the air, in the Tee Bar community;
We cleared the land and built a shack, and drilled a well, you see;
And built a fence around the tract, and a shed for our Model "T".

They built a school of brick so fine, and hired a teacher or three;
And sent us kids, four or five, the next to the youngest was me;
I finally got through the seventh grade, and to O'Donnell High I'd go,
An "A", and a "B", and some "C's" I made, barely made the grade, you know.

But I had a lot of fun those days, enjoyed my classmates, too;
There was Billy Joe, and Elvin Ray, to mention just a few;
Junior, H.M., George and Marie, Alton, Rex, Wanda and J.C.;
And a few good friends that played hookie with me.

My teachers, I guess I'll never forget, S.F. Johnson ran the show;
Red Conger carried the whip, you can bet, and Miss Nunnally, a fine person to know;
There was Vandergriff, Trice and DeBusk, and Snodgrass, all were good sports;
Their lives and influence was a must, Mrs. Cathey, none better than her sort.

Miss Guthrie needed no club or whip, when those dark eyes scanned the hall;
We knew right then to button our lip, but she was the best of them all;
I said that learning was not the way, to make a success of my life;
I met a sweet girl at Phillip's Cafe, as soon as I could, I made her my wife.

Our first-born son in forty-eight, the only one we ever had;
I said, "That's enough", to my lifetime mate, he looks too much like his dad;
God up above has been good to me, to Rita (my wife), and to Ron;
Georgia, his wife, is a teacher, you see, and if I may say so, a good one.

This is not the end of the story, you know, I'll live to a hundred and seven;
Then I'll retire and finally go, and manage a Seven-Eleven;
So long, ex-classmates, friend or foe, I've had my say, so now I'll go;
Hi-Ho Silver, up and away, see you on our hundredth anniversary.

Herbert Eugene Ward
Graduating Class of 1942
O'Donnell, Texas

FAMILY GROUP No. _____

Husband's Full Name HERBERT EUGENE WARD

This Information Obtained From:

Husband's Data	Day Month Year	City, Town or Place	County or Province, etc.	State or Country	Add. Info. on Husband
Birth	20 OCT 1922	KNOX CITY	KNOX	TEX.	
Chr'nd					
Mar.	30 Mar 1947	O'DONNELL	LYNN	TEX.	
Death					
Burial					

Places of Residence

Occupation _____ Church Affiliation PROTESTANT Military Rec. _____

Other wives, if any. No. (1) (2) etc. Make separate sheet for each mar.

His Father THOMAS MARVIN WARD   Mother's Maiden Name MINNIE VIOLA ALTOM

Wife's Full Maiden Name CLORITA ELIZABETH SHOULDERS

Wife's Data	Day Month Year	City, Town or Place	County or Province, etc.	State or Country	Add. Info. on Wife
Birth	11 FEB 1927	DENTON	DENTON	TEX.	
Chr'nd					
Death					
Burial					

Compiler _____ Places of Residence

Address _____ Occupation if other than Housewife _____ Church Affiliation PROTESTANT

City, State _____ Other husbands, if any. No. (1) (2) etc.

Date _____ Her Father CLAUDE SHOLDERS   Mother's Maiden Name ELIZABETH LOVEDAY

Sex	Children's Names in Full (Arrange in order of birth)	Children's Data	Day Month Year	City, Town or Place	County or Province, etc.	State or Country	Add. Info. on Children
M	1. RONNIE GENE	Birth	28 MAY 1948	LAMESA	DAWSON	TEX	
	Full Name of Spouse	Mar.	29 JUL 1972	ARLINGTON	TARRANT	TEX.	
	GEORGIA ANN WOODARD	Death					
		Burial					

The Ward Family History
Page 118

FAMILY GROUP No. ___

Husband's Full Name: TOMMY JACK WARD

Husband's Data	Day Month Year	City, Town or Place	County or Province, etc.	State or Country	Add. Info. on Husband
Birth	11 NOV 1935	O'DONNELL	LYNN	TEX.	
Chr'nd					
Mar.	NOV 1962	LAS VEGAS	CLARK	NEV.	
Death					
Burial					

Places of Residence:
Occupation: Church Affiliation: PRESBYTERIAN Military Rec.: ARMY 57/60
Other wives, if any: GIL
His Father: T.M. WARD Mother's Maiden Name: EDWINA COY WESTFALL

Wife's Full Maiden Name: LIMON

Wife's Data	Day Month Year	City, Town or Place	County or Province, etc.	State or Country	Add. Info. on Wife
Birth	04 JUL 1942	MINILLA	LUZON	PHILIPPINES	
Chr'nd					
Death					
Burial					

Places of Residence:
Occupation if other than Housewife: Church Affiliation: ROMAN CATHOLIC
Other husbands, if any:
Her Father: Mother's Maiden Name:

Children

Sex	#	Children's Names in Full	Event	Day Month Year	City, Town or Place	County or Province	State or Country
F	1	APRIL LEANNE	Birth	24 MAR 1964	LAS VEGAS	CLARK	NEV.
M	2	SHAWN THOMAS	Birth	24 SEP 1966	LAS VEGAS	CLARK	NEV.
M	3	MATTHEW	Birth	20 NOV 1979	LAS VEGAS	CLARK	NEV.

The Ward Family History

FAMILY GROUP No. _____ **Husband's Full Name** MARVIN JOE WARD

Husband's Data	Day Month Year	City, Town or Place	County or Province, etc.	State or Country	Add. Info. on Husband
Birth	12 DEC 1936	O'DONNELL	LYNN	TEX.	
Chr'nd					
Mar.	18 JUN 1960	DENVER CITY	YOAKUM	TEX.	
Death					
Burial					

Places of Residence: DENVER CITY, LUBBOCK, SALT LAKE CITY, CALIFORNIA
Occupation: WAREHOUSE MGR.   Church Affiliation: PROTESTANT   Military Rec.: U.S. ARMY

His Father: T. M. WARD   Mother's Maiden Name: EDWINA COY WESTFALL

Wife's Full Maiden Name MODENA ANN WRIGHT

Wife's Data	Day Month Year	City, Town or Place	County or Province, etc.	State or Country	Add. Info. on Wife
Birth	25 SEP 1940	SEAGRAVES	GAINS	TEX.	
Chr'nd					
Death					
Burial					

Places of Residence: SEAGRAVES, DENVER CITY, LUBBOCK
Occupation if other than Housewife: _____   Church Affiliation: PROTESTANT

Her Father: YANCY LEON WRIGHT   Mother's Maiden Name: MINNIE PIPKIN

Sex	Children's Names in Full	Children's Data	Day Month Year	City, Town or Place	County or Province, etc.	State or Country
M	1. YANCY DEAN Spouse: SHERRI DARNELL SADDLER	Birth Mar. Death Burial	25 JAN 1963 28 DEC 1981	DENVER CITY LUBBOCK	YOAKUM LUBBOCK	TEX. TEX.

FAMILY GROUP No. ___

Husband's Full Name YANCY DEAN WARD

This Information Obtained From:

Husband's Data	Day Month Year	City, Town or Place	County or Province, etc.	State or Country	Add. Info. on Husband
Birth	25 JAN 1963	DENVER CITY	YOAKUM	TEX.	
Chr'nd					
Mar.	28 DEC 1981	LUBBOCK	LUBBOCK	TEX.	
Death					
Burial					

Places of Residence DENVER CITY, LUBBOCK TEXAS
Occupation MECHANIC   Church Affiliation PROTESTANT   Military Rec.
His Father MARVIN JOE WARD   Mother's Maiden Name MODENA ANN WRIGHT

Wife's Full Maiden Name SHERRI DARNELL SADDLER

Wife's Data	Day Month Year	City, Town or Place	County or Province, etc.	State or Country	Add. Info. on Wife
Birth	28 SEP 1965	LUBBOCK	LUBBOCK	TEX.	
Chr'nd					
Death					
Burial					

Places of Residence LUBBOCK
Occupation if other than Housewife   Church Affiliation
Her Father J. D. SADDLER   Mother's Maiden Name MELTON

Sex	#	Children's Names in Full	Event	Day Month Year	City, Town or Place	County or Province, etc.	State or Country
M	1	JOSEPH DEAN	Birth	30 SEP 1984	LUBBOCK	LUBBOCK	TEX.
M	2	ANTHONY LEON	Birth	16 DEC 1986	LUBBOCK	LUBBOCK	TEX.

RECORD OF BIRTHS NOT PREVIOUSLY REGISTERED

STATE OF TEXAS — TEXAS DEPARTMENT OF HEALTH
DELAYED CERTIFICATE OF BIRTH

Certificate No. 371178

REGISTRANT
1. Name: Juanita Lee Ward
2. Date of Birth: 9-15-25
3. Color or Race: White
4. Sex: Female
5a. City or Town of Birth: O'Donnell, Rural
5b. County of Birth: Lynn, County, Texas

FATHER
6. Full Name: Thomas Marvin Ward
7. State or Country of Father's Birth: United States

MOTHER
8. Maiden Name: Minnie Viola Alton
9. State or Country of Mother's Birth: Arkansas

AFFIDAVIT
10. Signature of Registrant: Juanita Lee Rodriguez
11. Present Address of Registrant: 2011 - 5 St. Greeley, Colo.
12. Signature of Notary Public: [signed]
13. Notary Public Commission Expires: October 20, 1981

Subscribed and sworn to before me on April 20, 1979

SUPPORTING DOCUMENT 1
- Type of Document: Cert. Copy of Birth Cert. of Child #808 (8-6-1949)
- Date of Birth: 23 yrs.
- Place of Birth: Texas
- By Whom Issued and Signed: Local Registrar, Greeley, Colorado
- Full Name of Mother: Not Stated
- Date Issued: 3-1-1979
- Date Original Entry: 8-11-1949
- Name of Father: Not Stated

SUPPORTING DOCUMENT 2
- Type of Document: Cert. Copy of Birth Cert. of Child #1074 (10-18-1955)
- Date of Birth: 30 yrs.
- Place of Birth: Texas
- By Whom Issued and Signed: Local Registrar, Greeley, Colorado
- Full Name of Mother: Not Stated
- Date Issued: 3-1-1979
- Date Original Entry: 10-22-1955
- Name of Father: Not Stated

SUPPORTING DOCUMENT 3
- Type of Document: Cert. Copy of Birth Cert. of Child #91 (1-24-1962)
- Date of Birth: 36 yrs.
- Place of Birth: Texas
- By Whom Issued and Signed: Local Registrar, Greeley, Colorado
- Full Name of Mother: Not Stated
- Date Issued: 3-1-1979
- Date Original Entry: 1-29-1962
- Name of Father: Not Stated

SUPPORTING DOCUMENT 4
- Type of Document: Aff. of Older Sister, Mrs. Willie Jewel Atkinson, N.P., Baker, Box 207, La Pryor, Texas, Zavala County, Texas
- Date of Birth: 9-15-1925
- Place of Birth: Texas
- Full Name of Mother: Minnie Viola Alton
- Date Rec'd: 4-25-1979
- Date Original Entry: 2-8-1979
- Name of Father: Thomas Marvin Ward

State Registrar: [signed]
Evidence Reviewed By: [signed]
Date Filed: APR 30 1979

Juanita L. Rodriquez

Mrs. Juanita L. Rodriquez of Greeley, died Friday, August 3, 1979, at her home.

She was born September 15, 1925, at O'Donnell, Texas, to Thomas M. and Minnie V. (Alton) Ward.

On August 6, 1945, she was married to Ernest Rodriquez in Denver.

She grew up at O'Donnell and moved to Denver at the time of her marriage and to Greeley later that same year. She was a member of the Greeley Baptist Temple.

Survivors are her husband, Ernest of Greeley; two daughters, Miss Mary and Mrs. Mohammed (Ruby) Ashkanani, both of Greeey; two sons, Ernest Jr. of Evans and Robert W. of Greeley; a sister, Mrs. Melvin Acres of La Pryor, Texas; four brothers, Eugene Ward of Fort Worth, Texas, E. C. Ward of Uvalde, Texas, T. M. and Jim Ward, both of Seagraves, Texas, and a granddaughter, Lori R. Rodriquez of Evans. One brother is deceased.

OBSEQUIES
Were Held For

Juanita L. Rodriquez

on
Tuesday, August 7, 1979
at 10:00 A.M.

from
Adamson Memorial Chapel

in charge of
The Rev. Frank Teal

ORGANIST
Mrs. Wallace Roberts

SOLOIST
Mr. Merrill P. Womach

SONGS
How Great Thou Art
Beyond The Sunset

Interment Linn Grove Cemetery

PALLBEARERS
Elmo Jenkins
Marty Coheo
Carl McDonell
Bill McKenzie
Wiliam Agens
Joe LaMar

Family Group Record

FAMILY GROUP No. _____

Husband's Full Name: ERNEST RODRIQUEZ

Husband's Data	Day	Month	Year	City, Town or Place	County or Province, etc.	State or Country	Add. Info. on Husband
Birth							
Chr'nd							
Mar.	06	AUG	1945	DENVER	ARAPAHOE	COL.	
Death							
Burial							

Places of Residence:
Occupation: ____ Church Affiliation: ____ Military Rec.: ____
His Father: ____ Mother's Maiden Name: ____

Wife's Full Maiden Name: JUANITA LEE WARD

Wife's Data	Day	Month	Year	City, Town or Place	County or Province, etc.	State or Country	Add. Info. on Wife
Birth	15	SEP	1925	O'DONNELL	LYNN	TEX.	
Chr'nd							
Death	03	AUG	1979	GREELEY	WELD	COL.	
Burial	07	AUG	1979	LINN GROVE CEMETERY	GREELEY,	COL.	

Places of Residence:
Occupation if other than Housewife: ____ Church Affiliation: BAPTIST
Her Father: THOMAS MARVIN WARD Mother's Maiden Name: MINNIE VIOLA ALTON

Children

Sex	#	Children's Names in Full	Data	Day	Month	Year	City, Town or Place	Add. Info.
	1	ROBERT W.	Birth / Mar. / Death / Burial					
	2	ERNEST JR.	Birth / Mar. / Death / Burial					1 CHILD LOPI R RODRIQUE
	3	RUBY — Spouse: MOHAMMED ASHKANANI	Birth / Mar. / Death / Burial					
	4	MARY	Birth / Mar. / Death / Burial					
	5							
	6							
	7							
	8							
	9							
	10							

FLORENCE WARD

Daughter of James Alexander Lacy Ward and Rebecca Jane (Baker) Ward.

Florence

Died 27 Oct 1981

McKenna

Mrs. Gladys McKenna, 78, died in the I.O.O.F. Home Tuesday morning, after a long illness.

Mrs. McKenna was born May 13, 1903, reared in Milford and attended the Milford schools. She has been a nurse in the Ennis Municipal Hospital for several years and later was a nurse in Gaston Episcopal Hospital in Dallas for thirty years before retiring in 1972. July 29, 1981 she came to Ennis to make her home in the I.O.O.F. and Rebekah Home. Mrs. McKenna was a member of the Elmira Rebekah Lodge in Dallas and the Baptist Church in Franklin.

Surviving her are two sons Harrell E. Johnson of Franklin and Kenneth L. Johnson of Mesquite; one daughter, Mrs. Chlotea Harrison of Dallas; fourteen grandchildren; a number of great-grandchildren; two sisters, Mrs. Beatrice Taylor of Dallas and Mrs. Addis Ruekle of San Antonio; and two brothers, James E. Goodman of DeSota and W.H. Goodman of Calistoga, California.

Funeral service will be held at 2 p.m. Thursday in the Keever Chapel with the Rev. Doyle Caldwell of Franklin officiating. Interment will be in the Milford Cemetery.

Family Group Record

FAMILY GROUP No. _____

Husband's Full Name: CARL JOHNSON

Husband's Data	Day Month Year	City, Town or Place	County or Province, etc.	State or Country	Add. Info. on Husband
Birth					
Chr'nd					
Mar.	16 APR 1919				
Death					
Burial					

Places of Residence:
Occupation: | Church Affiliation: | Military Rec.:
Other wives, if any:

His Father: | Mother's Maiden Name:

Wife's Full Maiden Name: GLADYS IOMA HAND

Wife's Data	Day Month Year	City, Town or Place	County or Province, etc.	State or Country	Add. Info. on Wife
Birth	13 MAY 1903				
Chr'nd					
Death	27 Oct 1981	ENNIS	ELLIS	TEX.	
Burial		MILFORD	ELLIS	TEX.	

Places of Residence:
Occupation if other than Housewife: NURSE | Church Affiliation: BAPTIST
Other husbands, if any: (2) McKENNA

Her Father: WILBER H HAND | Mother's Maiden Name: FLORENCE E.B. WARD

Children

Sex	Children's Names in Full	Data	Day Month Year	City, Town or Place	County or Province	State or Country	Add. Info. on Children
M 1	JAMES OTIS — Spouse: FRANCIS FRANK	Birth	15 MAR 1922				(2) Wife EDITH HOVER
		Mar.	194_				
		Death	17 DEC 1972	DALLAS	DALLAS	TEX.	DIED OF CANCER
		Burial					
M 2	HARRELL EUGENE — Spouse: ANITA BURLESON	Birth	17 JUL 1925				
		Mar.	17 OCT 1947				
		Death					
		Burial					
F 3	CHLOTEA ELIZABETH — Spouse: JOE HARRISON	Birth	03 DEC 1928				
		Mar.	10 MAY 1947				
		Death					
		Burial					
M 4	KENNETH LAVERN — Spouse: MYRTLE HAYES	Birth	24 DEC 1931				CANADIAN
		Mar.	30 NOV 1952	DALLAS	DALLAS	TEX.	
		Death					
		Burial					

Family Group Record

FAMILY GROUP No. _____

This Information Obtained From: _____

Husband's Full Name: JAMES OTIS JOHNSON

Husband's Data	Day Month Year	City, Town or Place	County or Province, etc.	State or Country	Add. Info. on Husb.
Birth	15 MAR 1922			TEX.	
Chr'nd					
Mar.	194_				
Death	17 DEC 1972	DALLAS	DALLAS	TEX.	
Burial					

Places of Residence:
Occupation: — Church Affiliation: — Military Rec.:
Other wives, if any, No. (1) (2) etc.: (2) EDITH HOUER
His Father: CARL JOHNSON   Mother's Maiden Name: GLADIS IONA HAND

Wife's Full Maiden Name: FRANCIS FRANK

Wife's Data	Day Month Year	City, Town or Place	County or Province, etc.	State or Country	Add. Info. on Wife
Birth					
Chr'nd					
Death					
Burial					

Places of Residence:
Occupation if other than Housewife: — Church Affiliation:
Other husbands, if any, No. (1) (2) etc.:
Her Father: _____   Mother's Maiden Name: _____

Compiler: _____
Address: _____
City, State: _____
Date: _____

Children

Sex	#	Children's Names in Full	Event	Day Month Year	City, Town or Place	County or Province	State or Country	Add. Info. on Children
F	1	SANDRA	Birth	09 DEC 1944				
		Full Name of Spouse	Mar. / Death / Burial					
	2		Birth / Mar. / Death / Burial					
	3		Birth / Mar. / Death / Burial					
	4		Birth / Mar. / Death / Burial					
	5		Birth / Mar. / Death / Burial					
	6		Birth / Mar. / Death / Burial					
	7		Birth / Mar. / Death / Burial					
	8		Birth / Mar. / Death / Burial					
	9		Birth / Mar. / Death / Burial					
	10		Birth / Mar. / Death / Burial					

*If married more than once No. each mar. (1) (2) etc. and list in "Add. info. on children" column. Use reverse side for additional children, other notes, references or information.

The Ward Family History
Page 128

FAMILY GROUP No. _____

Husband's Full Name: JAMES OTIS JOHNSON

This Information Obtained From: _____

Husband's Data	Day Month Year	City, Town or Place	County or Province, etc.	State or Country	Add. Info. on Husband
Birth	15 MAR 1922				
Chr'nd					
Mar.	06 JAN 1950				
Death	17 DEC 1972	DALLAS	DALLAS	TEX.	
Burial					

Places of Residence:
Occupation: _____ Church Affiliation: _____ Military Rec.: _____

Other wives, if any: (1) FRANCIS FRANK

His Father: CARL JOHNSON Mother's Maiden Name: GLADIS IONA HAND

Wife's Full Maiden Name: EDITH HOUER

Wife's Data	Day Month Year	City, Town or Place	County or Province, etc.	State or Country	Add. Info. on Wife
Birth					SHE HAD A SON
Chr'nd					BILLY WHEN SHE
Death					MARRIED
Burial					

Compiler: _____
Address: _____
City, State: _____
Date: _____

Places of Residence: _____
Occupation if other than Housewife: _____ Church Affiliation: _____

Her Father: _____ Mother's Maiden Name: _____

Sex	Children's Names in Full (Arrange in order of birth)	Children's Data	Day Month Year	City, Town or Place	County or Province, etc.	State or Country	Add. Info. on Children
M	1 BRUCE WAYNE	Birth	20 AUG 1951				
	Full Name of Spouse	Mar.					
		Death					
		Burial					
F	2 BARBARA JO	Birth	14 MAY 1952				
	Full Name of Spouse	Mar.					
		Death					
		Burial					
	3	Birth					
	Full Name of Spouse	Mar.					
		Death					
		Burial					
	4	Birth					
	Full Name of Spouse	Mar.					
		Death					
		Burial					
	5	Birth					
	Full Name of Spouse	Mar.					
		Death					
		Burial					
	6	Birth					
	Full Name of Spouse	Mar.					
		Death					
		Burial					
	7	Birth					
	Full Name of Spouse	Mar.					
		Death					
		Burial					
	8	Birth					
	Full Name of Spouse	Mar.					
		Death					
		Burial					
	9	Birth					
	Full Name of Spouse	Mar.					
		Death					
		Burial					
	10	Birth					
	Full Name of Spouse	Mar.					
		Death					
		Burial					

FAMILY GROUP No. _____

Husband's Full Name: HARRELL EUGENE JOHNSON

Husband's Data	Day Month Year	City, Town or Place	County or Province, etc.	State or Country	Add. Info. on Husband
Birth	17 JUL 1925				DIVORCED 1S. WIFE IN 1966
Chr'nd					
Mar.	17 OCT 1947	DALLAS	DALLAS	TEX.	
Death					
Burial					

Places of Residence

Occupation — Church Affiliation — Military Rec.

Other wives: (2) MARY JO BARNET

His Father: CARL JOHNSON — Mother's Maiden Name: GLADIS IONA HAND

Wife's Full Maiden Name: ANITA BURLESON

Wife's Data	Day Month Year	City, Town or Place	County or Province, etc.	State or Country	Add. Info. on Wife
Birth					
Chr'nd					
Death	08 DEC 1971				
Burial					

Her Father: — Mother's Maiden Name:

Children

Sex	#	Name	Event	Day Month Year	City	County	State	Add. Info.
F	1	TERE LYNN (Spouse: DAVID deBOARD)	Birth	19 DEC 1951				
			Mar.	01 MAR 1968	FRANKLIN	ROBERTSON	TEX.	
			Death					
			Burial					
M	2	HARRELL EUGENE JR.	Birth	30 APR 1953				
			Mar.					
			Death	26 DEC 1953				DIED FROM A FALL.
			Burial					
M	3	BOBBY JACK (Spouse: LAUONNE)	Birth	18 APR 1956				
			Mar.					
			Death					
			Burial					

FAMILY GROUP No. ___

This Information Obtained From:

Husband's Full Name DAVID deROARDNSON

Husband's Data	Day Month Year	City, Town or Place	County or Province, etc.	State or Country	Add. Info. on Husband
Birth					
Chr'nd					
Mar.	01 MAR 1968	FRANKLIN	ROBERTSON	TEX.	
Death					
Burial					

Places of Residence
Occupation   Church Affiliation   Military Rec.
Other wives, if any. No. (1) (2) etc. Make separate sheet for each mar.

His Father ___   Mother's Maiden Name ___

Wife's Full Maiden Name TERE LYNN JOHNSON

Wife's Data	Day Month Year	City, Town or Place	County or Province, etc.	State or Country	Add. Info. on Wife
Birth	19 DEC 1951				
Chr'nd					
Death					
Burial					

Compiler
Address
City, State
Date

Places of Residence
Occupation if other than Housewife   Church Affiliation
Other husbands, if any. No. (1) (2) etc. (2) CECIL ELLIS (3) JIM SCEBECK

Her Father HARRELL E. JOHNSON   Mother's Maiden Name ANITA BURLESON

Sex	Children's Names in Full (Arrange in order of birth)	Children's Data	Day Month Year	City, Town or Place	County or Province, etc.	State or Country	Add. Info. on Children
F	1 KRISTY	Birth	18 MAR 1969				
	Full Name of Spouse	Mar. / Death / Burial					
	2	Birth / Mar. / Death / Burial					
	3	Birth / Mar. / Death / Burial					
	4	Birth / Mar. / Death / Burial					
	5	Birth / Mar. / Death / Burial					
	6	Birth / Mar. / Death / Burial					
	7	Birth / Mar. / Death / Burial					
	8	Birth / Mar. / Death / Burial					
	9	Birth / Mar. / Death / Burial					
	10	Birth / Mar. / Death / Burial					

*If married more than once No. each mar. (1) (2) etc. and list in "Add. info. on children" column. Use reverse side for additional children, other notes, references or information.

FAMILY GROUP No. ____

Husband's Full Name CECIL ELLIS

This Information Obtained From:

Husband's Data	Day Month Year	City, Town or Place	County or Province, etc.	State or Country	Add. Info. on Husband
Birth					
Chr'nd					
Mar.					
Death					
Burial					

Places of Residence

Occupation _____ Church Affiliation _____ Military Rec.

Other wives, if any. No. (1) (2) etc. Make separate sheet for each mar.

His Father _____ Mother's Maiden Name _____

Wife's Full Maiden Name TERE LYNN JOHNSON

Wife's Data	Day Month Year	City, Town or Place	County or Province, etc.	State or Country	Add. Info. on Wife
Birth	19 DEC 1951				
Chr'nd					
Death					
Burial					

Places of Residence

Occupation if other than Housewife _____ Church Affiliation

Other husbands, if any. No. (1) (2) etc. (1) DAVID DeBOARD (3) JIM SCEBECK

Her Father HARRELL E. JOHNSON   Mother's Maiden Name ANITA BURLESON

Sex	Children's Names in Full (Arrange in order of birth)	Children's Data	Day Month Year	City, Town or Place	County or Province, etc.	State or Country	Add. Info. on Children
M	1 BRANDI JOE	Birth	24 May 1972	WACO	McLENNAN	TEX.	
	Full Name of Spouse	Mar.					
		Death					
		Burial					
	2	Birth					
	Full Name of Spouse	Mar.					
		Death					
		Burial					
	3	Birth					
	Full Name of Spouse	Mar.					
		Death					
		Burial					
	4	Birth					
	Full Name of Spouse	Mar.					
		Death					
		Burial					
	5	Birth					
	Full Name of Spouse	Mar.					
		Death					
		Burial					
	6	Birth					
	Full Name of Spouse	Mar.					
		Death					
		Burial					
	7	Birth					
	Full Name of Spouse	Mar.					
		Death					
		Burial					
	8	Birth					
	Full Name of Spouse	Mar.					
		Death					
		Burial					
	9	Birth					
	Full Name of Spouse	Mar.					
		Death					
		Burial					
	10	Birth					
	Full Name of Spouse	Mar.					
		Death					
		Burial					

The Ward Family History

FAMILY GROUP No. _____

Husband's Full Name JIM SCEBECK

Husband's Data	Day Month Year	City, Town or Place	County or Province, etc.	State or Country	Add. Info. on Husband
Birth					
Chr'nd					
Mar.		WACO	McLENNAN	TEX.	
Death					
Burial					

Places of Residence
Occupation   Church Affiliation   Military Rec.
Other wives, if any.
His Father   Mother's Maiden Name

Wife's Full Maiden Name TERE LYNN JOHNSON

Wife's Data	Day Month Year	City, Town or Place	County or Province, etc.	State or Country	Add. Info. on Wife
Birth	19 DEC 1951				
Chr'nd					
Death					
Burial					

Places of Residence
Occupation if other than Housewife   Church Affiliation
Other husbands, if any: (1) DAVID deBOARD (2) CECIL ELLIS
Her Father HARRELL E. JOHNSON   Mother's Maiden Name ANITA BURLESON

Sex	Children's Names in Full	Children's Data	Day Month Year	City, Town or Place	County or Province, etc.	State or Country	Add. Info. on Children
F	1 FARRAH DAWN	Birth	19 DEC 1976	WACO	McLENNAN	TEX.	
M	2 JEREMIAH JOHN	Birth	28 JAN 1979	WACO	McLENNAN	TEX.	
M	3	Birth	28 JAN 1979	WACO	McLENNAN	TEX.	

Family Group Record

Husband's Full Name: BOBBY JACK JOHNSON

Husband's Data	Day Month Year	City, Town or Place	County or Province, etc.	State or Country	Add. Info. on Husband
Birth	18 APR 1956				
Chr'nd					
Mar.					
Death					
Burial					

Places of Residence:
Occupation: Church Affiliation: Military Rec.: MARINES

His Father: HARRELL E. JOHNSON   Mother's Maiden Name: ANITA BURLESON

Wife's Full Maiden Name: LAUONNE

Wife's Data	Day Month Year	City, Town or Place	County or Province, etc.	State or Country	Add. Info. on Wife
Birth					
Chr'nd					
Death					
Burial					

Places of Residence:
Occupation if other than Housewife: Church Affiliation:

Her Father: Mother's Maiden Name:

Children

Sex	#	Name	Event	Day Month Year	City, Town or Place	County	State
M	1	ROBERT AUBERY	Birth	29 NOV 1978	GUAM MARINE BASE		
F	2	STACY LORAINE	Birth	04 JUL 1983	AVON PARK	HIGHLANDS	FLA.

The Ward Family History
Page 134

FAMILY GROUP No. _____

Husband's Full Name: WILBER H. HAND

This Information Obtained From:

Husband's Data	Day Month Year	City, Town or Place	County or Province, etc.	State or Country	Add. Info. on Husb.
Birth					
Chr'nd					
Mar.	25 APR 1901	ABILENE	TAYLOR	TEX.	
Death					
Burial					

Places of Residence:
Occupation: Church Affiliation: Military Rec.:
Other wives, if any. No. (1) (2) etc.

His Father: Mother's Maiden Name:

Wife's Full Maiden Name: FLORENCE ELIZABETH BELL WARD

Wife's Data	Day Month Year	City, Town or Place	County or Province, etc.	State or Country	Add. Info. on Wife
Birth	12 APR 1881	PARKER	JOHNSON	TEX.	
Chr'nd					
Death	30 AUG 1945	MILFORD	ELLIS	TEX.	
Burial	1945	MILFORD	ELLIS	TEX.	

Places of Residence:
Occupation if other than Housewife: Church Affiliation:
Other husbands, if any. No. (1) (2) etc. (2) WILLIAM HARRISON GOODMAN

Her Father: J.A.L. WARD   Mother's Maiden Name: REBECKA J. BAKER

Children

Sex	Children's Names in Full	Children's Data	Day Month Year	City, Town or Place	County, State
1	GLADYS IOMA — Spouse: CARL JOHNSON	Birth / Mar.	13 MAY 1903 / 16 APR 1919		

FAMILY GROUP No. _____

Husband's Full Name: HARRELL EUGENE JOHNSON

Husband's Data	Day Month Year	City, Town or Place	County or Province, etc.	State or Country	Add. Info. on Husband
Birth	17 JUL 1925				
Chr'nd					
Mar.	13 AUG 1966				
Death					
Burial					

Places of Residence

Occupation   Church Affiliation   Military Rec.

Other wives, if any. No. (1) (2) etc. Make separate sheet for each mar.: (1) ANITA BURLESON

His Father: CARL JOHNSON   Mother's Maiden Name: GLADIS IONA HAND

Wife's Full Maiden Name: MARY JO BARNET WALKER

Wife's Data	Day Month Year	City, Town or Place	County or Province, etc.	State or Country	Add. Info. on Wife
Birth					SHE HAD A BOY
Chr'nd					AND A GIRL
Death					WHEN SHE
Burial					MARRIED.

Places of Residence

Occupation if other than Housewife

Other husbands, if any. No. (1) (2) etc.   Church Affiliation

Her Father   Mother's Maiden Name

Sex	Children's Names in Full		Day Month Year	City, Town or Place	County or Province, etc.	State or Country	Add. Info. on Children
F 1	REBECCA RENE	Birth	31 JUL 1967				
	Full Name of Spouse	Mar. / Death / Burial					
F 2	MARY FRANCIS	Birth	29 JUN 1972				
	Full Name of Spouse	Mar. / Death / Burial					
3							
4							
5							
6							
7							
8							
9							
10							

FAMILY GROUP No.

Husband's Full Name: JOE HARRISON

Husband's Data	Day Month Year	City, Town or Place	County or Province, etc.	State or Country	Add. Info. on Husband
Birth					
Chr'nd					
Mar.	10 May 1947	ENNIS	ELLIS	TEX.	
Death					
Burial					

Places of Residence:
Occupation: Church Affiliation CATHOLIC   Military Rec.
Other wives, if any.
His Father: Mother's Maiden Name:

Wife's Full Maiden Name: CHLOTEA ELIZABETH JOHNSON

Wife's Data	Day Month Year	City, Town or Place	County or Province, etc.	State or Country	Add. Info. on Wife
Birth	03 DEC 1928				
Chr'nd					
Death					
Burial					

Places of Residence:
Occupation if other than Housewife: Church Affiliation CATHOLIC
Her Father: CARL JOHNSON   Mother's Maiden Name: GLADIS IONA HAND

Children

Sex	#	Name	Event	Day Month Year
M	1	JOE CARL	Birth	12 DEC 1947
M	2	MICHEAL WAYNE	Birth	27 NOV 1950
M	3	RUSSEL DEAN	Birth	21 JUL 1952

FAMILY GROUP No. ___

Husband's Full Name: KENNETH LAVERN JOHNSON

Husband's Data	Day Month Year	City, Town or Place	County or Province, etc.	State or Country	Add. Info. on Husband
Birth	24 DEC 1931				
Chr'nd					
Mar.	30 NOV 1952			MAINE	
Death					
Burial					

Places of Residence:
Occupation: Church Affiliation: Military Rec. AIR FORCE
Other wives, if any. No. (1) (2) etc. Make separate sheet for each mar.

His Father: CARL JOHNSON   **Mother's Maiden Name:** GLADIS IONA HAND

Wife's Full Maiden Name: MYRTLE HAYES

Wife's Data	Day Month Year	City, Town or Place	County or Province, etc.	State or Country	Add. Info. on Wife
Birth					CANADIAN
Chr'nd					
Death					
Burial					

Places of Residence:
Occupation if other than Housewife: Church Affiliation:
Other husbands, if any. No. (1) (2) etc. Make separate sheet for each mar.

Her Father: ___   **Mother's Maiden Name:** ___

Sex	Children's Names in Full (Arrange in order of birth) / Full Name of Spouse	Children's Data	Day Month Year	City, Town or Place	County or Province, etc.	State or Country	Add. Info. on Children
M	1. PETER KENNETH / TRESA WEST	Birth	31 DEC 1953			MAINE	
		Mar.	21 MAR 1985		DALLAS	TEX.	
		Death					
		Burial					
F	2. TOMI LYNN / DUG SHEHAN	Birth	11 AUG 1956	WACO	McLENNAN	TEX.	DIVORCED J_
		Mar.	08 MAR 1979	MESQUITE	DALLAS	TEX.	1982. NOW _
		Death					DALLAS ATT.
		Burial					
M	3. PAUL JAMES / STEPHANIE McCLURE	Birth	21 FEB 1959			MAINE	
		Mar.	13 Sep 1986	DALLAS	DALLAS	TEX.	
		Death					
		Burial					
M	4. RANDY LEE / LISA HARRILL	Birth	25 MAR 1963	LORING A.F.B.		MAINE	
		Mar.	07 JUN 1986	DALLAS	DALLAS	TEX.	
		Death					
		Burial					

Family Group Record

FAMILY GROUP No. ___

Husband's Full Name: JOE CARL HARRISON

Husband's Data	Day Month Year	City, Town or Place	County or Province, etc.	State or Country	Add. Info. on Husband
Birth	12 DEC 1947				
Chr'nd					
Mar.					
Death					
Burial					

Places of Residence:
Occupation: | Church Affiliation: | Military Rec.:
Other wives, if any.
His Father: | Mother's Maiden Name:

Wife's Full Maiden Name:

Wife's Data	Day Month Year	City, Town or Place	County or Province, etc.	State or Country	Add. Info. on Wife
Birth					
Chr'nd					
Death					
Burial					

Places of Residence:
Occupation if other than Housewife: | Church Affiliation:
Other husbands, if any.
Her Father: | Mother's Maiden Name:

Children

(Children 1–10: all entries blank)

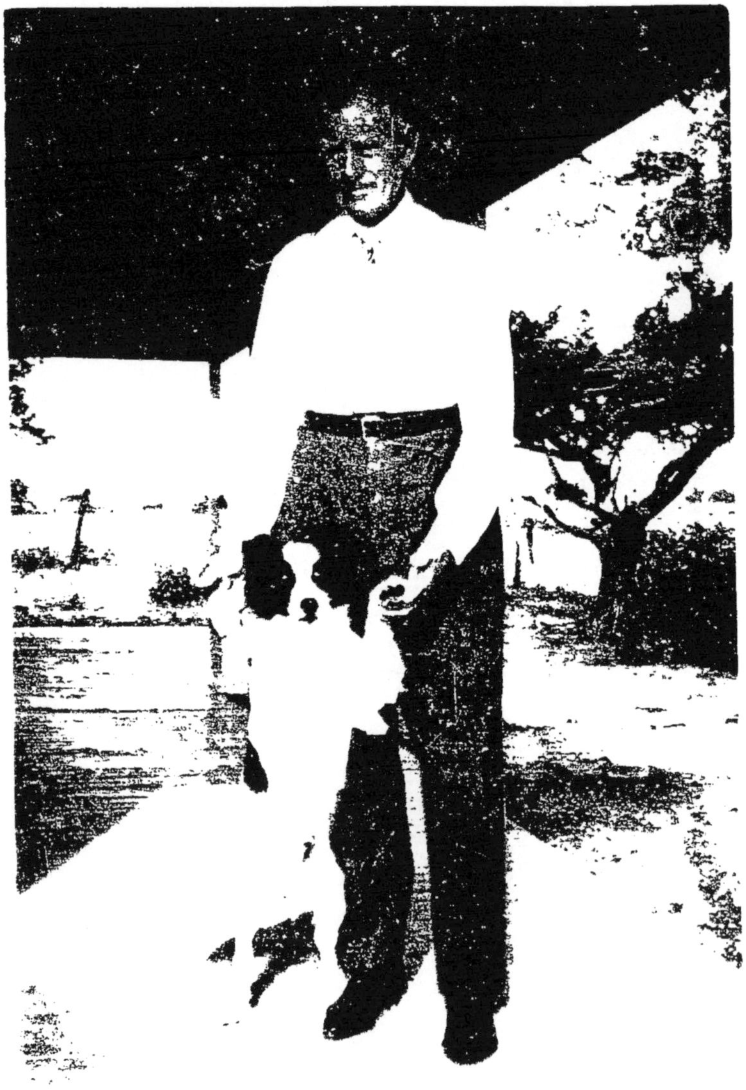

FAMILY GROUP No. ___

Husband's Full Name WILLIAM HARRISON GOODMAN SR.

Husband's Data	Day Month Year	City, Town or Place	County or Province, etc.	State or Country	Add. Info. on Husband
Birth	9 JUL 1875	TICKLEFOOT	GRIMES	TEX.	SON OF A METHODIST PREACHER
Chr'nd					
Mar.	10 JAN 1912	HILSBORO	HILL	TEX.	
Death	26 OCT 1956	MILFORD	ELLIS	TEX.	
Burial	1956	MILFORD	ELLIS	TEX.	

Places of Residence

Occupation FARMER   Church Affiliation METHODIST   Military Rec.

His Father JOHN EDWIN GOODMAN   Mother's Maiden Name ANNA BELL

Wife's Full Maiden Name FLORENCE ELIZABETH BELL WARD

Wife's Data	Day Month Year	City, Town or Place	County or Province, etc.	State or Country	Add. Info. on Wife
Birth	12 APR 1881	PLUTO	ELLIS	TEX.	MUSIC TEACHER
Chr'nd					
Death	30 AUG 1945	MILFORD	ELLIS	TEX.	
Burial	1945	MILFORD	ELLIS	TEX.	

Places of Residence

Occupation if other than Housewife   Church Affiliation METHODIST

Other husbands: (1) WILBER H. HAND

Her Father J.A.L. WARD   Mother's Maiden Name REBECCA JANE BAKER

Children

1. ADDIS NAOMI — Spouse: NORMAN LLOYD RUEKLE
- Birth: 11 OCT 1912, PLUTO, ELLIS, TEX.
- Mar.: 15 May 1948, MILFORD, ELLIS, TEX.

2. BEATRICE IONE — Spouse: JAMES LOYD TAYLOR
- Birth: 3 DEC 1914, PLUTO, ELLIS, TEX.
- Mar.: 1 APR 1941

3. WILLIAM HARRISON JR.
- Birth: 20 SEP 1918, PLUTO, ELLIS, TEX.
- Mar.: 13 MAR 1944

4. JAMES EDWIN — Spouse: ROSE NELL CRUMP
- Birth: 18 JAN 1923, PLUTO, ELLIS, TEX.
- Mar.: 5 JUN 1946

Florence & Will Goodman
Taken April 12, 1942
on Florence Birthday

Rebecca Ward
(Baker)
nee
Rebecca B Ward

Addis (Goodman)
Ruehle
Age 30

FAMILY GROUP No. ___

This Information Obtained From:

Husband's Full Name: NORMAN ALFRED RUEKEL

Husband's Data	Day Month Year	City, Town or Place	County or Province, etc.	State or Country	Add. Info. on H
Birth		NEW BRAUNFELS	COMAL	TEX.	
Chr'nd					
Mar.	15 MAY 1948	MILFORD	ELLIS	TEX.	
Death	22 MAY 1975	SAN ANTONIA	BEXAR	TEX	
Burial		NEW BRAUNFELS	COMEL	TEX.	

Places of Residence:
Occupation: Church Affiliation: Military Rec.:
Other wives, if any. No. (1) (2) etc.

His Father: Mother's Maiden Name:

Wife's Full Maiden Name: ADDIS NAOMI GOODMAN

Wife's Data	Day Month Year	City, Town or Place	County or Province, etc.	State or Country	Add. Info. on Wife
Birth	11 Oct 1912	PLUTO	ELLIS	TEX	
Chr'nd					
Death					
Burial					

Compiler: Places of Residence:
Address: Occupation if other than Housewife: Church Affiliation: METHODIST
City, State: Other husbands, if any. No. (1) (2) etc.
Date: Her Father: W.H GOODMAN SR.   Mother's Maiden Name: FLORENCE E. B. WARD

Sex	Children's Names in Full (Arrange in order of birth)	Children's Data	Day Month Year	City, Town or Place	County or Province, etc.	State or Country	Add. Info. on Children
1	NO ISSUE	Birth / Mar. / Death / Burial					
2		Birth / Mar. / Death / Burial					
3		Birth / Mar. / Death / Burial					
4		Birth / Mar. / Death / Burial					
5		Birth / Mar. / Death / Burial					
6		Birth / Mar. / Death / Burial					
7		Birth / Mar. / Death / Burial					
8		Birth / Mar. / Death / Burial					
9		Birth / Mar. / Death / Burial					
10		Birth / Mar. / Death / Burial					

FAMILY GROUP No. ___

Husband's Full Name: JAMES LLOYD TAYLOR SR.

Husband's Data	Day Month Year	City, Town or Place	County or Province, etc.	State or Country	Add. Info. on Husband
Birth	27 FEB 1908	NAIL		OK.	
Chr'nd					
Mar.	01 APR 1941	DURANT	BRYAN	OK.	
Death	24 JAN 1981	DALLAS	DALLAS	TEX.	
Burial		ENNIS MURTLE GROVE CEMITARY		TEX.	

Places of Residence:
Occupation: Church Affiliation: Military Rec.:
His Father: Mother's Maiden Name:

Wife's Full Maiden Name: BEATRICE IONA GOODMAN

Wife's Data	Day Month Year	City, Town or Place	County or Province, etc.	State or Country	Add. Info. on Wife
Birth	3 DEC 1914	MILFORD	ELLIS	TEX.	
Chr'nd					
Death					
Burial					

Places of Residence:
Occupation if other than Housewife: Church Affiliation:
Her Father: W. H. GOODMAN SR.   Mother's Maiden Name: FLORENCE E. B. WARD

Sex	Children's Names in Full	Children's Data	Day Month Year	City, Town or Place	County or Province, etc.	State or Country	Add. Info. on Children
M	1. ADDIS RAY	Birth	03 DEC 1941	ENNIS	ELLIS	TEX.	
	Full Name of Spouse:	Mar.					
		Death	03 DEC 1941	ENNIS	ELLIS	TEX.	
		Burial		ENNIS	ELLIS	TEX.	
M	2. JAMES LLOYD JR.	Birth	19 JUL 1945	ENIS	ELLIS	TEX	
	Full Name of Spouse: REBECCA LYNN WALL	Mar.	14 NOV 1964	DALLAS	DALLAS	TEX.	
		Death					
		Burial					
	3. WILLIAM ROSS	Birth	1 AUG 1947	DALLAS	DALLAS	TEX.	
	Full Name of Spouse: BRENDA MAXWELL	Mar.	21 SEP 1967	DALLAS	DALLAS	TEX.	
		Death					
		Burial					

FAMILY GROUP No.

Husband's Full Name: JAMES LLOYD TAYLOR JR.

Husband's Data	Day Month Year	City, Town or Place	County or Province, etc.	State or Country	Add. Info. on Husband
Birth	19 JUL 1945	ENIS	ELLIS	TEX.	
Chr'nd					
Mar.	14 NOV 1964	DALLAS	DALLAS	TEX.	
Death					
Burial					

Places of Residence

Occupation | Church Affiliation | Military Rec.

His Father: JAMES LLOYD TAYLOR SR. Mother's Maiden Name: BEATRICE IONA GOODMAN

Wife's Full Maiden Name: REBECCA LYNN WALL

Wife's Data	Day Month Year	City, Town or Place	County or Province, etc.	State or Country	Add. Info. on Wife
Birth					
Chr'nd					
Death					
Burial					

Places of Residence

Occupation if other than Housewife | Church Affiliation

Her Father | Mother's Maiden Name

Sex	Children's Names in Full	Children's Data	Day Month Year	City, Town or Place	County or Province, etc.	State or Country
M	1. MARK	Birth	04 JUN 1965	DALLAS	DALLAS	TEX.

The Ward Family History
Page 146

FAMILY GROUP No. _____ **Husband's Full Name** WILLIAM ROSS TAYLOR

This Information Obtained From:

Husband's Data	Day	Month	Year	City, Town or Place	County or Province, etc.	State or Country	Add. Info. on Husband
Birth	01	AUG	1947	DALLAS	DALLAS	TEX.	
Chr'nd							
Mar.	21	SEP	1967	DALLAS	DALLAS	TEX.	
Death							
Burial							

Places of Residence

Occupation _____ Church Affiliation _____ Military Rec. _____

Other wives, if any. No. (1) (2) etc. (2) PAULA PATERSON (3) PAT CHILDRESS HARRISON

His Father JAMES LLOYD TAYLOR SR. Mother's Maiden Name BEATRICE IONA GOODMAN

Wife's Full Maiden Name BRENDA MAXWELL

Wife's Data	Day	Month	Year	City, Town or Place	County or Province, etc.	State or Country	Add. Info. on Wife
Birth							
Chr'nd							
Death							
Burial							

Places of Residence

Occupation if other than Housewife _____ Church Affiliation _____

Other husbands, if any. No. (1) (2) etc.

Her Father _____ Mother's Maiden Name _____

Sex	#	Children's Names in Full	Children's Data	Day	Month	Year	City, Town or Place	County or Province, etc.	State or Country
F	1	CLAUDIA ANGELIQUE	Birth	13	MAR	1968	DALLAS	DALLAS	TEX.

FAMILY GROUP No. ___

Husband's Full Name: WILLIAM ROSS TAYLOR

Husband's Data	Day Month Year	City, Town or Place	County or Province, etc.	State or Country	Add. Info. on Husband
Birth	01 AUG 1947	DALLAS	DALLAS	TEX	
Chr'nd					
Mar.	07 MAR 1970	DALLAS	DALLAS	TEX.	
Death					
Burial					

Places of Residence:
Occupation: Church Affiliation: Military Rec.:
Other wives, if any. No. (1) (2) etc.: (1) BRENDA MAXWELL (3) PAT CHILDRESS HARRISON
His Father: JAMES LLOYD TAYLOR SR. Mother's Maiden Name: BEATRICE IONA GOODMAN

Wife's Full Maiden Name: PAULA PATERSON

Wife's Data	Day Month Year	City, Town or Place	County or Province, etc.	State or Country	Add. Info. on Wife
Birth					
Chr'nd					
Death					
Burial					

Places of Residence:
Occupation if other than Housewife: Church Affiliation:
Other husbands, if any. No. (1) (2) etc.:
Her Father: Mother's Maiden Name:

Sex	Children's Names in Full	Children's Data	Day Month Year	City, Town or Place	County or Province, etc.	State or Country	Add. Info. on Children
M	1. TIMOTHY	Birth	20 AUG 1970	DALLAS	DALLAS	TEX	
		Mar.					
		Death					
		Burial					

The Ward Family History
Page 148

FAMILY GROUP No. _____

Husband's Full Name: WILLIAM ROSS TAYLOR

This information Obtained From:

Husband's Data	Day Month Year	City, Town or Place	County or Province, etc.	State or Country	Add. Info. on Husband
Birth	01 AUG 1947	DALLAS	DALLAS	TEX.	
Chr'nd					
Mar.	21 OCT 1983	DALLAS	DALLAS	TEX	
Death					
Burial					

Places of Residence
Occupation — Church Affiliation — Military Rec.
Other wives, if any: (1) BRENDA MAXWELL (2) PAULA PATERSON
His Father: JAMES LLOYD TAYLOR SR.   Mother's Maiden Name: BEATRICE IONA GOODMAN

Wife's Full Maiden Name: PAT CHILDRESS HARRISON

Wife's Data	Day Month Year	City, Town or Place	County or Province, etc.	State or Country	Add. Info. on Wife
Birth					
Chr'nd		DIVORCED IN 1987			
Death					
Burial					

Places of Residence
Occupation if other than Housewife — Church Affiliation
Other husbands, if any:
Her Father —   Mother's Maiden Name

The Ward Family History
Page 149

FAMILY GROUP No. _____

This information Obtained From: _____

Husband's Full Name: WILLIAM HARRISON GOODMAN JR.

Husband's Data	Day Month Year	City, Town or Place	County or Province, etc.	State or Country	Add. Info. on Husband
Birth	20 SEP 1918	SAN FRANCISCO		CAL.	
Chr'nd					
Mar.	13 MAR 1944	SAN FRANCISCO		CAL.	
Death					
Burial					

Places of Residence:
Occupation: **Church Affiliation:** **Military Rec.:**
Other wives, if any: (2) WANDA CARPENTER (3) MARY L.S.W. SMITH
His Father: W. H. GOODMAN SR. **Mother's Maiden Name:** FLORANCE E. B. WARD

Wife's Full Maiden Name: DOROTHY BAHNSEN

Wife's Data	Day Month Year	City, Town or Place	County or Province, etc.	State or Country	Add. Info. on Wife
Birth					
Chr'nd					
Death	DIVORCED		1960		
Burial					

Compiler: **Places of Residence:**
Address: **Occupation if other than Housewife:** **Church Affiliation:**
City, State: **Other husbands, if any:**
Date: **Her Father:** **Mother's Maiden Name:**

Children

Sex	Children's Names in Full	Children's Data	Day Month Year	City, Town or Place	County or Province, etc.	State or Country	Add. Info. on Children
	1. MELISSA RUTH	Birth	14 NOV 1953	SAN FRANCISCO		CAL	
	Full Name of Spouse	Mar.					
		Death	ADOPTED (STILL LIVED IN CAL IN 1988)				
		Burial					

FAMILY GROUP No. ___

Husband's Full Name: WILLIAM HARRISON GOODMAN JR.

Husband's Data	Day Month Year	City, Town or Place	County or Province, etc.	State or Country	Add. Info. on Husb.
Birth	20 SEP 1918	MILFORD (PLUTO)	ELLIS	TEX.	
Chr'nd					
Mar.	8 SEP 1961				
Death					
Burial					

Places of Residence:
Occupation: **Church Affiliation:** **Military Rec.:**
Other wives, if any. No. (1) (2) etc.: (1) D. M. BAHNSEN (3) MARY L.S.W. SMITH
His Father: W. H. GOODMAN SR. **Mother's Maiden Name:** FLORENCE E. B. WARD

Wife's Full Maiden Name: WANDA CARPENTER

Wife's Data	Day Month Year	City, Town or Place	County or Province, etc.	State or Country	Add. Info. on Wife
Birth					
Chr'nd					
Death		DIVORCED IN 1963			
Burial					

Places of Residence:
Occupation if other than Housewife: **Church Affiliation:**
Other husbands, if any. No. (1) (2) etc.
Her Father: **Mother's Maiden Name:**

The Ward Family History
Page 151

FAMILY GROUP No. _____

This Information Obtained From: _____

Husband's Full Name: WILLIAM HARRISON GOODMAN JR.

Husband's Data	Day Month Year	City, Town or Place	County or Province, etc.	State or Country	Add. Info. on Husb.
Birth	20 SEP 1918	MILFORD	ELLIS	TEX.	
Chr'nd					
Mar.	22 MAY 1965	RENO	STOREY	NEV.	
Death					
Burial					

IN 1988 WAS LIVING IN VALLANT OK.

Places of Residence:
Occupation: **Church Affiliation:** **Military Rec.:**
Other wives, if any. No. (1) (2) etc. (1) D.M. BAHSEN (2) WANDA CARPENTER
His Father: W. H. GOODMAN SR   **Mother's Maiden Name:** FLORENCE E. B. WARD

Wife's Full Maiden Name: MARY LUCILLE SMART WELCH SMITH

Wife's Data	Day Month Year	City, Town or Place	County or Province, etc.	State or Country	Add. Info. on Wife
Birth					
Chr'nd					
Death					
Burial					

Compiler:
Address:
City, State:
Date:

Places of Residence:
Occupation if other than Housewife: **Church Affiliation:**
Other husbands, if any. No. (1) (2) etc.
Her Father: **Mother's Maiden Name:**

Sex	Children's Names in Full (Arrange in order of birth)	Children's Data	Day Month Year	City, Town or Place	County or Province, etc.	State or Country	Add. Info. on Children
1	Full Name of Spouse	Birth / Mar. / Death / Burial					
2	Full Name of Spouse	Birth / Mar. / Death / Burial					
3	Full Name of Spouse	Birth / Mar. / Death / Burial					
4	Full Name of Spouse	Birth / Mar. / Death / Burial					
5	Full Name of Spouse	Birth / Mar. / Death / Burial					
6	Full Name of Spouse	Birth / Mar. / Death / Burial					
7	Full Name of Spouse	Birth / Mar. / Death / Burial					
8	Full Name of Spouse	Birth / Mar. / Death / Burial					
9	Full Name of Spouse	Birth / Mar. / Death / Burial					
10	Full Name of Spouse	Birth / Mar. / Death / Burial					

FAMILY GROUP No. ___

Husband's Full Name JAMES EDWIN GOODMAN

Husband's Data	Day Month Year	City, Town or Place	County or Province, etc.	State or Country	Add. Info. on Husband
Birth	18 JAN 1923	MILFORD (PLUTO) ELLIS		TEX.	
Chr'nd					
Mar.	5 JUN 1946	NATCHITOCHES	NATCHITOCHES, LA.		
Death					
Burial					

Places of Residence

Occupation — Church Affiliation — Military Rec.

His Father **W. H. GOODMAN SR** Mother's Maiden Name **FLORENCE E. B. WARD**

Wife's Full Maiden Name ROSE NELL CRUMP

Wife's Data	Day Month Year	City, Town or Place	County or Province, etc.	State or Country	Add. Info. on Wife
Birth	13 OCT 1926	NATCHITOCHES	NATCHITOCHES LA.		
Chr'nd					
Death					
Burial					

Places of Residence

Occupation if other than Housewife — Church Affiliation

Her Father — Mother's Maiden Name

Children

1. NO ISSUE

Henry Ward and his wife, Allie, and daughter, Inez

Henry was the son of James A. Lacy Ward (Lacy and John William Ward were brothers)

Henry B. Ward *13 aug 71*

ROTAN (RNS) — Henry B. Ward, 88, died at 10 a.m. Friday in Holiday Lodge Nursing Home in Hamlin following a lengthy illness.

Funeral will be at 2 p.m. Sunday in Sylvester Methodist Church.

Burial will be in Sylvester Cemetery with Weathersbee Funeral Home of Rotan in charge.

Born Nov. 8, 1882, in Knox County, he was a retired Sylvester farmer. He came to the Sylvester area in 1924. He was a member of the Methodist Church.

Survivors are his wife of Hamlin; five daughters, Mrs. J. O. Spikes of Abilene, Mrs. Henrietta Worthy of Seguin, Mrs. A. T. Williams of Odessa, Mrs. Roy Kiser of Sylvester, and Mrs. Harry Suter of Gautier, Miss.; one nephew, Jim Ward of Seminole; eight grandchildren and nine great-grandchildren.

TEXAS DEPARTMENT OF HEALTH
BUREAU OF VITAL STATISTICS
CERTIFICATE OF BIRTH

1. Place of Birth
   STATE OF TEXAS
   COUNTY OF ELLIS
   City or Precinct No. **Waxahachie**

2. Full Name of Child: **Allie J. Smith**

3. Sex: **fem**
4. Twin, Triplet, Other:
5. Number in Order of Birth:
6. Legitimate? **yes**
7. Date of Birth: **April 17, 1889**

FATHER

8. Full Name: **Willis Huddleston Smith**
9. Residence at Time of This Birth: **Waxahachie, Texas**
10. Color or Race: **White**
11. Age at Time of This Birth: **38** Years
12. Birthplace (State or Country): **Tennessee**
13A. Trade, Profession or Kind of Work Done: **Farming**
13B. Industry or Business in Which Engaged: **FARM**

MOTHER

14. Full Maiden Name: **Nancy Mary Wise**
15. Residence At Time of This Birth: **Waxahachie, Texas**
16. Color or Race: **white**
17. Age at Time of This Birth: **36** Years
18. Birthplace (State or Country): **Kentucky**
19A. Trade, Profession or Kind of Work Done: **Housewife**
19B. Industry or Business in Which Engaged: **Home**

20. Number of Children Born to This Mother, Including This Birth: **9**
21. Number of Children Born to This Mother and Now Living: **9**
22. What Prophylactic Was Used to Prevent Ophthalmia Neonatorum?

I hereby certify to the birth of this child who was born alive at _____ M. on the date stated above.

23. Signature of Physician or Other Person: **Mrs. Lesse L. Luther**   Address: **1908 Fillmore Wichita Falls, Tex.**

AFFIDAVIT A

STATE OF TEXAS
COUNTY OF **Wichita**

Before me on this day appeared **Mrs. Lessie L. Luther** known to me to be the person who signed the certificate attached hereto, who on oath deposes and says that the facts stated in the foregoing birth certificate of **Allie J. Smith** (Name Appearing on Certificate) are true and correct to the best of her knowledge and belief, and that she was acquainted with the facts at the time of the event.

Signed: **Mrs. Lesse L. Luther**

Sworn to and subscribed before me, this **8** day of **July**, 19**53**

Velma Clark

(Seal)   Notary Public in and for **Wichita** County, Texas.

AFFIDAVIT B

STATE OF TEXAS
COUNTY OF **Wichita**

Before me on this day appeared **Mrs. C. C. Barton** known to me to be the person who signed this affidavit, who on oath deposes and says that the facts stated in the foregoing birth certificate of **Allie J. Smith** (Name Appearing on Certificate) are true and correct to the best of her knowledge and belief, and that she is acquainted with the facts and that she is not related to the individual by blood or marriage.

Signed: **Mrs. C. C. Barton**

Sworn to and subscribed before me, this **8** day of **July**, 19**53**

Velma Clark

(Seal)   Notary Public in and for **Wichita** County, Texas.

STATE OF TEXAS
COUNTY OF ELLIS

THE CITIZENSHIP OF **Allie J. Smith** and the truthfulness of the statements made in the above Birth Certificate have been established to the satisfaction of this Court, as required by H. B. No. 614, and amendments thereto.

IT IS ORDERED that this record be **accepted** and filed in the State Bureau of Vital Statistics.

Signed: **Lem Wray**

Date **July 21**, 19**53**   County Judge of Ellis County, Texas.

Filed for record the **21st** day of **July**, 19**53**

Recorded this **21st** day of **July**, 19**53**   **Chas. W. Huff**

By **Faye Washington**, Deputy.   County Clerk of Ellis County, Texas.

A-1578—Certified Copy of Marriage Record—Class 4

CERTIFIED COPY OF MARRIAGE RECORD

THE STATE OF TEXAS
COUNTY OF TAYLOR } No. ----

To any regularly Licensed or Ordained Minister of the Gospel, Jewish Rabbi, Judge of the District or County Court, or any Justice of the Peace, in and for the State of Texas—GREETING:

YOU ARE HEREBY AUTHORIZED TO SOLEMNIZE THE RITES OF MATRIMONY

Between Mr. H. B. Ward and Miss Allie J. Smith

and make due return to the Clerk of the County Court of said County within sixty days thereafter, certifying your action under this License.

Witness my offical signature and seal of office at office in Abilene, Texas, the 17 day of May, 19 05.

(SEAL)

S. H. Garrison, Clerk
of the County Court, Taylor County, Texas

Seal

By _____, Deputy

I, A. J. Leach, hereby certify that on the 21 day of May, 19 05 I united in Marriage Mr. H. B. Ward and Miss Allie J. Smith the parties above named.

Witness my hand this 22 day of May, 19 05.

A. J. Leach
Minister of the Gospel

Returned and filed for record the 23 day of May, 19 05

and recorded the 23 day of May, 19 05

S. H. Garrison, County Clerk

By _____, Deputy

THE STATE OF TEXAS
COUNTY OF TAYLOR }

I, Mrs. Chester Hutcheson, Clerk of the County Court of Taylor County, Texas, do hereby certify that the above and foregoing is a full, true and correct copy of the Marriage License issued to Mr. H. B. Ward and Miss Allie J. Smith and the return of the person who solemnized the rites of matrimony between said parties as the same appears of record in my office, in volume 4 on page 81, of the Marriage Records of said County, and I am lawful possessor and custodian of said record.

Given under my hand and offical seal, at office in Abilene, Texas, this the 1 day of June, 19 54.

(SEAL)

Mrs. Chester Hutcheson, Clerk
of the County Court, Taylor County, Texas

By _____, Deputy

FAMILY GROUP No. ___

This Information Obtained From:

Husband's Full Name: HENRY BASCUM WARD

Husband's Data	Day Month Year	City, Town or Place	County or Province, etc.	State or Country	Add. Info. on Husband
Birth	8 NOV 1882	PARKER	JOHNSON	TEX.	
Chr'nd					
Mar.	17 MAY 1905	TRENT	TAYLOR	TEX	
Death	13 AUG 1971	HAMLIN	JONES	TEX	
Burial	15 Aug 1971	SYLVESTER	FISHER	TEX.	

Places of Residence:
Occupation: FARMER Church Affiliation: Methodist Military Rec.

His Father: J.A.L. WARD   Mother's Maiden Name: REBECKA JANE BAKER

Wife's Full Maiden Name: ALLIE J. SMITH

Wife's Data	Day Month Year	City, Town or Place	County or Province, etc.	State or Country	Add. Info. on Wife
Birth	17 APR 1889	WAXAHACHIE	ELLIS	TEX.	
Chr'nd					
Death	17 JAN 1978	HAMLIN	JONES	TEX.	
Burial	19 JAN 1978	TRENT	TAYLOR	TEX.	

Places of Residence:
Occupation if other than Housewife: Church Affiliation: METHODIST

Her Father: WILLIE HUDLESTON SMITH   Mother's Maiden Name: NANCY MARY WISE (36)

Children

Sex	Children's Names in Full		Day Month Year	City, Town or Place	County or Province, etc.	State or Country
1	NAOMI INEZ / Spouse: JOSEPH OTTIS SPIKES	Birth	27 SEP 1906	STIFF	HASKELL	TEX.
		Mar.	10 DEC 1927	ROSCOE	NOLAN	TEX
		Death				
		Burial				
2	FLORANCE HENRIETTA / Spouse: ROY WORTHY	Birth	14 FEB	BENJAMIN	KNOX	TEX.
		Mar.				
		Death				
		Burial				
3	MARTHA REBECKA / Spouse: A. THURSTON WILLIAMS	Birth	17 AUG 1911	SYLVESTER	FISHER	TEX.
		Mar.	03 JUL 1931			
		Death				
		Burial				
4	BIRDIE ESTELLE / Spouse: ROY KISER	Birth	28 APR 1913	ROBY	FISHER	TEX
		Mar.				
		Death				
		Burial				
5	ELIZABETH CORINNE / Spouse: JOSEPH F. THOMPSON	Birth	8 FEB 1928	ROSCOE	NOLAN	TEX.
		Mar.	12 DEC 1945	ABILENE	TAYLOR	TEX.
		Death				
		Burial				

ABILENE, TEXAS, MONDAY MORNING, DECEMBER 19, 1977

Deaths & Funer

Dec. 20 1977

Funerals Today

Joseph Otis Spikes, 78, of 5350 Harwood at 2 p.m. at Elliott-Hamil Chapel of Faith, U.S. Highway 277; burial in Elmwood Memorial Park.

Joseph Spikes

Joseph Otis Spikes, 78, of 5350 Harwood, a retired technical sergeant, was dead on arival at Dyess AFB Hospital at 9:10 a.m. Sunday of natural causes. Services will be 2 p.m. Tuesday at 2 p.m. Tuesday at Elliott-Hamil Chapel of Faith, U.S. 277.

The Rev. Marshall Stewart, pastor of the First Nazarene Church in Hamlin, will officiate. Military graveside services will be in Elmwood Memorial Park.

Born March 18, 1899, at Ferris, he enlisted in the Navy in 1916. He served in the Navy, Army and Air Force, before retiring in 1964 as an Air Force technical sergeant. He was a veteran of World War I and World War II and was a member of VFW Post No. 12 in Abilene. He was a member of Elmwood West United Methodist church. He married Naomi Inez Ward Dec. 10, 1927, in Roscoe. In 1964, they moved from Moses Lake, Wash., to Abilene where he worked for the Holiday Inn and Sheraton Inn.

Survivors include his wife; a brother, Tom of Fontana, Calif.; and a sister, Lyna Payne of 1717 Chesnut.

MR., MRS. SPIKES
...wed 50 years

J. O. SPIKES

Mr. and Mrs. J.O. Spikes will celebrate their golden wedding anniversary with a reception at their home, 5350 Harwood, from 2 until 6 p.m. Sunday. The party will be hosted by their sisters, Mrs. Beth Suter, Mrs. A. T. Williams and Mrs. Stella Kiser.

Spikes was 22 and Mrs. Spikes was 14 when the couple first met in 1920 in Knox City.

At the time of their marriage Spikes had already served in the U. S. Army and the U. S. Navy. He started his military career in 1916 at the age of 17 when he spent eight months patrolling the border between Mexico and Texas trying to keep Pancho Villa and other renegades from crossing over into the U. S.

Spikes retired from the U. S. Air Force in 1964 as a technical sergeant. He started his military career at a time when covered wagons and horse drawn cannons were in vogue. When he retired intercontinental missiles and long-range bombers were standard equipment.

They are members of the Methodist Church.

LARSON LEDGER   Tuesday, Mar. 31, 1964

A Colorful Career Draws To A Close

By A1C Charles L. Sherrill

Like the face of history, the face of TSgt. Joseph Spikes has been marked by time. The piercing blue eyes, set deeply in that rugged, line-etched face, have seen hell. They've seen the United States military progress from covered wagons and horse-drawn cannons to supersonic aircraft and radar-controlled weapon systems.

Born in 1898 near a little town in northeast Texas, Sergeant Spikes was transported to his first military assignment in a covered wagon. In 1916, he spent his first eight months in uniform patrolling the Mexican border with the then federalized Texas National Guard. Sergeant Spikes recalls, "We had our hands full trying to keep Pancho Villa and his tribe of renegades on their side of the Rio Grande."

Reminiscing about the months he spent defending the Texas border, Sergeant Spikes says, "Our deputy commander was Gen. George E. Patton. At that time there was also a first lieutenant named Dwight D. Eisenhower serving in San Antonio, Tex."

Shortly after the United States entered World War I, Sergeant Spikes found himself in the thick of the French Campaign. During 1917 and 1918 he crossed France, inch by inch, most of the time crawling through trenches and under barbed wire.

"I remember one particularly horrible night. I was called out of our front-line trench to check the rear ranks. When I returned, 28 men who had fought beside me for months were dead. A barrage of mortar shells had fallen directly into our trench. That was my closest brush with death."

For heroic action in France, Sergeant Spikes received one of his most prized citations, the French Fourragere. This red and green cord, slung over the left shoulder, was awarded by the French government to members of the Second Army Division, for gallantry in action.

After the war, he filled civilian shoes for a short time, but soon became restless and enlisted in the Navy. Beginning in 1923, he spent four years at Pearl Harbor. During this time, he was a member of the party that rescued the crew of one of the first sea planes ever to attempt a non-stop flight from San Francisco to Honolulu.

In 1926, Sergeant Spikes was sent on temporary duty to participate in the Nicaraguan Campaign. During a portion of this time he was stationed aboard the U.S.S. Savannah.

With an honorable discharge from the Navy in his pocket, Sergeant spikes again became a civilian Texan. He lived the life of a salesman, in Lubbock, Tex., until the Japanese attack on Pearl Harbor, when he again answered the call to the colors.

He spent most of the war in Dodge City Kan., as non-commissioned officer in charge of base Flight Radio. From his desk there, Sergeant Spikes followed the course of the war on the Normandy front with intense interest. "I've been all through there," he said proudly.

At the end of World War II, Sergeant Spikes received his third honorable discharge. This time, however, he decided that he had found a home in the military.

After his fourth enlistment, in 1946, he was sent to Smoky Hill Army Air Field, Kan., as a B-29 radio repairman. He was stationed at Smoky Hill, since renamed Schilling AFB, when the Strategic Air Command was first organized.

In the winter of 1946, Sergeant Spikes was a member of a crew sent to Alaska on a cold weather research expedition, designated Operation Deep Freeze. His reaction to that experience was: "I'm a Texan, and Alaska is no place for Texans. The temperature dipped back and forth between 35 and 55 below zero."

The biggest mix-up of Sergeant Spikes' career arose shortly after his 60th birthday. While stationed in Salina, Kan., he went home one afternoon to find greetings from the Salina County Draft Board in his mail box.

Sergeant Spikes came to Larson in April of last year, from Hunter AFB, Ga. His assignment here as chief supply inspector, in the 462d Supply Squadron, marked his second tour of duty in a unit designated 462d. You see, during World War II, he was assigned to the 462d Bombardment Group. This was the highly decorated unit in honor of which the 4170th Strategic Aerospace Wing was redesignated 462d, in January, 1963.

With all of the memories this 66-year-old citizen-airman has accumulated in his past 48 years in and out of the military, today will probably be one of the most memorable of his career. For TSgt. Joseph O. Spikes, today will be the culmination—today he retires after a total of 29 years in the Army, Navy and Air Force. He is believed to be one of the last World War I veterans still on active duty in the Air Force.

As he's done a half dozen times in the past, Sergeant Spikes plans to return to his native Texas. But, again, he says he might not stay there. He and his wife, Naomi, plan to go first to her home town, Abilene. From there, the Sergeant says, they have no definite plans.

THIS IS HOW the typical American soldier looked shortly before World War I. TSgt. Joseph Spikes (center) recalls that this picture of he and his buddies from Company 4, 144th Infantry, of the Texas National Guard, was taken in Forth Worth, Tex., in 1917.

THE WAR HAD ENDED, and Joe Spikes was ready to return to his homeland. Among his belongings he carried this photo, taken in Roane, France, in 1918.

DURING TSGT. JOSEPH SPIKES' first days in the Texas National Guard, 48 years ago, he found himself surrounded by covered wagons and horse-drawn cannons. Today, he retires from a military that relies upon intercontinental missiles and long-range bombers to provide America's first line of defense.

FAMILY GROUP

Husband's Full Name: JOSEPH OTTIS SPIKES

Husband's Data	Day Month Year	City, Town or Place	County or Province, etc.	State or Country	Add. Info. on Husband
Birth					Served 30 years in the Military
Chr'nd					
Mar.	10 MAR 1927	ROSCO	NOLAN	TEX	
Death		ABILENE	TAYLOR	TEX.	
Burial		ABILENE	TAYLOR	TEX.	

Places of Residence:
Occupation: Church Affiliation: Military Rec. AIRFORCE
His Father: Mother's Maiden Name:

Wife's Full Maiden Name: NAOMI INEZ WARD

Wife's Data	Day Month Year	City, Town or Place	County or Province, etc.	State or Country	Add. Info. on Wife
Birth	27 SEP 1906	CLIFF	HASKELL	TEX.	
Chr'nd					
Death					
Burial					

Places of Residence:
Occupation if other than Housewife: Church Affiliation:
Her Father: HENRY BASCUM WARD Mother's Maiden Name: ALLIE J. SMITH

Children

1. NO ISSUES

FAMILY GROUP No.

Husband's Full Name: AVERY THURSTON WILLIAMS

Husband's Data

	Day Month Year	City, Town or Place	County or Province, etc.	State or Country
Birth	21 JUN 1909	DE LEON	COMANCHE	TEX.
Chr'nd				
Mar.	03 JUL 1931			
Death	09 JAN 1973	ODESA	ECTOR	TEX.
Burial	13 JAN 1973	SYLVESTER	FISHER	TEX.

Places of Residence:
Occupation: TEACHER Church Affiliation: BAPTIST Military Rec.:

His Father: ALLEN B. T. WILLIAMS Mother's Maiden Name: WILLIE MAE HINES

Wife's Full Maiden Name: MARTHA REBECKA WARD

Wife's Data

	Day Month Year	City, Town or Place	County or Province, etc.	State or Country
Birth	17 AUG 1911	SYLVESTER	FISHER	TEX.
Chr'nd				
Death				
Burial				

Places of Residence:
Occupation if other than Housewife: Church Affiliation: BAPTIST

Her Father: HENRY BASCOM WARD Mother's Maiden Name: ALLIE J. SMITH

Children

1. (M) HENRY ALLEN
Spouse: DORTHY SUE WOOD

	Day Month Year	City, Town or Place	County or Province, etc.	State or Country
Birth	19 AUG 1932	SYLVESTER	FISHER	TEX.
Mar.	19 FEB 1950	SAN ANTONIO	BEXAR	TEX.
Death				
Burial				

FAMILY GROUP No. _____

Husband's Full Name HENRY ALLEN THURSTON

Husband's Data	Day Month Year	City, Town or Place	County or Province, etc.	State or Country	Add. Info. on Husband
Birth	19 AUG 1932	SYLVESTER	JONES	TEX.	
Chr'nd					
Mar.	25 NOV 1950	SAN ANTONIO	BEXAR	TEX.	
Death					
Burial					

Places of Residence

Occupation OIL CONSULTANT Church Affiliation BAPTIST Military Rec.

His Father AVERY THURSTON WILLIAM Mother's Maiden Name MARTHA REBECKA WARD

Wife's Full Maiden Name DORTHY SUE WOOD

Wife's Data	Day Month Year	City, Town or Place	County or Province, etc.	State or Country	Add. Info. on Wife
Birth	28 NOV 1932				
Chr'nd					
Death					
Burial					

Places of Residence

Occupation if other than Housewife Church Affiliation BAPTIST

Her Father Mother's Maiden Name

Sex	Children's Names in Full	Children's Data	Day Month Year	City, Town or Place	County or Province, etc.	State or Country
F	1. ALANA CORINNE Spouse: ROBERT MACK GIPSON	Birth Mar. Death Burial	21 AUG 1953 16 SEP 1972	KILLEEN	BELL	TEX
M	2. KEVIN LEN Spouse: DENISE BRIDGES WILLIAMS	Birth Mar. Death Burial	21 SEP 1956 30 May 1983	SAN ANTONIA	BEXAR	TEX

FAMILY GROUP No. _____

Husband's Full Name: JOSEPH E. THOMPSON

Husband's Data	Day Month Year	City, Town or Place	County or Province, etc.	State or Country	Add. Info. on Husband
Birth	1906				
Chr'nd					
Mar.	12 DEC 1945	ABILENE	TAYLOR	TEX.	
Death					
Burial					

Places of Residence:
Occupation: Church Affiliation: Military Rec.:
Other wives, if any:
His Father: Mother's Maiden Name:

Wife's Full Maiden Name: ELIZABETH CORINNE WARD

Wife's Data	Day Month Year	City, Town or Place	County or Province, etc.	State or Country	Add. Info. on Wife
Birth	08 FEB 1928	ROSCO	NOLAN	TEX.	
Chr'nd					
Death					
Burial					

Places of Residence:
Occupation if other than Housewife: Church Affiliation:
Other husbands: (2) C. SMITH (3) HARRY F. SUTER
Her Father: HENRY BASCUM WARD Mother's Maiden Name: ALLIE J. SMITH

Sex	Children's Names in Full	Data	Day Month Year	City, Town or Place	County or Province, etc.	State or Country
F	1. SAMMIE CORINNE — Spouse: GUSTEN GUY BEARD	Birth	01 FEB 1948	LUBBOCK	LUBBOCK	TEX.
		Mar.	02 AUG 1968			
		Death				
		Burial				

FAMILY GROUP

Husband's Full Name: GUSTIN GUY BEARD (GUS)

Occupation: BUS DRIVER

Wife's Full Maiden Name: SAMMIE CORINNE THOMPSON (SAM)

	Day	Month	Year	City, Town or Place	County	State
Birth	14	JAN	1948	LUBBOCK	LUBBOCK	TEX.

Her Father: JOSEPH E. THOMPSON
Mother's Maiden Name: ELIZABETH CORINNE WA[RD]

Children

Sex	Name	Event	Date
M	1. MATTHEW GRANT	Birth	04 SEP 1971
M	2. DANIEL SHANE	Birth	18 SEP 1974

Family Group Record

Husband's Full Name: FRANK DORNELL LANE

Husband's Data	Day	Month	Year	City, Town or Place	County or Province, etc.	State or Country	Add. Info. on Husband
Birth							
Chr'nd							
Mar.							
Death							
Burial							

Places of Residence:
Occupation: Church Affiliation: Military Rec.:
Other wives, if any. No. (1) (2) etc. Make separate sheet for each mar.
His Father: Mother's Maiden Name:

Wife's Full Maiden Name: DIXIE GWENNE SUTER

Wife's Data	Day	Month	Year	City, Town or Place	County or Province, etc.	State or Country	Add. Info. on Wife
Birth	19	OCT	1958			MISS.	
Chr'nd							
Death							
Burial							

Places of Residence:
Occupation if other than Housewife: Church Affiliation:
Other husbands, if any. No. (1) (2) etc.
Her Father: HARRY FULLER SUTER JR.   Mother's Maiden Name: ELIZABETH C. WARD

Children

Sex	#	Children's Names in Full	Event	Day	Month	Year	City, Town or Place	State or Country
M	1	MYKAEL DORNELL	Birth	26	OCT	1984		
M	2	CHANCE JEROEN	Birth	03	NOV	1987		

The Ward Family History — Page 166

J. W. Ward Services Held Sat. In Goree

Funeral for John Walter Ward, 86, was held Saturday at 2:30 p.m., February 28, 1971, in the First United Methodist Church with the Rev. Marvin James, pastor, officiating, assisted by the Rev. Bennie Hagen of Eastland.

Mr. Ward died in the Knox County Hospital Thursday morning after a short illness.

Burial was in the Johnson Memorial Cemetery under direction of McCauley-Smith Funeral Home.

Mr. Ward was born in Johnson County November 14, 1884 and married Nellie A. Douglas in Merkel August 8, 1905. They moved to Knox County in 1961. He was a retired farmer.

Survivors include his wife; three daughters, Mrs. Goldie Brown of Goree, Mrs. Opal Draper of Dallas and Mrs. Alyne Parham of Munday; two sons, Ernest of Knox City and Alton of Munday; 17 grandchildren; 25 great-grandchildren; one sister, Mrs. Stella Swain of Anaheim, Calif.; two brothers, Henry of Hamlin and Ocie of Palmer.

Pallbearers were Ronnie Ward, Bobby Ward, Jerry Brown, Randall Brown, David Parham, Gary Draper, Gerald Draper, O'Darrell Draper. Honorary pallbearers were Ray Lynn Parham, Dennis Parham, Ralph Studer, Bill Caddell, Harlan Draper.

FAMILY GROUP No. ___

Husband's Full Name JOHN WALTER WARD

Husband's Data	Day	Month	Year	City, Town or Place	County or Province, etc.	State or Country	Add. Info. on Husband
Birth	14	NOV	1884	PARKER	JOHNSON	TEX.	
Chr'nd							
Mar.	08	AUG	1905	MERKEL	TAYLOR	TEX.	
Death	28	FEB	1971	KNOX CITY	KNOX	TEX.	
Burial				JOHNSON MEMORIAL CEMETERY			

Places of Residence
Occupation FARMER Church Affiliation METHODIST Military Rec.

His Father JAMES A. L. WARD Mother's Maiden Name REBECKA J. BAKER

Wife's Full Maiden Name NELLIE OPLAS DOUGLAS

Wife's Data	Day	Month	Year	City, Town or Place	County or Province, etc.	State or Country	Add. Info. on Wife
Birth							
Chr'nd							
Death							
Burial							

Places of Residence
Occupation if other than Housewife Church Affiliation

Her Father Mother's Maiden Name

Sex	Children's Names in Full	Children's Data	Day	Month	Year	City, Town or Place	County or Province, etc.	State or Country
1	GOLDIE ANN / Spouse: JOE ALTON BROWN	Birth	25	JUL	1906	ABILENE	TAYLOR	TEX.
		Mar.	01	SEP	1931	KNOX CITY	KNOX	TEX.
		Death						
		Burial						
2	OPAL / Spouse: DRAPER	Birth	14	NOV	1909			
		Mar.						
		Death						
		Burial						
3	EARNEST J / Spouse: DOLLIE MARGARET WEST	Birth	17	MAY	1912			TEX.
		Mar.				OLNEY	YOUNG	TEX.
		Death						
		Burial						
4	ALTON	Birth			1921			
		Mar.						
		Death	19	SEP	1980			
		Burial						
5	ALYNE / Spouse: PARHAM	Birth						
		Mar.						
		Death						
		Burial						

The Ward Family History
Family Group Record

FAMILY GROUP No. _____

Husband's Full Name: JOE ALTON BROWN

Husband's Data	Day Month Year	City, Town or Place	County or Province, etc.	State or Country
Birth	29 JAN 1906	MERIDAN	BOSQUE CO.	TEXAS
Chr'nd				
Mar.	1 SEPT 1931	KNOX CITY	KNOX CO.	TEXAS
Death	26 APR 1982	WICHITA FALLS	ARCHER CO.	TEXAS
Burial	28 APR 1982	GOREE	KNOX CO.	TEXAS

Occupation: FARMER **Church Affiliation:** METHODIST **Military Rec.:**

His Father: TOM BROWN **Mother's Maiden Name:** MOLLY WARREN

Wife's Full Maiden Name: GOLDIE ANN WARD

Wife's Data	Day Month Year	City, Town or Place	County or Province, etc.	State or Country
Birth	25 JULY 1906	ABILENE	TAYLOR CO	TEXAS
Chr'nd				
Death				
Burial				

Church Affiliation: METHODIST

Her Father: JOHN WALTER WARD **Mother's Maiden Name:** NILLIE OPLAS DOUGLAS

Children

1. M — JERRY LYNN (Spouse: LYNDA KAY GRISSOM)
- Birth: 23 JULY 1940, HASKEL, HASKEL CO., TEXAS
- Mar.: 3 APRIL 1961, MUNDAY, KNOX CO., TEXAS

2. M — RANDALL RAY (Spouse: PEGGY BOOE)
- Birth: 7 OCT 1942, GOREE, KNOX CO, TEXAS
- Mar.: 6 SEPT 1963, MUNDAY, KNOX CO., TEXAS

3. F — JOEANN (Spouse: MARVIN K. PATTERSON)
- Birth: 15 NOV 1944, GOREE, KNOX CO., TEXAS
- Mar.: 8 NOV 1968, GOREE, KNOX CO., TEXAS

FAMILY GROUP No.

Husband's Full Name: JERRY LYNN BROWN

Husband's Data	Day Month Year	City, Town or Place	County or Province, etc.	State or Country	Add. Info. on Husband
Birth	23 JULY 1940	HASKEL	HASKEL CO.	TEXAS	
Chr'nd					
Mar.	3 APRIL 1964	MUNDAY	KNOX CO.	TEXAS	
Death					
Burial					

Places of Residence:
Occupation: Church Affiliation: Military Rec.:

His Father: JOE ALTON BROWN Mother's Maiden Name: GOLDIE ANN WARD

Wife's Full Maiden Name: LINDA KAY GRISSOM

Wife's Data	Day Month Year	City, Town or Place	County or Province, etc.	State or Country	Add. Info. on Wife
Birth					
Chr'nd					
Death					
Burial					

Places of Residence:
Occupation if other than Housewife: Church Affiliation:

Her Father: Mother's Maiden Name:

Children

Sex	#	Child's Name	Event	Day Month Year
	1	MONTY BRAD	Birth	24 JUNE 1965
	2	KIMBERLY JOE	Birth	2 JAN 1970

FAMILY GROUP No. _____

Husband's Full Name: RANDALL RAY BROWN

Husband's Data	Day	Month	Year	City, Town or Place	County or Province, etc.	State or Country	Add. Info. on Husband
Birth	7	OCT	1942	GOREE	KNOX CO.	TEXAS	
Chr'nd							
Mar.	6	SEP	1963	MUNDAY	KNOX CO	TEXAS	
Death							
Burial							

Places of Residence
Occupation   Church Affiliation   Military Rec.
Other wives, if any. No. (1) (2) etc.

His Father: JOE ALTON BROWN   **Mother's Maiden Name:** GOLDIE ANN WARD

Wife's Full Maiden Name: PEGGY BOOE

Wife's Data	Day	Month	Year	City, Town or Place	County or Province, etc.	State or Country	Add. Info. on Wife
Birth							
Chr'nd							
Death							
Burial							

Places of Residence
Occupation if other than Housewife   Church Affiliation
Other husbands, if any. No. (1) (2) etc.

Her Father: _____   **Mother's Maiden Name:** _____

Children

Sex	#	Children's Names in Full	Event	Day	Month	Year	City, Town or Place	County	State
	1	AMY MELINDA	Birth	1	APRIL	1967			
	2	LANCE MICHEAL	Birth	11	MAY	1969			

FAMILY GROUP No. _____

Husband's Full Name MARVIN KENNETH PATTERSON

This Information Obtained From:

Husband's Data	Day	Month	Year	City, Town or Place	County or Province, etc.	State or Country	Add. Info. on Husband
Birth							
Chr'nd							
Mar.	8	NOV	1968	GOREE	KNOX CO.	TEXAS	
Death							
Burial							

Places of Residence

Occupation   Church Affiliation   Military Rec.

Other wives, if any, No. (1) (2) etc.

His Father _____   Mother's Maiden Name _____

Wife's Full Maiden Name JO ANN BROWN

Wife's Data	Day	Month	Year	City, Town or Place	County or Province, etc.	State or Country	Add. Info. on Wife
Birth	15	NOV	1944	GOREE	KNOX CO T	TEXAS	
Chr'nd							
Death							
Burial							

Compiler

Address

City, State

Date

Places of Residence

Occupation if other than Housewife   Church Affiliation

Other husbands, if any, No. (1) (2) etc.

Her Father JOE ALTON BROWN   Mother's Maiden Name GOLDIE ANN WARD

Sex	Children's Names in Full (Arrange in order of birth)		Day	Month	Year	City, Town or Place	County or Province, etc.	State or Country	Add. Info. on Children
1	KENNY LYNN	Birth	13	DEC	1972				
	Full Name of Spouse	Mar.							
		Death							
		Burial							
2		Birth							
	Full Name of Spouse	Mar.							
		Death							
		Burial							
3		Birth							
	Full Name of Spouse	Mar.							
		Death							
		Burial							
4		Birth							
	Full Name of Spouse	Mar.							
		Death							
		Burial							
5		Birth							
	Full Name of Spouse	Mar.							
		Death							
		Burial							
6		Birth							
	Full Name of Spouse	Mar.							
		Death							
		Burial							
7		Birth							
	Full Name of Spouse	Mar.							
		Death							
		Burial							
8		Birth							
	Full Name of Spouse	Mar.							
		Death							
		Burial							
9		Birth							
	Full Name of Spouse	Mar.							
		Death							
		Burial							
10		Birth							
	Full Name of Spouse	Mar.							
		Death							
		Burial							

*If married more than once No. each mar. (1) (2) etc. and list in "Add. info. on children" column. Use reverse side for additional children, other notes, references or information.

FAMILY GROUP No. _____

Husband's Full Name: ERNEST J. WARD

This Information Obtained From:

Husband's Data	Day Month Year	City, Town or Place	County or Province, etc.	State or Country	Add. Info. on Husb.
Birth	17 MAY 1912	ABILENE	TAYLOR	TEX.	
Chr'nd					
Mar.		OLNEY	YOUNG	TEX.	
Death					
Burial					

Places of Residence:
Occupation: GRO. STORE **Church Affiliation:** **Military Rec.:**
Other wives, if any, No. (1) (2) etc. Make separate sheet for each mar.

His Father: JOHN WALTER WARD **Mother's Maiden Name:** NELLIE OPLAS DOUGL[AS]

Wife's Full Maiden Name: DOLLIE MARGARET WEST

Wife's Data	Day Month Year	City, Town or Place	County or Province, etc.	State or Country	Add. Info. on Wife
Birth	08 MAR 1921				
Chr'nd					
Death					
Burial					

Compiler:
Address:
City, State:
Date:

Places of Residence:
Occupation if other than Housewife: GRO. OWNER **Church Affiliation:**
Other husbands, if any, No. (1) (2) etc. Make separate sheet for each mar.
WILLIAM[S]

Her Father: LUTHER LLOYD WEST **Mother's Maiden Name:** MARGARET ELIZABETH

Sex	Children's Names in Full (Arrange in order of birth)	Children's Data	Day Month Year	City, Town or Place	County or Province, etc.	State or Country	Add. Info. on Childr.
	1. Full Name of Spouse	Birth / Mar. / Death / Burial					
	2. Full Name of Spouse	Birth / Mar. / Death / Burial					
	3. Full Name of Spouse	Birth / Mar. / Death / Burial					
	4. Full Name of Spouse	Birth / Mar. / Death / Burial					
	5. Full Name of Spouse	Birth / Mar. / Death / Burial					
	6. Full Name of Spouse	Birth / Mar. / Death / Burial					
	7. Full Name of Spouse	Birth / Mar. / Death / Burial					
	8. Full Name of Spouse	Birth / Mar. / Death / Burial					
	9. Full Name of Spouse	Birth / Mar. / Death / Burial					
	10. Full Name of Spouse	Birth / Mar. / Death / Burial					

*If married more than once No. each mar. (1) (2) etc. and list in "Add. info. on children" column. Use reverse side for additional children, other notes, references or information.

Funeral and Obituary Notice printed in
THE ABILENE REPORTER NEWS
Abilene, Texas

In Memoriam

Entered Into Eternal Rest
MAY 2 2 1971

Lacy Ocia Ward

PALMER — Lacy Ocia Ward, 84, father of an Abilene man, died Saturday at 6:20 p.m. in an Ennis nursing home after a long illness.

Funeral will be at 3:30 p.m. Monday in the Palmer First Baptist Church with the Rev. W. P. Murchison, pastor, officiating, assisted by the Rev. Joe Pendleton and the Rev. Harold Burns.

Burial will be in the Palmer Cemetery under direction of Bunch Funeral Home.

Mr. Ward was born Nov. 11, 1886, in Cleburne, and spent most of his life as a farmer in the Palmer area.

He belonged to the Palmer First Baptist Church.

He married Stella Fowler.

Survivors are his wife of Palmer; three sons, T. J. of Abilene, Grady of Fort Worth and A. C. of Dallas; two daughters, Mrs. Claude Riley of Ennis and Mrs. Charles Green of Ferris; 10 grandchildren; 13 great-grandchildren; one brother, Henry of Hamlin.

One daughter, Mrs. Gertrude Billups, preceded him in death in 1968.

JULY 3, 1980

A Memorial Tribute

By Lloyd Fowler

A little less than a century ago the family of James A.L. Ward and Rebecca (Baker) Ward, were blessed by an addition of a baby boy, born Nov. 11, 1886 in the town of Cleburne, Texas. They gave him the name Lacy Ocia Ward. There were eight children in all, five boys: T.M., Henry, Herman, John and Lacy Ocia. The sisters being Florence, Beulah and Stella. Lacy Ocia of whom this tribute is dedicated, along with his wife, Stella, lived in Cleburne while growing up as young people.

At the age of twenty-one he was married to Miss Stella Lee Fowler, the daughter of Thomas Jefferson and Fredonia Fowler, also a native of Cleburne, Texas. She was about one year and one month younger than her husband, her birthdate being October 19, 1887.

They first lived in Newport, Texas for a few years, then moved into the Palmer community during the year 1916. They were engaged in the farming business most of their lifetime; however during the war years Mr. Ward became involved in other occupations for short periods of time. At one time he served as city nightwatchman. Stella, his wife, came from a rather large family, the Fowler family, with five brothers and five sisters namely: Elmer, Roy, William, Arthur and Omer were the brothers. The sisters were Clyde (Mrs. Alexander), Mrs. Jewel Cleveland, Dennora, Mrs. Ruby Laningham and Mrs. Clara Tackett. Mrs. Clara Tackett of Ennis being the surviving sister. Mr. and Mrs. Ward at an earlier date lived out in the Dalton Community, being engaged in farming. I believe this was on the old L.B. Griffith farm (not sure). Then sometime later they moved out on the Dr. Wadley farm, west of Palmer, on the old Palmer to Rockett road. The latter part of their farming career they moved to what was called the Ebenezer community, about three miles southwest of town, out on the old Risinger farm. From the time they had moved from Newport, Tex. into the Palmer Community, they were blessed with five fine children; namely: Gertrude Ward (Billups), deceased; T.J. of Abilene, Texas; Grady of Fort Worth, Texas; Gracie Ward (Green) of Ferris and Addison of Cedar Creek. Not sure that all the children were born in Palmer. After all the children had married and left home they shared much of their time with Grandmother Fredonia Fowler, who lived with them up until her death. Grandma Fowler was known to be one of sweetest persons who ever lived. If she ever got angry, she never showed it, with always a kind and good word about everyone. I still have the letter that she had written me while over-seas, with a prayer that I return safely home after the war. Yes, she was a great woman. Lacy Ocia Ward was better known, and was most times called by his initials, L.O. Some knew him as

Oce Ward. If he had a nickname, as most Palmer people did, I don't recall hearing one. These two fine people were my own aunt and uncle. Although this good uncle of mine enjoyed his work as a farmer, and the other jobs that ne performed, he just as equally enjoyed one particular sport, and that was fishing. For those who knew him, and that was just about everyone, they could expect him to stop and show the channel catfish or drums, which he had just caught the night before, or that day, from the old Chambers Creek fishing hole. It just always happened to be my good pleasure and opportunity to go along with Uncle Oce on these overnight fishing trips. It seemed that we had very much in common along this line. The particular style of fishing we used was the throw-line method, along with the single hook, tight-line, with small crawfish for bait on the throw-lines and Red-Horse minnows on the tight lines. Nylon lines were always used, least a big fish might break away. We would stop along the way and catch the crawfish from out of stock tanks, or ditches. Seldom did we fail to catch some fish; however, there was just one time that I remember, and I'm sure T.J. will also remember when we all three went to the old Trinity river, near Bristol, Tex. Well to make a long story short, the river was level full at the banks with muddy water, caused by a rise from upstream, making it impossible to do any fishing. Anyway Uncle Oce knew exactly where one of the Davis boys kept his fish-box, with live fish of which were for sale. Since we were hungry for fish, and there was some available, we built a campfire and cooked and ate fish. I think it was a Carp, not the best by any means, but we ate fish. Uncle Oce settled with the fisherman at a later date, so far as paying for fish fry. Yes, Uncle Oce Ward and I went on many fishing trips, most of the times at Chambers Creek. Two of my buddies will also remember going along at times. None other than A.B. Sealy and Raymond Caldwell, just ask them about how we used to catch those channel cats. My daddy enjoyed going fishing also as much as anyone, if not more so. Although Aunt Stella seldom went along, she never complained about out going. She always prepared a grub-book of food, and wished us much good luck. Later they bought the old Shingle Shack Cafe, and coverted it into a residence, where they lived for several years. Both Mr. and Mrs. Ward were members of the First Baptist Church in Palmer. Also he was a member of the Odd Fellows Lodge. Uncle Oce looked on the positive side of life. He enjoyed taking the lead and doing what he could for anyone who needed help. He enjoyed playing jokes on his friends, always with a ready answer for most anything. Uncle Oce Ward departed his life here May 22, 1971, his wife and children surviving, along with many, many friends. Aunt Stella continued to live in Palmer up until her death. Both have and will be missed, but will never be forgotten, in the generations to come.

They celebrated their 50th wedding anniversary in 1956, at the Fellowship Hall First Baptist Church in Palmer. They enjoyed sixty-four years and five months of happy married life, and attended many special reunions of the family together.

The Ward Family History
Page 177

FAMILY GROUP No.

Husband's Full Name: LACY OCIA WARD

Husband's Data	Day Month Year	City, Town or Place	County or Province, etc.	State or Country	Add. Info. on Husband
Birth	11 NOV 1886	PARKER	JOHNSON	TEX.	
Chr'nd					
Mar.	23 DEC 1906	CLEBURN	JOHNSON	TEX.	
Death	22 MAY 1971	ENNIS	ELLIS	TEX.	
Burial	24 MAY 1971	PALMER CEMETERY, ELLIS		TEX.	

Places of Residence:
Occupation: FARMER Church Affiliation: BAPTIST Military Rec.
His Father: J.A.L. WARD Mother's Maiden Name: REBECKA JANE BAKER

Wife's Full Maiden Name: STELLA LEE FOWLER

Wife's Data	Day Month Year	City, Town or Place	County or Province, etc.	State or Country	Add. Info. on Wife
Birth	19 Oct 1887	CLEBURN	JOHNSON	TEX.	
Chr'nd					
Death	14 DEC 1972	FERRIS	ELLIS	TEX.	
Burial	16 DEC 1972	PALMER CEM.	ELLIS	TEX.	

Places of Residence:
Occupation if other than Housewife: Church Affiliation: BAPTIST
Her Father: THOMAS JEFFERSON FOWLER Mother's Maiden Name: FREDONIA

Children

Sex	Children's Names in Full (Arrange in order of birth) / Spouse	Data	Day Month Year	City, Town or Place	County or Province, etc.	State or Country
F	1. GERTRUDE VIOLA / TRUETT BILLUPS	Birth	01 NOV 1907	CLIFF	HASKELL	TEX.
		Mar.	09 Jan 1929	PALMER	ELLIS	TEX.
		Death	27 Mar 1968	WAXAHACHIE	ELLIS	TEX
		Burial		BELLS CHAPEL ROCKET	ELLIS	TEX.
M	2. THOMAS JAMES (T. J.) / ETTA MAE HOBBS	Birth	16 JAN 1910	CLIFF	HASKELL	TEX.
		Mar.	15 APR 1934	PALMER	ELLIS	TEX.
		Death				
		Burial				
F	3. JEWELL O. / E. T. CLOUSE	Birth	31 DEC 1911	NEWPORT	CLAY	TEX.
		Mar.	12 FEB 1934	PALMER	ELLIS	TEX.
		Death				
		Burial				
F	4. GRACY LEONA / CHARLES GREEN	Birth	08 MAY 1914	NEWPORT	CLAY	TEX.
		Mar.	04 SEP 1937	ENNIS	ELLIS	TEX.
		Death				
		Burial				
M	5. GRADY LEON / LORENE WHITLOCK	Birth	08 MAY 1914	NEWPORT	CLAY	TEX.
		Mar.	22 MAY 1933			
		Death	22 SEP 1983	FT. RORTH	TARRANT	TEX.
		Burial		LAUREL LAND CEM. FT. WORTH, TARRANT		TEX.
M	6. ADDISON CLARENCE / CLEOPAL MERLE MARCRUM	Birth	28 JUN 1917	DALTON	ELLIS	TEX.
		Mar.	25 APR 1936	WAXACHACHI	ELLIS	TEX.
		Death				
		Burial				

FAMILY GROUP No. _____

Husband's Full Name: LACEY OCIA WARD

Husband's Data	Day Month Year	City, Town or Place	County or Province, etc.	State or Country
Birth	11 NOV 1886	PARKER	JOHNSON	TEX.
Chr'nd				
Mar.	1906	CLEBURN	JOHNSON	TEX.
Death	27 MAY 1971			
Burial				

Places of Residence:
Occupation: Church Affiliation: Military Rec.:

His Father: J.A.L. WARD **Mother's Maiden Name:** REBECKA JANE BAKER

Wife's Full Maiden Name: STELLA LEE FOWLER

Wife's Data	Day Month Year	City, Town or Place	County or Province, etc.	State or Country
Birth	19 Oct 1887	CLEBURN	JOHNSON	TEX.
Chr'nd				
Death				
Burial				

Her Father: THOMAS JEFFERSON FOWLER **Mother's Maiden Name:** FREDONIA

Sex	Children's Names in Full	Spouse	Birth
F	1. GERTRUDE	TRUETT BILLUPS	
M	2. THOMAS JAMES (T. J.)	MAY HOBBS	16 JAN 1910
F	3. JEWELL O.	CLAUD CLOUSE	31 DEC 1911
F	4. GRACY		08 MAY 1914
M	5. GRADY		08 MAY 1914
M	6. ADDISON		

			TEXAS	
M216	HEAD OF FAMILY	Ward, Henry Elmer	E.D. 240	SHEET 33
COLOR W	AGE 25	BIRTHPLACE Tex	VOL. 86	
COUNTY Jones		CITY		

OTHER MEMBERS OF FAMILY

NAME	RELATION-SHIP	AGE	BIRTHPLACE
Beulah	W	23	
Lacy L	D	5	
Baxter B	D	2	
Leonard	S	4/12	

U.S. DEPARTMENT OF COMMERCE — BUREAU OF THE CENSUS
1910 CENSUS INDEX — FAMILY

Edward Washburn and **Beulah** (Ward) Washburn. **Beulah** is the daughter of James Alexander Lacy Ward and Rebecca Jane (Baker) Ward

Edward   Beulah

Thirteenth Census Of The United States (1910 Census)

State: TEXAS | County: JONES | Township or other Division of County: JUSHIA | Enumeration Date: 20 APRIL | Roll: ___ | Sheet: 133 | Dist. ___

Location & Personal Description

Line	House number city or town	Number of dwelling house	Number of family	NAME	RELATION	Sex	Color	Age	Marital Status	Yrs. present marr.	Children born	Children living	Place of birth	Father's birthplace	Mother's birthplace
1		133	133	MASHBURN, EDWIN	Head	M	W	25	M	6			GEORGIA	GEORGIA	GEORGIA
2				BULAH	WIFE	F	W	23	M	6	3	3	TEXAS	LOUISIANA	TEN.
3				LACY ILLA	DAUGHTER	F	W	5	S				TEXAS	GEORGIA	TEXAS
4				KATIE BELL	DAUGHTER	F	W	2	S				TEXAS	GEORGIA	TEXAS
5				LEONORD	SON	M	W	4/12	S				TEXAS	GEORGIA	TEXAS
6															
7															
8															

Citizenship, Occupation, Education, Ownership

Line	Language	Occupation (Trade)	Industry	Employer/Employee	Out of work April 15, 1910	Weeks out of work 1909	Read	Write	Attended school since Sept. 1, 1909	Owned/rented	Owned free or mortgaged	Farm or house	Remarks
1	ENGLISH	SALESMAN	RETAIL GROCERY	W	NO	0	YES	YES	NO	R		H	
2	ENGLISH						YES	YES	NO				
3													
4													
5													
6													
7													
8													

FAMILY GROUP No. ___

Husband's Full Name: CHARLES EDMOND MASHBURN

Husband's Data	Day Month Year	City, Town or Place	County or Province, etc.	State or Country	Add. Info. on Husb
Birth	26 SEP 1883			GR.	
Chr'nd					
Mar.					
Death	1921	STITH	JONES	TX.	
Burial		STITH	JONES	TX.	

Places of Residence:
Occupation: GRO. SALES   Church Affiliation: Military Rec.:
Other wives, if any, No. (1) (2) etc.

His Father: J. W. MASBBURN   Mother's Maiden Name: S. C. WHITMIRE

Wife's Full Maiden Name: ALA BULAH WARD

Wife's Data	Day Month Year	City, Town or Place	County or Province, etc.	State or Country	Add. Info. on Wife
Birth	08 FEB 1889	PARKER	JOHNSON	TX.	
Chr'nd					
Death					
Burial		KNOX CITY	KNOX	TX.	

Places of Residence:
Occupation if other than Housewife: Church Affiliation:
Other husbands, if any, No. (1) (2) etc.   2-CAGLE 3-LANDRETH 4-HELMS

Her Father: JAMES A. L. WARD   Mother's Maiden Name: REBECCA J. BAKER

Sex	Children's Names in Full	Children's Data	Day Month Year	City, Town or Place	County or Province, etc.	State or Country	Add. Info. on Child
F	1 ILA LACY — Spouse: LUTHER REECE WOOLEY	Birth	04 NOV 1904	KNOX CITY	KNOX	TX.	
		Mar.	1924				
		Death					
		Burial					
F	2 KATIE BELL	Birth	04 AUG 1907	STITH	JONES	TX.	
		Mar.					
		Death					
		Burial					
M	3 LENARD	Birth	12 DEC 1909	STITH	JONES	TX.	
		Mar.					
		Death					
		Burial		STITH	JONES	TX.	
M	4 ROBERT	Birth	01 NOV 1911	STITH	JONES	TX.	
		Mar.					
		Death					
		Burial					
M	5 EDMOND CHARLES (BUD) — Spouse: EVA EDELINE GILLESPIE	Birth	31 JAN 1913	STITH	JONES	TX.	
		Mar.	13 APR 1935	SWEETWATER	NOLAN	TX.	
		Death					
		Burial					
M	6 EDWARD CHARLES (DUD)	Birth	31 JAN 1913	STITH	JONES	TX.	
		Mar.					
		Death	19 FEB 1968	FORT WORTH	TARANT	TX.	
		Burial		FORT WORTH	TARANT	TX.	
F	7 REBECKA BULA	Birth	22 MAY 1916	SWEETWATER	NOLAN	TX.	
		Mar.					
		Death					
		Burial					
	8 BILLIE	Birth	29 JAN 1919	SWEETWATER	NOLAN	TX.	
		Mar.					
		Death				CAL.	
		Burial					

FAMILY GROUP No. ___

Husband's Full Name LUTHER REECE WOOLEY

This Information Obtained From:

Husband's Data	Day Month Year	City, Town or Place	County or Province, etc.	State or Country	Add. Info. on Husband
Birth	27 JAN 1896	MARLIN	FALLS	TEX.	
Chr'nd					
Mar.	1924	BENJAMIN	KNOX	TEX.	
Death	17 OCT 1984	KNOX CITY	KNOX	TEX.	
Burial	19 OCT 1984	KNOX CITY	KNOX	TEX.	

Marshal L. Wooley
3324 LA SALL
COLORADO SPRINGS. COL
85909
Phone 303-633-6155

Places of Residence

Occupation RANCHER   Church Affiliation 4 SQUARE   Military Rec.

His Father JAMES R. WOOLEY   Mother's Maiden Name NANNY

Wife's Full Maiden Name LACEY ILLA WARD

Wife's Data	Day Month Year	City, Town or Place	County or Province, etc.	State or Country	Add. Info. on Wife
Birth	04 NOV 1904	KNOX CITY	KNOX	TEX.	
Chr'nd					
Death					
Burial					

Compiler Alvin L. Ward
Address P.O. Box 1756
City, State Denver City, Tx.
Date 14 Sept 1989

Places of Residence

Occupation if other than Housewife   Church Affiliation 4 SQUARE

Her Father EDWIN MASHBURN   Mother's Maiden Name BULAH WARD

Sex	Children's Names in Full (Arrange in order of birth)	Children's Data	Day Month Year	City, Town or Place	County or Province, etc.	State or Country	Add. Info. on Children
M	1 MARSHAL L.	Birth	18 AUG				
	Full Name of Spouse	Mar.					
		Death					
		Burial					
	2 WILLIAM	Birth	18 AUG				
	Full Name of Spouse	Mar.					
		Death					
		Burial					

The Ward Family History

FAMILY GROUP No. _____

Husband's Full Name EDMOND CHARLES MASHBURN

Husband's Data	Day Month Year	City, Town or Place	County or Province, etc.	State or Country	Add. Info. on Husband
Birth	31 JAN 1913	STITH	JONES	TX.	
Chr'nd					
Mar.	13 APR 1935	SWEETWATER	NOLAN	TX.	
Death					
Burial					

Places of Residence
Occupation Church Affiliation C. OF CHRIST Military Rec.

His Father CHARLES E. MASHBURN Mother's Maiden Name BUELAH WARD

Wife's Full Maiden Name EVA ADELINE GILLESPIE

Wife's Data	Day Month Year	City, Town or Place	County or Province, etc.	State or Country	Add. Info. on Wife
Birth	12 NOV 1916	RANKIN	TRAVIS	TX.	
Chr'nd					
Death	09 APR 1983	LAS VEGAS	CLARK	NV.	
Burial		LAS VEGAS	CLARK	NV.	

Places of Residence
Occupation if other than Housewife Church Affiliation BAPTIST

Her Father BENJAMINE GILLESPI Mother's Maiden Name

Sex	Children's Names in Full	Event	Day Month Year	City, Town or Place	County or Province	State or Country
F	1. MINNIE M. — Spouse: JAMES R. EBARD	Birth / Mar.	03 JUL 1936 / 03 JUL 1954	SWEETWATER / LAS VEGAS	NOLAN / CLARK	TX. / NV.
F	2. JACQUELINE A. — Spouse: THOMAS EATON	Birth	23 DEC 1940	BLYTHE	RIVERSIDE	CAL.
F	3. JEANETTE — Spouse: ROBERT L. SIMPSON	Birth / Mar.	06 MAR 1946 / 28 NOV 1962	SWEETWATER	NOLAN	TX.
M	4. WILLIAM E — Spouse: DELORES	Birth	23 OCT 1963	SWEETWATER	NOLAN	TX.

The Ward Family History
Page 185

TEXAS STATE DEPARTMENT OF HEALTH
BUREAU OF VITAL STATISTICS
STANDARD CERTIFICATE OF DEATH

Registrar's No. 75

1. PLACE OF DEATH
   STATE OF TEXAS
   COUNTY OF: Nolan
   CITY OR PRECINCT NO.: Sweetwater, Texas

2. FULL NAME OF DECEASED: Mr. W.W. Cagle

PERSONAL AND STATISTICAL PARTICULARS

3. SEX: Male
4. COLOR OR RACE: White
5. Single / Widowed / Married: Married
5a. HUSBAND of (or) WIFE of: Mrs. W.W. Cagle
6. DATE OF BIRTH: April 4, 1889
7. AGE: 44 Years, 6 Months, 10 Days

12. BIRTHPLACE: Texas
13. NAME (Father): Don't know
14. BIRTHPLACE (Father): Don't know
15. MAIDEN NAME (Mother): Don't know
16. BIRTHPLACE (Mother): Don't know

17. INFORMANT: Mrs. W.W. Cagle, Sweetwater, Texas
18. BURIAL, CREMATION, OR REMOVAL: Sweetwater, Tex. — Date: Oct. 17, 1933
19. UNDERTAKER: S.M. Johnston, Sweetwater, Texas
20. FILE DATE AND SIGNATURE OF REGISTRAR: Nov. 4, 1933 — E.W. Prothro

MEDICAL CERTIFICATE OF DEATH

21. DATE OF DEATH: Oct. 17, 1933
22. I HEREBY CERTIFY, That I attended deceased from Oct. 1, 1933 to Oct. 7, 1933. I last saw h__ alive on Oct. 7, 1933; death is said to have occurred on the date stated above, at 1:00 A.m.

The principal cause of death and related causes of importance were as follows: I did not see him till had hemorrhage on date above given said to have a typhoid origin.

Other contributory causes of importance: None that I know of.

Name of operation: none
What test confirmed diagnosis? ___ Was there an autopsy? no

23. If death was due to external causes (violence) fill in also the following:
    Accident, suicide, or homicide: ___
    Date of injury: ___

24. Was disease or injury in any way related to occupation of deceased? no

(Signed) A.A. Chapman, M.D.
(Address) Sweetwater, Texas

FAMILY GROUP No. ____

Husband's Full Name: WILLIAM WESLEY CAGLE

Husband's Data	Day	Month	Year	City, Town or Place	County or Province, etc.	State or Country	Add. Info.
Birth							
Chr'nd							
Mar.							
Death							
Burial							

Places of Residence:
Occupation: Church Affiliation: Military Rec.:
Other wives, if any. No. (1) (2) etc.
His Father: Mother's Maiden Name:

Wife's Full Maiden Name: BEULAH WARD

Wife's Data	Day	Month	Year	City, Town or Place	County or Province, etc.	State or Country	Add. Info. on Wife
Birth	8	FEB	1889	PARKER	JOHNSON	TEX.	
Chr'nd							
Death							
Burial				KNOX CITY	KNOX	TEX.	

Places of Residence:
Occupation if other than Housewife: Church Affiliation:
Other husbands, if any. No. (1)(2) etc.: (1) EDWIN MASHBURN (3) HELMS
Her Father: J.A.L. WARD   Mother's Maiden Name: REBECK J. BAKER

Sex	Children's Names in Full	Children's Data	Day	Month	Year	City, Town or Place	County or Province, etc.	State or Country
M	1 JOHN WESLEY	Birth	11	MAR	1926	SWEETWATER	NOLAN	TEX.
		Mar.						
		Death						
		Burial						
M	2 WILLIAM HERSHEL	Birth						
		Mar.						
		Death						
		Burial						

FAMILY GROUP No. ___

Husband's Full Name JOHN WILLIAM (BILL) SWAIN

This Information Obtained From:

Husband's Data	Day	Month	Year	City, Town or Place	County or Province, etc.	State or Country	Add. Info. on Husband
Birth							
Chr'nd							
Mar.							
Death							
Burial							

Places of Residence

Occupation _____ Church Affiliation _____ Military Rec.

Other wives, if any, No. (1) (2) etc. Make separate sheet for each mar.

His Father _____ Mother's Maiden Name _____

Wife's Full Maiden Name STELLA WARD

Wife's Data	Day	Month	Year	City, Town or Place	County or Province, etc.	State or Country	Add. Info. on Wife
Birth			1894	PARKER	JOHNSON	TEX.	
Chr'nd							
Death	15	MAY	1971				
Burial							

Compiler _____
Address _____
City, State _____
Date _____

Places of Residence
Occupation if other than Housewife _____ Church Affiliation _____
Other husbands, if any, No. (1) (2) etc.

Her Father J.A.L. WARD _____ Mother's Maiden Name REBECKA JANE WARD

Sex	Children's Names in Full (Arrange in order of birth)	Children's Data	Day	Month	Year	City, Town or Place	County or Province, etc.	State or Country	Add. Info. on Children
1	BERNICE	Birth						TEX.	
	Full Name of Spouse	Mar. / Death / Burial							
2	J. W. JR.	Birth						CAL.	
	Full Name of Spouse	Mar. / Death / Burial							
3	DWIGHT	Birth						CAL.	
	Full Name of Spouse	Mar. / Death / Burial							

James Herman and Stella Ward - Children of J.A.L. Ward and Rebecca Jane Baker Ward.

Kennedy, Cleburne, Texas.

Herman   Stella

Mrs. Ila Ward Dies At Age 73
01 Jun 1971

Mrs. Ila Katie Ward, 73, a native of Eastland County, died about 6 p.m. Tuesday in a Plainview nursing home.

Funeral services are scheduled for 4:30 p.m. Thursday in Ninth and Columbia Street Church of Christ with Gene Polvado, minister, and Rev. Eddie Freeman, pastor, Date Street Baptist Church, officiating. Burial will be in Parklawn Memorial Gardens with Lemons Funeral Home in charge of arrangements.

Mrs. Ward moved to Plainview from Snyder in 1923 to Ranger in 1939 and to Belton in 1961 from Sweetwater and recently had made her home in Plainview with her son. She had lived in the nursing home about a month.

A member of the Belton Church of Christ, Mrs. Ward was born March 1, 1898 in Eastland County.

She is survived by a son, Weldon Way of Plainview; three daughters, Mrs. Emil Staub of Peoria, Ill., Mrs. Troy Hill of Amarillo and Mrs. C. E. Wheeler of Belton; four brothers, Sterling Reynolds of Lubbock; Cullen Reynolds of McAllen, William Reynolds of San Gabriel, Calif. and L. J. Reynolds of Denver, Colo., two sisters, Mrs. L. L. Snead of Plainview and Mrs. Pallie Way of Victoria; 10 grandchildren; 20 great-grandchildren and one great-great-grandchild.

James H. (Jack) Ward Died Today
13 Jan 1939

James H. (Jack) Ward, 41, died early this morning at his home in Seth Ward addition after a week's illness. Funeral services will be tomorrow afternoon at 3 o'clock at the Roy G. Wood chapel with Dr. E. A. Reed, pastor of the First Methodist Church, officiating. Burial will be here.

Jack Ward was born Aug. 8, 1897 in Jones County, Texas, and moved to Plainview 20 years ago from Floydada. He was a farmer and a musician, having been with Terry Bros. Orchestra.

Surviving are his wife, child, Betty Jo, three daughters, Mrs. Estelle Barbee, Weldon and Christine Way, all of Plainview; three brothers, John Henry Ward of Munday, Ward of Corsicana; and sisters, Mrs. Florence Good Itasca, Mrs. Beulah Kagle of Sweetwater, and Mrs. Estelle of Pasadena, Calif.

Last Rites Held For (Jack) Ward

Funeral services for James H. (Jack) Ward were conducted yesterday afternoon at the Roy G. Wood chapel by Dr. E. A. Reed, pastor of the First Methodist Church, and burial followed in the I.O.O.F. cemetery.

Pallbearers were: Clyde Terry, William Terry, Wayne Locke, J. H. Rainer, Calvin Cook, and Warren Gregory.

Flower bearers were Mrs. Z. T. Garner, Mrs. Ray Couch, and Mrs. Jack Wizner.

Mr. Ward died Friday morning at his home in Seth Ward addition. He moved here 20 years ago from Floydada.

FAMILY GROUP No. ___

This Information Obtained From:

Husband's Full Name: James Herman (Jack) WARD

Husband's Data	Day Month Year	City, Town or Place	County or Province, etc.	State or Country	Add. Info. on Husb.
Birth	08 Aug 1896	Parker	Johnson	Tex.	
Chr'nd					
Mar.					
Death	13 Jan 1939	Plainview	Hale	Tex.	
Burial		Plainview	Hale	Tex.	

Places of Residence: Plainview Hermleigh Snyder
Occupation: Farmer **Church Affiliation:** Methodist **Military Rec.**

His Father: J. A. T. WARD **Mother's Maiden Name:** Rebecca Jane BAKER

Wife's Full Maiden Name: Ila Katie REYNOLDS

Wife's Data	Day Month Year	City, Town or Place	County or Province, etc.	State or Country	Add. Info. on Wife
Birth	01 Mar 1898	Desdemon	Eastland	Tex.	
Chr'nd					
Death	01 Jun 1971	Plainview	Hale	Tex.	
Burial		Plainview	Hale	Tex.	

Compiler **Places of Residence**
Address **Occupation if other than Housewife** **Church Affiliation:** Church of Christ
City, State Other husbands, if any. (1) J author Way
Date **Her Father:** John W. REYNOLDS **Mother's Maiden Name:** Sidney E. Warren

Sex	Children's Names in Full (Arrange in order of birth)	Children's Data	Day Month Year	City, Town or Place	County or Province, etc.	State or Country	Add. Info. on Child
M/F	1 Betty Jo — Claude F. (Jack) Wheel	Birth	11 Dec 1927	Plainview	Hale	Tex.	
		Mar.	31 May 1947	Hobbs	Lee	N.M.	
		Death					
		Burial					
	2	Birth					
		Mar.					
		Death					
		Burial					
F	3 Estelle — Emil STAUB	Birth	12 Apr 1916	RANGER	Eastland	Tex.	Step child
		Mar.	Jun 1945	Abilene	Taylor	Tex.	
		Death					
		Burial					
M	4 Weldon A. — F. Maurine Garner	Birth	16 APR 1919	Snyder	Scurry	Tex.	Step child
		Mar.	7 Nov 1937	Plainview	Hale	Tex.	
		Death					
		Burial					
F	5 Christine A. — Troy Hill	Birth	11 Jun 1923	Snyder	Scurry	Tex.	Step child
		Mar.	Jul 1950	Amarillo	Randall	Tex.	
		Death	22 Nov 1981	Amarillo	Randall	Tex.	
		Burial		Amarillo	Randall	Tex.	

FAMILY GROUP No. _____

Husband's Full Name Michael C. GULLEY

Husband's Data	Day Month Year	City, Town or Place	County or Province, etc.	State or Country	Add. Info. on Husband
Birth					
Chr'nd					
Mar.	20 Jul 1974	Belton	Bell	Tex.	
Death					
Burial					

Places of Residence

Occupation — Church Affiliation — Military Rec.

Other wives, if any. No. (1) (2) etc. Make separate sheet for each mar.

His Father — Mother's Maiden Name

Wife's Full Maiden Name Pamela Sue WHEELER

Wife's Data	Day Month Year	City, Town or Place	County or Province, etc.	State or Country	Add. Info. on Wife
Birth	02 Mar 1956	Sweetwater	Nolen	Tex.	
Chr'nd					
Death					
Burial					

Places of Residence

Occupation if other than Housewife — Church Affiliation

Her Father Claude Elvis WHEELER — Mother's Maiden Name Betty Jo WARD

Sex	Children's Names in Full	Children's Data	Day Month Year	City, Town or Place	County or Province, etc.	State or Country
M	1. David Michael	Birth	25 Oct 1978			
M	2. Patrick Wayne	Birth	22 Aug 1982			
	3.					
	4.					
	5.					
	6.					
	7.					
	8.					
	9.					
	10.					

FAMILY GROUP No.

Husband's Full Name: Billy Jack Wheeler

Husband's Data	Day Month Year	City, Town or Place	County or Province, etc.	State or Country	Add. Info. on Husband
Birth	18 Jul 1959	Sweetwater	Nolan	Tex.	
Chr'nd					
Mar.	10 Apr 1987	Belton	Bell	Tex.	
Death					
Burial					

Places of Residence:
Occupation: Church Affiliation: Military Rec.:

His Father: Claude Elvis WHEELER   Mother's Maiden Name: Betty Jo WARD

Wife's Full Maiden Name: Penny Lee WHITLEY

Wife's Data	Day Month Year	City, Town or Place	County or Province, etc.	State or Country	Add. Info. on Wife
Birth					
Chr'nd					
Death					
Burial					

Compiler: Places of Residence:
Address: Occupation if other than Housewife: Church Affiliation:
City, State:
Date: Her Father: Mother's Maiden Name:

Children

Sex	#	Name	Event	Day Month Year	Add. Info.
M	1	Cory Jack	Birth	03 Jul 1977	
F	2	Amanda Nicole	Birth	31 Oct 1979	
m	3	Joshua Lee	Birth	06 Jul 1985	Step son
M	4	Jason Allen	Birth	09 Oct 1987	

FAMILY GROUP No. ____

Husband's Full Name: Claude Elvis (Jack) WHEELER

Husband's Data	Day Month Year	City, Town or Place	County or Province, etc.	State or Country	Add. Info. on Husband
Birth	26 Jan 1923	Ranger	Eastland	Tex.	
Chr'nd					
Mar.	31 May 1947	Hobbs	Lea	N.M.	
Death					
Burial					

Places of Residence: Belton, Sweetwater, Ft. Worth, Ranger
Occupation: Machinist   **Church Affiliation:** Baptist   **Military Rec.:** U.S.N.

His Father: Toney B. WHEELER   **Mother's Maiden Name:** Mattie Lee Sharp

Wife's Full Maiden Name: Betty Jo WARD

Wife's Data	Day Month Year	City, Town or Place	County or Province, etc.	State or Country	Add. Info. on Wife
Birth	11 Dec 1927	Plainview	Hale	Tex.	
Chr'nd					
Death					
Burial					

Places of Residence: Plainview, Sweetwater, Ft. Worth, Ranger, Belton
Occupation if other than Housewife: **Church Affiliation:** Church of Christ

Her Father: James Herman WARD   **Mother's Maiden Name:** Ila Katie REYNOLDS

Children

Sex	#	Children's Names in Full / Spouse	Event	Day Month Year	City, Town or Place	County or Province, etc.	State or Country	Add. Info. on Children
M	1	Larry Weldon / Clarinda Ann CULP	Birth	09 Oct 1953	Ft. Worth	Tarrent	Tex.	
			Mar.	25 Jun 1971	Belton	Bell	Tex	
F	2	Pamela Sue / Michael C. Gulley	Birth	02 Mar 1956	Sweetwater	Nolan	Tex.	
			Mar.	20 Jul 1974	Belton	Bell	Tex.	
M	3	Billy Jack / Penny Lee WHITLEY	Birth	18 Jul 1959	Sweetwater	Nolan	Tex.	
			Mar.	10 Apr 1987	Belton	Bell	Tex	2nd wife

The Ward Family History

FAMILY GROUP No. _____ **Husband's Full Name** Larry Weldon WHEELER

Husband's Data	Day Month Year	City, Town or Place	County or Province, etc.	State or Country	Add. Info. on Husband
Birth	09 Oct 1953	Ft. Worth	Tarrent	Tex.	
Chr'nd					
Mar.	25 Jun 1971	Belton	Bell	Tex.	
Death					
Burial					

Places of Residence
Occupation   Church Affiliation   Military Rec.

His Father: Claud Elvis Wheeler   Mother's Maiden Name: Betty Jo WARD

Wife's Full Maiden Name Clarinda Ann Culp

Wife's Data	Day Month Year	City, Town or Place	County or Province, etc.	State or Country	Add. Info. on Wife
Birth					
Chr'nd					
Death					
Burial					

Her Father: _____   Mother's Maiden Name: _____

Children

Sex	Child's Name	Event	Day Month Year
M	1. Jeremy Lynn	Birth	22 Apr 1974
F	2. Tessa Renee	Birth	23 Oct 1983

WILL HARRIS & ELKANEA AND THEIR CHILDREN

Will Harris and Elkanea Ann (Ward) Harris and their children.

The youngest children in the picture are twin boys, Douglas and Duran.

DOUGLAS and DURAN HARRIS

Twin sons of Will Harris and Elkanea Ann (Ward) Harris.

Mrs. E. A. Harris, wife of Wm. Harris, died at her home, three miles northwest of Covington May 23rd, 1928, at 9:20 a. m. Deceased leaves to mourn her loss, her husband and five children, three boys and two girls, George, Robert, Duren, Miss Essie Harris, all of Covington, and Mrs. Oscar Woods of McAdo, Texas, and several brothers and sisters. The deceased was born in Louisiana August 24th, 1861 and moved to Texas with her parents in early childhood. Although Mrs. Harris' death was not unexpected it was a great shock to her many friends when the word came that she lived no more. Bro. Ervin of Hillsboro had charge of the services. The pallbearers were: Will Goodman, Joe Bean, Joe Taylor, Henry Johnson, Rev. McDonald, Mr. Clements. Brown Rees Co., Itasca, were in charge of arrangements.

Dearest mother, thou hath left us,
  And our loss we deeply feel.
But 'tis God that has bereft us.
  He can all our sorrows heal.

Yet again we hope to meet thee,
  When the day of life has fled,
When in heaven in joy to greet thee
  Where no farewell tear is shed.

FAMILY GROUP No. _____ **Husband's Full Name** WILLIAM HARRIS

This information Obtained From:

Husband's Data	Day Month Year	City, Town or Place	County or Province, etc.	State or Country	Add. Info. on Husband
Birth	JUL 1858			TEX.	
Chr'nd					
Mar.	12 Jul 1880			TEX.	
Death					
Burial					

We know that this family had 11 children that were born to them by the time of the 1910 Census. By 28 Douglas had died. The 1900 Census List the 3rd child as Marvin F. 11 yrs old. In 1910 the 3rd child is Robert, who is 21 Years old. Also the 1928 Obit list the son as Robert. I am of the opinion that his name is Robert. Why in 1900 He is Marvin F. I do not know, unless he had three names

Places of Residence

Occupation   Church Affiliation   Military Rec.

Other wives, if any. No. (1) (2) etc.

His Father   Mother's Maiden Name

Wife's Full Maiden Name ELCANZIE A. WARD (CANZIE)

Wife's Data	Day Month Year	City, Town or Place	County or Province, etc.	State or Country	Add. Info. on Wife
Birth	24 AUG 1861		HEMPSTEAD	ARK.	
Chr'nd					
Death	23 MAY 1928	COVINGTON	HILL	TEX.	
Burial					

Compiler
Address
City, State
Date

Places of Residence
Occupation if other than Housewife   Church Affiliation
Other husbands, if any, No. (1) (2) etc.

Her Father MARVIN FULLER WARD   Mother's Maiden Name ELIZABETH JANE ROSE

Sex	Children's Names in Full	Children's Data	Day Month Year	City, Town or Place	County or Province, etc.	State or Country	Add. Info. on Children
M	1 GEORGE	Birth	JUN 1881	COVINGTON	HILL	TEX.	
		Mar.					
		Death					
		Burial					
F	2 ELIZABETH PEARL / OSCAR WOODS	Birth	MAR 1884	COVINGTON	HILL	TEX.	
		Mar.					
		Death					
		Burial					
M	3 MARVIN F. (ROBERT)	Birth	NOV 1888	COVINGTON	HILL	TEX.	
		Mar.					
		Death					
		Burial					
M	4 DOUGLAS	Birth	DEC 1897	COVINGTON	HILL	TEX.	
		Mar.					
		Death		COVINGTON	HILL	TEX.	
		Burial					
M	5 DUREN	Birth	DEC 1897	COVINGTON	HILL	TEX.	
		Mar.					
		Death					
		Burial					
M	6 CARL	Birth	1902	COVINGTON	HILL	TEX.	
		Mar.					
		Death					
		Burial					
F	7 ESSIE	Birth	1905	COVINGTON	HILL	TEX	
		Mar.					
		Death					
		Burial					
	8	Birth					
		Mar.					
		Death					
		Burial					
	9	Birth					
		Mar.					
		Death					
		Burial					
	10	Birth					
		Mar.					
		Death					
		Burial					

*If married more than once No. each mar. (1) (2) etc. and list in "Add. info. on children" column. Use reverse side for additional children, other notes, references or information.

The Ward Family History
Page 200

FAMILY GROUP No. _____

Husband's Full Name OSCAR V. WOODS

This Information Obtained From:

It seems that this family is like the Harris family as this is from the 1910 Census and they have lost one child by now.

Husband's Data	Day	Month	Year	City, Town or Place	County or Province, etc.	State or Country	Add. Info. on Husband
Birth			1879			TEX.	
Chr'nd							
Mar.							
Death							
Burial							

Places of Residence:
Occupation: FARMER Church Affiliation: Military Rec.:
Other wives, if any, No. (1) (2) etc. Make separate sheet for each mar.
His Father: Mother's Maiden Name:

Wife's Full Maiden Name ELIZABETH PEARL HARRIS

Wife's Data	Day	Month	Year	City, Town or Place	County or Province, etc.	State or Country	Add. Info. on Wife
Birth		MAR	1884	COVINGTON	HILL	TEX.	
Chr'nd							
Death							
Burial							

Places of Residence:
Occupation if other than Housewife: Church Affiliation:
Other husbands, if any, No. (1) (2) etc. Make separate sheet for each mar.
Her Father: WILLIAM HARRIS Mother's Maiden Name: ELCANZIE A. WARD

Sex	Children's Names in Full (Arrange in order of birth)	Children's Data	Day	Month	Year	City, Town or Place	County or Province, etc.	State or Country	Add. Info. on Children
M	1 DEWEY L.	Birth			1905				
	Full Name of Spouse	Mar.							
		Death							
		Burial							
M	2 JOHN F.	Birth							
	Full Name of Spouse	Mar.							
		Death							
		Burial							
	3	Birth							
	Full Name of Spouse	Mar.							
		Death							
		Burial							
	4	Birth							
	Full Name of Spouse	Mar.							
		Death							
		Burial							
	5	Birth							
	Full Name of Spouse	Mar.							
		Death							
		Burial							
	6	Birth							
	Full Name of Spouse	Mar.							
		Death							
		Burial							
	7	Birth							
	Full Name of Spouse	Mar.							
		Death							
		Burial							
	8	Birth							
	Full Name of Spouse	Mar.							
		Death							
		Burial							
	9	Birth							
	Full Name of Spouse	Mar.							
		Death							
		Burial							
	10	Birth							
	Full Name of Spouse	Mar.							
		Death							
		Burial							

The Ward Family History
Page 201

John William WARD

Docia Hewit

John William WARD

John William and Lucia Ward family, and the first six of their ten children.

Back row - left to right: Oscar Samuel - George Jarvin - John Ira.
Front: (?)...William Byron - Vancie Bell - Lucia and Elmer

The Mena Weekly Star

John William Ward

WARD FUNERAL MONDAY AT HATFIELD

Funeral service for John W. Ward, who died Saturday at his home east of Hatfield, was held Monday afternoon at 4 o'clock at the Hatfield Methodist church with the Rev. Vinson, pastor, officiating. Burial at the Hatfield cemetery was directed by the Geyer Funeral home. The pallbearers were Amos Musgrave, Tut Harris, Joe Lane, James Rogers, Roy Parsons and Elmer Hasting.

Mr. Ward was a native of Texas but had been a resident of Polk county for the past 20 years. He was a farmer by vocation, was a member of the Methodist church and the Masonic and W.O.W. fraternities. He was preceded in death by his wife in 1937, and is survived by one daughter, Mrs. S. W. Almonrode, Hatfield; nine sons, Monroe Ward, Knox City, Texas; J. I. Ward, Pocahontas, Miss.; Oscar Ward, Morrilton, Ark.; Elmer Ward, Sweetwater, Texas; William Ward, Oklahoma City, Okla.; Fred and Dale Ward, Whittier, Calif.; Dewey Ward, Santa Monica, Calif.; Ollie Ward, Canoga Park, Calif.; one brother, M. N. Ward, Crane, Texas; eighteen grandchildren and one great grandchild.

Born: 29 Feb. 1864
Died: 30 Mar. 1940

Docia (Hewitt) Ward

Mrs. Docia Ward Dies at Farm Home.

Mrs. Docia Ward, wife of J. W. Ward, died from a long illness early Friday morning at their farm home on Six Mile creek. The family came here from Brownsfield, Texas, in 1920. Funeral services were held at the Methodist church Sunday afternoon, the Rev. J. W. Rushing, pastor, officiating.

Elder C. E. Burkeen had charge of the singing with the Geyer Funeral Home directing. Burial took place in Six Mile cemetery.

The deceased is survived by J. W. Ward, her husband, Hatfield; nine sons, M. M. Ward, Knox City, Texas, Ira Ward, Pocahontas, Miss., Oscar Ward, Hatfield, Elmer Ward, Sweetwater, Texas, W. B. Ward, Oklahoma City, Okla., Fred Ward, Dale Ward, Ollie Ward, Whittier, Calif., and Dewey Ward, San Francisco, Calif., and one daughter, Mrs. Nannie Almonrode, Hatfield, two brothers, J. A. Hewitt, Cleburn, Texas, and Fred Hewitt, Hatfield, and one sister, Bessie Willis, Booneville.

Mrs. Ward was born in Taylorville, Illinois, 69 years ago. She was married to J. W. Ward in 1885 at Rio Vista, Texas, and became a member of the Methodist church the same year.

Born: 04 Jan. 1868
Died: 15 Oct. 1937

Excerpt from a letter written at Anaheim, California, August 22, 1970, from Monroe Ward (age 83) to his sister, Nannie (Ward) Almonrode, who lived at Hatfield, Arkansas.

About our trip to Jones County:

As I remember, we left Johnson Co. in Dec. 1889. On Christmas day that year we were in a wagon yard at Eastland, I think. I remember some one shooting Roman Candles. Have one idea we pulled in to Abilene a few days later. As I remember we stayed in Abilene only a few days and headed North. Camped one day for dinner or something half way between Abilene and Anson in front of the house of a family by the name of Newberry. Mr Newberry wanted Dad and Uncle Fred to look at a piece of land (200 acres) about a mile west. They did and there's where we settled. About a half mile East of our place was a store and Post office and blacksmith shop. Hodges was the name of the place. I think we stayed in Jones County a couple of years, maybe a little longer. Could have been 4 years.

Note: They stayed about two years at Hodges. Willie Byron was the only child that was born in Jones County. By the time that Dewey was born in 1903, they were living in Knox County.

FAMILY GROUP NO.

Husband's Full Name: John William Ward

Husband's Data	Day Month Year	City, Town or Place	County or Province, etc.	State or Country	Add. Info. on Husband
Birth	29 Feb. 1864	Texarkana	Miller Co.	Arkansas	
Chr'nd					
Mar.	01 Aug. 1886		Johnson Co.	Texas	
Death	30 Mar. 1940	Hatfield	Polk	Arkansas	
Burial		Six Mile Cemetary, Hatfield, Arkansas			

Places of Residence: Texas - Arkansas
Occupation: Farmer
Church Affiliation: Methodist
His Father: Marvin Fuller WARD
Mother's Maiden Name: Elizabeth Jane ROSE

Wife's Full Maiden Name: Docia HEWITT

Wife's Data	Day Month Year	City, Town or Place	County or Province, etc.	State or Country	Add. Info. on Wife
Birth	04 Jan. 1868	Taylorville	Christian Co.	Illinois	
Chr'nd					
Death	15 Oct. 1937	Hatfield	Polk Co.	Arkansas	
Burial		Six Mile Cemetary, Hatfield, Arkansas			

Places of Residence: Illinois, Texas and Arkansas
Her Father: Frances Monroe Hewitt
Mother's Maiden Name: Nancy Francis Stanley

Children

#	Children's Name in Full / Spouse	Data	Day Month Year	City, Town or Place	County or Province, etc.	State or Country
1	Monroe Marvin Ward / Flora Vance	Birth	11 Aug. 1887	Rio Vista	Johnson Co.	Texas
		Mar.	14 Sept. 1913	Knox City	Knox Co.	Texas
		Death	25 May 1975	Anaheim	Orange Co.	Calif.
		Burial				
2	John Ira Ward / Leila Didlake	Birth	31 Oct. 1889	Rio Vista	Johnson Co.	Texas
		Mar.				
		Death	06 May 1951	Dallas	Dallas Co.	Texas
		Burial	10 May 1951	Jackson	Hinds Co.	Mississippi (Cedar Lawn)
3	Oscar Samuel Ward / Bess B. Richardson	Birth	28 Aug. 1891	Rio Vista	Johnson Co.	Texas
		Mar.	14 Apr. 1928	Hatfield	Polk Co.	Arkansas
		Death	23 Nov. 1983	Mena		
		Burial		Pine Crest Memorial Cemetary, Mena, Arkansas		
4	Nannie Bell Ward / Sherrod Wesley Almonrode	Birth	01 Oct. 1894	Rio Vista	Johnson Co.	Texas
		Mar.	24 Dec. 1914	Munday	Knox Co.	Texas
		Death	19 Aug. 1986	Mena	Polk	Arkansas
		Burial	21 Aug. 1986	Hatfield	Polk	Ar. (Six Mile Cemetery)
5	Elmer Ward / Mary Ann Griffith	Birth	16 Apr. 1897	Rio Vista	Johnson Co.	Texas
		Mar.	24 June 1917	Knox City	Knox Co.	Texas
		Death	04 Sep. 1957	Sweetwater		Texas
		Burial		Sweetwater Cemetary		
6	William Byron Ward / Julia Josephine Taylor	Birth	18 Aug. 1900	Hodges	Jones Co.	Texas
		Mar.	09 Jan. 1926	Guthrie		Oklahoma
		Death	04 Sep. 1983	Oklahoma City		"
		Burial				
7	Dewey Ward	Birth	24 June 1903	Knox City	Knox Co.	Texas
		Mar.				
		Death	14 Mar. 1974	Mena	Polk Co.	Ark.
		Burial		Rocky Cemetary - Mena RFD		
8	Fred Stanley Ward / Katie Stockton	Birth	04 Mar. 1906	Knox City		Texas
		Mar.				
		Death	12 Mar. 1984			
		Burial		Brea		California
9	Ole Arlington Ward / 1st Mildred Gaddis / 2nd Fay	Birth	23 June 1908	Knox City	Knox Co.	Texas
		Mar.				
		Death				
		Burial				
10	Olie Ward / 1. Ethel Reed / 2. Opal Irene Martin	Birth	21 Mar. 1911	Knox City	Knox Co.	Texas
		Mar.				
		Death				
		Burial				

FAMILY GROUP No. ___

Husband's Full Name: JOHN WILLIAM WARD

This Information Obtained From:

Husband's Data	Day Month Year	City, Town or Place	County or Province, etc.	State or Country	Add. Info.
Birth	29 FEB 1864	TEXARKANA	MILLER	ARK.	
Chr'nd					
Mar.	30 JUL 1886	RIO VISTA	JOHNSON	TEX.	
Death	30 MAR 1940	HATFIELD	POLK	ARK.	
Burial		SIX MILE CEMETERY			

Places of Residence:
Occupation: ___ Church Affiliation: METHODIST Military Rec.:
His Father: MARVIN FULLER WARD Mother's Maiden Name: ELIZABETH JANE ROSS

Wife's Full Maiden Name: LUCIA HEWITT

Wife's Data	Day Month Year	City, Town or Place	County or Province, etc.	State or Country	Add. Info. on Wife
Birth	04 JAN 1868	TAYLORVILLE	CHRISTIAN	ILL.	
Chr'nd					
Death	15 OCT 1937	HATFIELD	POLK	ARK.	
Burial		SIX MILE CEMETARY			

Compiler: Alvin L. Ward
Address: P.O. Box 1736
City, State: Denver City, Tx. 79360

Her Father: FRANCIS MONROE HEWITT Mother's Maiden Name: NANCY FRANCIS STANLE[Y]

Sex	Children's Names in Full (Arrange in order of birth)		Day Month Year	City, Town or Place	County or Province, etc.	State or Country
M	1. MONROE MARVIN Spouse: FLORA VANCE	Birth	11 AUG 1887	RIO VISTA	JOHNSON	TEX.
		Mar.	14 SEP 1913	KNOX CITY	KNOX	TEX.
		Death	25 MAY 1974	ANAHEIM	ORANGE	CAL.
		Burial		ANAHEIM CEMETERY		CAL.
	2. JOHN IRA Spouse: Leila DIDLAKE	Birth	31 OCT 1889	RIO VISTA	JOHNSON	TEX.
		Mar.				
		Death	06 MAY 1951	Dallas	Dallas	MIS.
		Burial	10 May 1951	Jackson	Hinds	Mis.
	3. OSCAR SAMUEL Spouse: BESS RICHARDSON	Birth	28 AUG 1891	RIO VISTA	JOHNSON	TEX.
		Mar.	14 APR 1920	HATFIELD	POLK	ARK.
		Death	23 NOV 1982	MENA	POLK	ARK.
		Burial		Pine Crest Memorial Cemetary, Mena, Ark.		
F	4. NANNIE BELL Spouse: SHERROD WESLEY ALMONROE	Birth	01 OCT 1894	RIO VISTA	JOHNSON	TEX.
		Mar.	24 DEC 1914	MUNDAY	KNOX	TEX.
		Death	19 Aug 1986	Mena	Polk	Ark.
		Burial		Six Mile Cemetary Hatfield Ark.		
	5. ELMER Spouse: MARY ANNE GRIFFITH	Birth	16 APR 1897	RIO VISTA	JOHNSON	TEX.
		Mar.	24 JUN 1917	BROWNFIELD	TERRY	TEX.
		Death	04 SEP 1957	SWEETWATER	NOLAN	TEX.
		Burial		SWEETWATER CEMETARY		
	6. WILLIAM BYRON Spouse: Julia Josephine TAYLOR	Birth	18 AUG 1900	Hodges	Jones	Tex.
		Mar.	09 Jan 1926	Guthrie	Logan	Ok.
		Death	04 SEP 1983	OKLAHOMA CITY	OKLAHOMA	OK.
		Burial				
	7. DEWEY NEVER MARRIED	Birth	24 JUN 1903	Knox City	Knox	Tex.
		Mar.	NEVER MARRIED			
		Death	14 MAR 1974	Mena	Polk	Ark.
		Burial		Rocky Cemetary Mena,		Ark.
	8. FRED STANLEY Spouse: Katie STOCKTON	Birth	04 MAR 1906	Knox City	Knox	Tex.
		Mar.				
		Death	12 Mar 1984			
		Burial		Brea	Orange	Cal.
	9. DALE ARLINGTON Spouse: Mildred GADDIS	Birth	23 JUN 1908	Knox City	Knox	Tex.
		Mar.				
		Death				
		Burial				
	10. OLIE	Birth	21 MAR 1911	Knox City	Knox	Tex.
		Mar.				
		Death				

Monroe Marvin WARD and Flora VANCE
Monroe was the 1st. child of John William and Jocia (Hewitt) Ward

FAMILY GROUP RECORD

HUSBAND Monroe Marvin WARD
Born: 11 AUG 1887 Place: Rio Vista, TEXAS
Married: 14 SEP 1913 Place: Knox City, TEXAS
Occupation: Carpenter
Church Affil.: Presbyterian
Died: 25 MAY 1975 Place: Anaheim, CALIF
Buried: Anaheim Cemetery Place: Anaheim, CALIF
Other wives:
Father: John William WARD (1864)
Mother (maiden name): Docia HEWITT (1868)

WIFE Flora VANCE
Born: 13 OCT 1891 Place: Memphis, TENN
Church Affil.: Presbyterian Occupation: Homemaker
Died: 04 MAY 1969 Place: Anaheim, CALIF
Buried: Anaheim Cemetery Place: Anaheim, CALIF
Other husbands: None
Father: Benjamin David VANCE
Mother (maiden name): Ida Geneva CALVERT

Name & Address of Person Filling Out This Sheet: Joyce (HENSON) TYSSEDAL

Sex M F	CHILDREN	BORN DATE & PLACE	MARRIED TO WHOM DATE & PLACE	DIED DATE & PLACE
1	Lura Ben WARD	22 OCT 1924 Knox City, TEXAS	Raymond Marion WILLIAMS 16 JULY 1945 Seymour, TEXAS	

Monroe and Flora

FAMILY GROUP RECORD

HUSBAND Raymond Marion WILLIAMS
Born: 29 NOV 1920 Place: Pacolet Mills, S.C.
Married: 16 JUL 1945 Place: Seymour, TEXAS
Occupation: Laboratory Technologist/Rancher
Church Affil.: Presbyterian
Died: _____ Place: _____
Buried: _____ Place: _____
Other wives: _____
Father: George Washington WILLIAMS
Mother (maiden name): Bessie HAMMETT

WIFE Lura Ben WARD
Born: 22 OCT 1924 Place: Knox City, TEXAS
Church Affil.: Presbyterian Occupation: Homemaker
Died: _____ Place: _____
Buried: _____ Place: _____
Other husbands: _____
Father: Monroe Marvin WARD (1887)
Mother (maiden name): Flora VANCE (1891)

NAME & ADDRESS OF PERSON FILLING OUT THIS SHEET: Joyce (HENSON) TYSSEDAL

Sex M/F	CHILDREN	BORN DATE & PLACE	MARRIED TO WHOM DATE & PLACE	DIED DATE & PLACE
F 1	Catherine Linn WILLIAMS	31 OCT 1950 Fullerton, Orange Co., CA		
F 2	Rebecca Ann WILLIAMS	18 OCT 1952 Reno, NEV	William Paul KRUEGER 15 JUL 1972 Anaheim, Orange Co, CA	
F 3	Rachel Flora WILLIAMS	26 FEB 1959 Anaheim, Orange Co., CA	James Clifton PRYOR 18 DEC 1982 Charleston, S.C.	
M 4	David Raymond WILLIAMS	23 DEC 1961 Anaheim, Orange Co., CA		

THE JOHN IRA WARD FAMILY

John Ira was the _second_ child of John William Ward and Docia (Hewitt) Ward

Ira   John Edward   Leila

A message from John Ira Ward to his parents, John William and Docia Ward, telling of the birth of his son, John Edward Ward.

ILLINOIS CENTRAL SYSTEM
FORM 19 — TRAIN ORDER No.

March 10, 1927

To All Concerned   At Pocahontas Station

> John Edward Ward arrived at 1:55 this AM and is doing fine, as is also Leila. Everything Hotsy-Totsy now.

Chief Train Dispatcher

CONDUCTOR AND ENGINEMAN MUST EACH HAVE A COPY OF THIS ORDER

MADE	TIME	DISPATCHER	OPERATOR
	M.		J. I. Ward

FAMILY GROUP NO.

Husband's Full Name: John Ira Ward

Husband's Data	Day Month Year	City, Town or Place	County or Province, etc.	State or Country	Add. Info. on Husband
Birth	31 Oct. 1889	Rio Vista	Johnson Co.,	Texas	
Chr'nd					
Mar.					
Death	06 May 1951	Dallas	Dallas Co.,	Texas	
Burial	10 May 1951	Jackson	Hinds Co.,	Mississippi	

Places of Residence: Texas & Mississippi
Occupation: Agent & Telegraph Opr.   **Church Affiliation:**   **Military Rec.:** Navy WWI
Other wives, if any: None
His Father: John William Ward   **Mother's Maiden Name:** Docia Hewitt

Wife's Full Maiden Name: Leila Didlake

Wife's Data	Day Month Year	City, Town or Place	County or Province, etc.	State or Country	Add. Info. on Wife
Birth		Crystal Springs,	Copiah Co.,	Miss.	
Chr'nd					
Death	02 Mar. 1984	Clinton,	Hinds	Mississippi	
Burial	05 Mar. 1984	Jackson	Hinds (Cedar Lawn Cemetery)		

Places of Residence: Crystal Springs, Pocahontas, Jackson & Clinton, Miss.
Occupation if other than housewife: **Church Affiliation:**
Other husbands, if any: None
Her Father: Samuel Didlake   **Mother's Maiden Name:** Eula Bullock

Sex	Children's Name in Full	Children's Data	Day Month Year	City, Town or Place	County or Province, etc.	State or Country
M	1. John Edward Ward — Spouse: Shirley McMahon	Birth	10 Mar. 1927	Pocahontas		Mississippi
		Mar.	25 June 1960	Jackson	Hinds	Mississippi
		Death				
		Burial				

John I. Ward Dies In Texas

John Ira Ward, 61, a resident of Pocahontas for the past 30 years, died late Sunday afternoon in Dallas, Texas. He had been in failing health for several months.

Mr. Ward was employed by the I. C. R. R. for 36 years, as telegraph operator at Canton, Miss. He was a member of Pearl Lodge number 23, and a veteran of World War I, having served in the U. S. Navy on ship Neptune.

He is survived by his wife, the former Leila Didlake of Jackson, and by a son, John Edward Ward of Camp Pickett, Va. He is also survived by a sister, Mrs. S. W. Almonrode, Hatfield, Ark., and eight brothers, M. M. Anaheim, Calif., Oscar and Dewey, both of Los Angeles, Calif., Dale, Norwalk, Calif., Fred, Fullerton, Calif., W. B., Oklahoma City, Okla., Elmer, Sweetwater, Texas and Olie, Houston, Texas.

His body arrived in Jackson Tuesday night, where funeral services were conducted at 2:00 p. m. Thursday, with Dr. Harold G. Basden and Dr. Henry M. Bullock officiating.

Interment was in Cedarlawn cemetery, with Masonic service at the graveside.

Pallbearers named are: A. Carter Blake, Jr., H. Grady Baker, Sr., both of Pocahontas, William Cockerham of Canton, W. J. Selman of Hazlehurst, E. M. Ervin and J. T. Marley of Jackson.

FAMILY GROUP RECORD

HUSBAND John Edward WARD
Born 10 March 1927 Place Pocahontas, Mississippi
Married 25 June 1960 Place Jackson, Hinds Co., Miss.
Occupation Merchant Seaman
Church Affil.
Died _____ Place _____
Buried _____ Place _____
Other wives
Father John Ira WARD (1889-1951)
Mother (maiden name) Leila ~~Edwards~~ Didlake

WIFE Shirley McMahon
Born 17 September 1929 Place Meridian, Lauderdale Co., Miss
Church Affil. Methodist Occupation Nurse
Died _____ Place _____
Buried _____ Place _____
Other husbands
Father
Mother (maiden name)

NAME & ADDRESS OF PERSON FILLING OUT THIS SHEET

Joyce (Henson) TYSSEDAL

Sex M/F	CHILDREN	BORN DATE & PLACE	MARRIED TO WHOM DATE & PLACE	DIED DATE & PLACE
M 1	John Alton Ward	28 Mar. 1961 Jackson Mississippi		
F 2	Sheryl Ann Ward	29 Oct. 1963 Jackson Mississippi		
3				
4				
5				
6				
7				
8				
9				
10				
11				
12				

FORM NO. FGR-B   PRINTED IN U.S.A.   **BLUE**   © GENEALOGY SYSTEMS OF AMERICA 1978

OSCAR SAMUEL WARD

Oscar was a veteran of World War 1 and served in England and France

3rd. child of John William and Docia Ward

Oscar
(1891-1982)

FAMILY GROUP RECORD

HUSBAND Oscar Samuel WARD
Born: 28 AUG 1891 Place: Rio Vista, TEXAS
Married: 14 APR 1928 Place: Hatfield, ARK
Occupation: _____
Church Affil.: _____
Died: 23 NOV 1982 Place: Mena, ARK
Buried: _____ Place: Mena, ARK
Other wives: _____
Father: John William WARD (1864)
Mother (maiden name): Docia HEWITT (1868)

WIFE Bess RICHARDSON
Born: 21 NOV 1902 Place: Hatfield, ARK
Church Affil.: Methodist Occupation: Homemaker
Died: _____ Place: _____
Buried: _____ Place: _____
Other husbands: _____
Father: William Isac RICHARDSON
Mother (maiden name): Julia Ann BARNES

NAME & ADDRESS OF PERSON FILLING OUT THIS SHEET:
Joyce (HENSON) TYSSEDAL

Sex M F	CHILDREN	BORN DATE & PLACE	MARRIED TO WHOM DATE & PLACE	DIED DATE & PLACE
1	Joyce Marie WARD	30 DEC 1928 Hatfield, ARK	George SHIPMAN 14 OCT 1945 Yuma, ARIZ	
2	John William WARD	31 JAN 1931 Hatfield, ARK	Dolores ROLLER Yuma, ARIZ	
3	~~Donnie WARD~~ Donald Oscar Ward	16 JAN 1937 Hatfield, ARK	Constance RICE NOV 1963 La Puente, CA	

FORM NO. FGR-8   PRINTED IN U.S.A.   BLUE   © GENEALOGY SYSTEMS OF AMERICA 1978

FAMILY GROUP RECORD

HUSBAND George Udell SHIPMAN
- Born: Sept. 1920 Place: OKLA.
- Married: Oct. 1945 Place: Yuma, ARIZ.
- Occupation:
- Church Affil.: Baptist
- Died: June 1969 Place: ~~Hatfield~~, ARK. Okla.
- Buried: 07 June 1969 Place: Hatfield, ARK.
- Other wives:
- Father: George SHIPMAN
- Mother (maiden name):

Name & Address of Person Filling Out This Sheet: Joyce (W)ENSO. TYSSEDAL

WIFE Joyce Marie WARD
- Born: 30 Dec. 1928 Place: Hatfield, ARK.
- Church Affil.: Methodist Occupation: Homemaker
- Died: 11 June 1987 Place: Bay City, Texas
- Buried: 16 June 1987 Place: Mena, Arkansas (Rocky Cem.)
- Other husbands:
- Father: Oscar Samuel WARD
- Mother (maiden name): Bess RICHARDSON

Sex M/F	CHILDREN	BORN DATE & PLACE	MARRIED TO WHOM DATE & PLACE	DIED DATE & PLACE
F 1	Stephanie Lynn SHIPMAN	14 Feb. 1947 Whittier, CA	LeRoy THACKER Nov. 1964 Mena, ARK.	
F 2	Melinda Susan SHIPMAN	28 Apr. 1951 CA	Rick KVEUM Apr. 1968 Mena, ARK.	
M 3	Johnnie Del SHIPMAN	18 Oct. 1953 CA		
F 4	Robin Joyce SHIPMAN	15 Aug. 1955 CA		

FAMILY GROUP RECORD

HUSBAND Leroy THACKER
Born 25 July 1943 Place Mena, (Polk) Arkansas
Married _____ Place _____
Occupation X-Ray Technician
Church Affil. Baptist
Died _____ Place _____
Buried _____ Place _____
Other wives _____
Father Lester THACKER
Mother (maiden name) Allene SCOTT

WIFE Stephanie Lynn SHIPMAN
Born 14 Feb. 1947 Place California
Church Affil. _____ Occupation _____
Died _____ Place _____
Buried _____ Place _____
Other husbands _____
Father George Udell SHIPMAN (1920-1969)
Mother (maiden name) Joyce Marie WARD (1928-1987)

Sex M F	CHILDREN	BORN DATE & PLACE	MARRIED TO WHOM DATE & PLACE	DIED DATE & PLACE
1	Kevin Mitchell THACKER	15 Mar. 1964 Mena, Arkansas		
2	Scott Lane THACKER	20 Jun. 1966 Mena, Arkansas	(buried in Rocky Cemetary)	21 Jun. 1966 Mena, Arkansas
3	Brent Leroy THACKER	03 Sep. 1967 Mena, Arkansas		
4	Dustin Matthew THACKER	01 Nov. 1968 Mena, Arkansas		
5	Terry Glenn THACKER	01 Mar. 1970 Mena, Arkansas		
6	Joshus Del THACKER	13 Mar. 1973 Mena, Arkansas		

FAMILY GROUP NO.

Husband's Full Name: Jonnie Del Shipman

Husband's Data	Day Month Year	City, Town or Place	County or Province, etc.	State or Country	Add. Info. on Husband
Birth	18 Oct. 1952		Los Angeles Co.	Calif.	
Chr'nd					
Mar.					
Death					
Burial					

Places of Residence: California - Oklahoma - Arkansas

His Father: George Udell Shipman **Mother's Maiden Name:** Joyce Marie Ward

Wife's Full Maiden Name:

Children

Sex	Child's Name	Event	Day Month Year	City, Town or Place	County	State
F	1. Amy Lynn Shipman	Birth	20 Sep. 1974	Tulsa	Tulsa Co.	Oklahoma
M	2. Eric Shipman	Birth	Feb. 1979	Tulsa	Tulsa Co.	Oklahoma

FAMILY GROUP NO.

Husband's Full Name: Rick Kveum

Places of Residence: Arkansas - Oklahoma

Wife's Full Maiden Name: Melinda Susan Shipman

	Day Month Year	City, Town or Place	County or Province, etc.	State or Country
Birth	28 Apr. 1951		Los Angeles Co.,	California

Other husbands, if any: Ronald Weekley

Her Father: George Udell Shipman
Mother's Maiden Name: Joyce Marie Ward

Children

Sex	Name	Event	Day Month Year	City, Town or Place	County	State	Add. Info.
M	1. Michael Shane Kveum						
F	2. Heather Welch	Birth		Mena	Polk Co.	Arkansas	Russell Welch is the father of Heather and Ariel
F	3. Ariel Welch	Birth		Mena	Polk Co.	Arkansas	

FAMILY GROUP NO.

Husband's Full Name

Wife's Full Maiden Name: Robin Joyce Shipman

Wife's Data	Day Month Year	City, Town or Place	County or Province, etc.	State or Country	Add. Info. on Wife
Birth	15 Aug. 1951			California	
Chr'nd					
Death					
Burial					

Places of Residence: California - Arkansas

Her Father: George Udell Shipman **Mother's Maiden Name:** Joyce Marie Ward

Sex	Children's Name in Full		Day Month Year
M	1. Jason	Birth	Apr. 1978
F	2. Amanda	Birth	24 Dec. 1981

Page 4—The Mena Star, Mena, Ark., Wednesday, June 17, 1987

IN LOVING MEMORY OF
Joyce Marie Shipman

BORN
December 30, 1928
Hatfield, Arkansas

PASSED AWAY
June 11, 1987
Bay City, Texas

SERVICES
Geyer-Quillin Chapel
Tuesday, June 16, 1987
10:00 A.M.

OFFICIATING
Rev. Charlie Talbott

FUNERAL DIRECTOR
Geyer-Quillin Funeral Home

INTERMENT
Rocky Cemetery

MRS. JOYCE MARIE SHIPMAN

Mrs. Joyce Marie Shipman, 58, of Mena, died Thursday in Bay City, Tex. She was born December 30, 1928 at Hatfield.

Funeral service was held at 10 Tuesday morning in the Geyer-Quillin Chapel with Rev. Charlie Talbott officiating. Interment was in the Rocky Cemetery under the direction of Geyer-Quillin Funeral Home.

Pallbearers were Kevin Thacker, Dustin Thacker, Terry Thacker, Eric Hughes, Marty Thacker, and Ron Thacker.

Mrs. Shipman was the daughter of the late Oscar Ward and Mrs. Bess Richardson Ward and was united in marriage to George U. Shipman on October 14, 1945 at Yuma, Ariz. He preceded her in death on June 3, 1969. She had made her home around the Mena area for the last 30 years. She was a housewife and a member of the Methodist faith.

Survivors are mother, Mrs. Bess Ward, Mena; one son, Jonnie Shipman, Mena; three daughters, Mrs. Stephanie Thacker, Mena, Mrs. Melinda Weekly, Marietta, Ohio, Miss Robin Shipman, Mena; two brothers, Bill Ward, Mena, Don Ward, Diamond Bar, Calif.; eight grandsons; eight granddaughters.

FAMILY GROUP RECORD

HUSBAND John William WARD
Born: 31 Jan. 1931 Place: Hatfield, Arkansas
Married: 19 March 1952 Place: Yuma, Arizona
Occupation: (U.S. Navy)
Church Affil.:
Died: Place:
Buried: Place:
Other wives:
Father: Oscar Samuel WARD (1891-1982)
Mother (maiden name): Bess RICHARDSON (1902-)

WIFE Dolores ROLLER
Born: 16 Oct. 1933 Place: St. Louis, Missouri
Church Affil.: Occupation: Office worker
Died: Place:
Buried: Place:
Other husbands:
Father: John Perry ROLLER
Mother (maiden name): Lorene SMITH

NAME & ADDRESS OF PERSON FILLING OUT THIS SHEET:
Joyce (Henson)
TYSSEDAL

Sex M/F	CHILDREN	BORN DATE & PLACE	MARRIED TO WHOM DATE & PLACE	DIED DATE & PLACE
1	Billy Ray WARD	20 Jun. 1953 Lynwood, California	Karen Ann Casagranda 16 Oct. 1976 Lynwood, California	
2	David Glen WARD	13 Jan. 1955 Lynwood, California		
3	Peggy JoAnn WARD	13 Jan. 1956 Lynwood, California		

FORM NO. FGR-8   PRINTED IN U.S.A.   BLUE   © GENEALOGY SYSTEMS OF AMERICA 1978

FAMILY GROUP RECORD

HUSBAND Billy Ray WARD
Born 20 June 1953 Place Lynwood, California
Married 16 Oct. 1976 Place Lynwood, California
Occupation
Church Affil.
Died _____ Place
Buried _____ Place
Other wives
Father John William WARD (1931-)
Mother (maiden name) Dolores ROLLER (1933-)

WIFE Karen Ann CASAGRANDA
Born _____ Place
Church Affil. _____ Occupation
Died _____ Place
Buried _____ Place
Other husbands
Father
Mother (maiden name)

NAME & ADDRESS OF PERSON FILLING OUT THIS SHEET

Relationship of above to Husband:
Relationship of above to Wife:
NAMES OF HUSBAND AND WIFE ON THIS CHART ARE THE SAME PERSONS AS NOS. ____ & ____ ON LINEAGE CHART NO

Sex M/F	CHILDREN	BORN DATE & PLACE	MARRIED TO WHOM DATE & PLACE	DIED DATE & PLACE
1	Brandon Ray WARD	08 Jul. 1981 Long Beach, California		
2	Nicollet Rene WARD	13 Nov. 1982 Long Beach, California		
3				
4				
5				
6				
7				
8				
9				
10				
11				
12				

FORM NO. FGR-B   PRINTED IN U.S.A.   **BLUE**   © GENEALOGY SYSTEMS OF AMERICA 1978

FAMILY GROUP RECORD

First Marriage.......

HUSBAND David Glen WARD
Born 13 Jan. 1955 Place Lynwood, California
Married ___ Place ___
Occupation ___
Church Affil. ___
Died ___ Place ___
Buried ___ Place ___
Other wives #-2 Gloria Hernandez
Father John William WARD (1931-)
Mother (maiden name) Dolores ROLLER (1933-)

WIFE Livia GALL (Divorced)
Born ___ Place ___
Church Affil. ___ Occupation ___
Died ___ Place ___
Buried ___ Place ___
Other husbands ___
Father Denes GALL
Mother (maiden name) Velma

Sex M/F	CHILDREN	BORN DATE & PLACE	MARRIED TO WHOM DATE & PLACE	DIED DATE & PLACE
1	David Glenn WARD	17 Aug. 1976 Long Beach, California		
2	Brock William WARD	19 Mar. 1978 Long Beach, California		
3				
4				
5				
6				
7				
8				
9				
10				
11				
12				

FORM NO. FGR-B   PRINTED IN U.S.A.   BLUE   © GENEALOGY SYSTEMS OF AMERICA 1978

FAMILY GROUP RECORD

Second Marriage........

HUSBAND David Glen WARD
Born ~~13 Jan~~ 1953 Place Lynwood, California
Married _____ Place _____
Occupation _____
Church Affil. _____
Died _____ Place _____
Buried _____ Place _____
Other wives #-1 Livia Gall (Divorced)
Father John William WARD (1931-)
Mother (maiden name) Dolores ROLLER (1933-)

WIFE Gloria HERNANDEZ
Born 09 July 1952 Place _____
Church Affil. _____ Occupation _____
Died _____ Place _____
Buried _____ Place _____
Other husbands _____
Father Cruz HERNANDEZ
Mother (maiden name) Hilda

Sex M F	CHILDREN	BORN DATE & PLACE	MARRIED TO WHOM DATE & PLACE	DIED DATE & PLACE
1	John Ryan WARD	30 Sep. 1984 Victorville, California		
2				
3				
4				
5				
6				
7				
8				
9				
10				
11				
12				

BLUE

FAMILY GROUP RECORD

First Marriage.......

HUSBAND Rocky MILLS
- Born _____
- Married 10 Aug. 1974 Place _____
- Occupation _____
- Church Affil. _____
- Died _____ Place _____
- Buried _____ Place _____
- Other wives _____
- Father _____
- Mother (maiden name) _____

WIFE Peggy JoAnn WARD
- Born 13 Jan. 1956 Place Lynwood, California
- Church Affil. _____ Occupation _____
- Died _____ Place _____
- Buried _____ Place _____
- Other husbands #-2 Douglas Roberts
- Father John William WARD (1931-)
- Mother (maiden name) Dolores ROLLER (1933-)

Sex M/F	CHILDREN	BORN DATE & PLACE	MARRIED TO WHOM DATE & PLACE	DIED DATE & PLACE
1	Justin Matthew MILLS	13 Dec. 1977 Long Beach, California		
2	Jeffrey Steven MILLS	20 Jan. 1979 Long Beach, California		
3				
4				
5				
6				
7				
8				
9				
10				
11				
12				

FORM NO. FGR-B   PRINTED IN U.S.A.   **BLUE**   © GENEALOGY SYSTEMS OF AMERICA 1978

The Ward Family History
Page 229

FAMILY GROUP RECORD

Second Marriage.......

HUSBAND Douglas ROBERTS
Born 03 Nov. 1955 Place Winfield, Kansas
Married _____ Place _____
Occupation _____
Church Affil. _____
Died _____ Place _____
Buried _____ Place _____
Other wives _____
Father James ROBERTS
Mother (maiden name) Sue

WIFE Peggy JoAnn WARD
Born 13 Jan. 1956 Place Lynwood, California
Church Affil. _____ Occupation _____
Died _____ Place _____
Buried _____ Place _____
Other husbands #-1 Rocky Mills
Father _____
Mother (maiden name) _____

NAME & ADDRESS OF PERSON FILLING OUT THIS SHEET

Relationship of above to Husband:

Relationship of above to Wife:

NAMES OF HUSBAND AND WIFE ON THIS CHART ARE THE SAME PERSONS AS NOS. ____ & ____ ON LINEAGE CHART NO. ____

Sex M/F	CHILDREN	BORN DATE & PLACE	MARRIED TO WHOM DATE & PLACE	DIED DATE & PLACE
1	Jamie Ward ROBERTS	03 Feb. 1982 Long Beach, California		
2				
3				
4				
5				
6				
7				
8				
9				
10				
11				
12				

FORM NO. FGR-B   PRINTED IN U.S.A.   **BLUE**   © GENEALOGY SYSTEMS OF AMERICA 1978

FAMILY GROUP RECORD

HUSBAND Donald ~~Oscar~~ WARD
Born __16 Jan. 1937__ Place __Hatfield, Arkansas__
Married __Nov. 1963__ Place __La Puente, California__
Occupation _____
Church Affil. _____
Died _____ Place _____
Buried _____ Place _____
Other wives _____
Father __Oscar Samuel WARD (1891-1982)__
Mother (maiden name) __Bess RICHARDSON (1902-   )__

WIFE __Constance RICE__
Born _____ Place _____
Church Affil. _____ Occupation _____
Died _____ Place _____
Buried _____ Place _____
Other husbands _____
Father _____
Mother (maiden name) _____

NAME & ADDRESS OF PERSON FILLING OUT THIS SHEET

Joyce (Henson) TYSSEDAL

Sex	CHILDREN	BORN DATE & PLACE	MARRIED TO WHOM DATE & PLACE	DIED DATE & PLACE

1. I have been unable to get Donald Oscar (Donnie) to send me his family group sheets. I know that he has a daughter named Lisa Bess, but do not know date of her birth - 1967 - 1968. He has one or two other children, I think, as well as several step children.

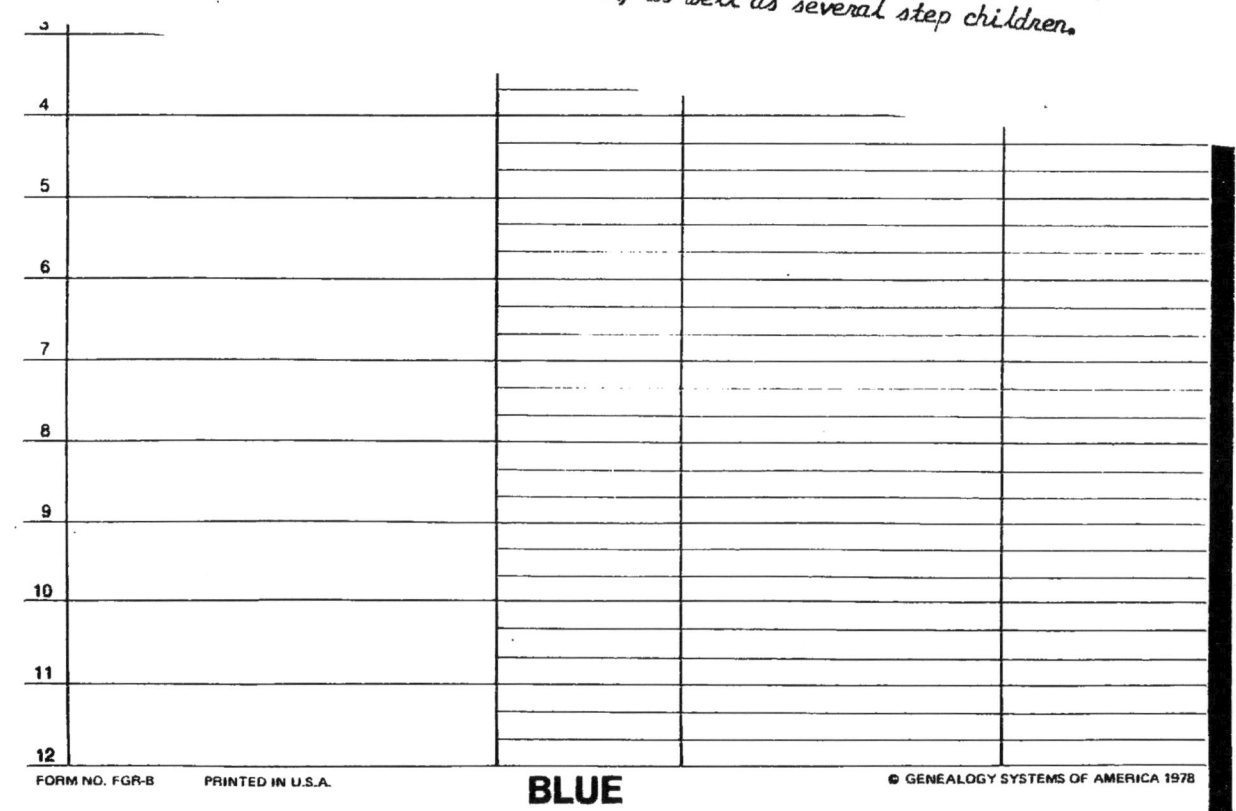

BLUE

SHERROD WESLEY ALMONRODE and NANNIE BELL (WARD) ALMONRODE

Nannie was the 4th child of J. J. and Docia Ward

Sherrod and Nannie in 1915

FAMILY GROUP RECORD

HUSBAND Sherrod Wesley ALMONRODE
- Born: 25 SEPT 1886 Place: Livingston, TN
- Married: 24 DEC 1914 Place: Munday, TX
- Occupation: Farmer
- Church Affil.: Methodist
- Died: 27 MAR 1968 Place: Mena, ARK
- Buried: Six Mile Cemetery Place: Hatfield, ARK
- Other wives:
- Father: William Winston ALMONRODE
- Mother (maiden name): Ella MURDOCK

WIFE Nannie Bell WARD
- Born: 01 OCT 1894 Place: Rio Vista, TX
- Church Affil.: Methodist Occupation: Homemaker
- Died: Place:
- Buried: Place:
- Other husbands:
- Father: John William WARD (1864)
- Mother (maiden name): Docia HEWITT (1868)

Name & Address of Person Filling Out This Sheet: Joyce (HENSON) TYSSEDAL

Sex M/F	Children	Born Date & Place	Married to Whom Date & Place	Died Date & Place
F	Ruby Cleo ALMONRODE	28 SEP 1916 Munday, TEXAS	Orvis Elmo MARTIN 01 JAN 1937 Hatfield, ARK	
M	Hollis K. ALMONRODE	27 JUL 1920 Livingston, TENN		05 NOV 1944 Udala, INDIA
F	Helen Pern ALMONRODE	15 OCT 1923 Hatfield, ARK	James B. CRAFTON 24 DEC 1952 Mena, ARK	
F	Dorothy Jo ALMONRODE	07 JUN 1927 Hatfield, ARK	Elbert Eugene FOLEY 20 DEC 1951 Mena, ARK	

SHERROD WESLEY ALMONRODE and NANNIE BELL WARD ALMONRODE

The children of Sherrod Wesley ALMONROE and Nannie Bell WARD

Ruby Cleo

Hollis K. 1920-1944

Helen P.

Dorothy Jo

HATFIELD
1968

Joe Lewis
Hatfield, Ark.

There was a large crowd at the funeral of S. W. Almonrode Saturday afternoon with a lot of beautiful floral offerings. He had been in Fort Smith and Mena hospitals nearly eight months. Rev. C. E. Lawrence and Rev. James Simpson conducted the funeral services at the Methodist Church.

19 August 1986

MRS. NANNIE BELL ALMONRODE

Mrs. Nannie Bell Almonrode, 91, of Hatfield, died Tuesday morning in a local nursing home. Funeral service will be held Thursday afternoon at 2 in the Hatfield United Methodist Church with Bro. Buz Lassiter and Bro. George Corbett officiating. Interment will be in the Six Mile Cemetery under the direction of Beasley-Wood Funeral Home.

S. W. ALMONRODE

Funeral service for Sherrod Wesley Almonrode, 81-year-old longtime resident of Hatfield, who died March 27, was held Saturday afternoon at 2:30 in the Hatfield Methodist Church, with the Rev. C. E. Lawrence and the Rev. James Simpson officiating. Interment was in the Six Mile Cemetery under the direction of the Beasley-Wood Funeral Home.

Casketbearers were Lonnie Baldwin, Herman Callahan, Gerald Johnson, Harold Wright, Charlie Nichols and Nolan Gann. Honorary casketbearers included L. M. Dover, J. T. Stockton, Lawrence Parsons, Roy Parsons, Joe Bob Lane, Lewis Joplin, Sammy Powell, Bennie Fisher, Charley Darr and Titus Manasco.

Mr. Almonrode was born Sept. 25, 1886, at Livingston, Tenn., his parents being the late Mr. and Mrs. William Almonrode. He was a member of the Hatfield Methodist Church and served for a number of years on the board of stewards. He was a retired farmer and was employed by the Watkins Mercantile Co. of Hatfield for several years. He was a board member for twenty years of the Polk County Farmers Assn. and served as president of the organization for eight years. He was also president of the Hatfield school board for many years. On Dec. 24, 1914, he was married at Munday, Texas, to Miss Nannie Ward, who survives him.

Other survivors include three daughters, Mrs. Ruby Martin, Hatfield, Mrs. Helen Crafton, Elsah, Ill., and Mrs. Jo Foley, Myrtle Beach, S. C.; two brothers, Walter Almonrode, Furlong, Pa., and H. D. Almonrode, Livingston, Tenn.; four sisters, Mrs. Jim Conaster and Mrs. D. T. Barnes, Livingston, Tenn., and Miss Dextor Almonrode and Mrs. Maurice Smith, Alpine, Tenn.; also seven grandchildren and one great-grandchild and several nieces and nephews. A son, Hollis K. Almonrode, a U. S. Army Air Force officer, was killed in action during World War II.

MRS. NANNIE BELL ALMONRODE

Mrs. Nannie Bell Almonrode, 91, of Hatfield, died Tuesday morning in a local nursing home. She was born October 1, 1894, at Rio Vista, Tex.

Funeral service was held Thursday afternoon at 2 in the Hatfield United Methodist Church with Bro. Buz Lassiter and Bro. George Corbett officiating. Interment was in the Six Mile Cemetery under the direction of Beasley-Wood Funeral Home.

Pallbearers were Lonnie Baldwin, Donald Myers, Lannie Richardson, Leroy Beck, Cecil Rose, and Forrest Martin.

Mrs. Almonrode was the daughter of the late John W. Ward and the late Mrs. Docia Hewitt Ward and was united in marriage to Sherrod W. Almonrode December 24, 1914, in Knox County, Tex. He preceded her in death March 27, 1968. She had made her home in Hatfield since 1920 and was a member of the Hatfield United Methodist Church.

Survivors are three daughters, Mrs. Ruby Martin, Hatfield; Mrs. Helen Crafton, Godfrey, Ill., Mrs. Jo Foley, Mena; two brothers, Dale Ward, West Fork, Olie Ward, Board Camp; seven grandchildren; nine great-grandchildren.

She was preceded in death by a son, Hollis Almonrode, in 1944.

FAMILY GROUP RECORD

HUSBAND Orvis Elmo MARTIN
- Born: 28 Sept. 1913 — Place: Hatfield, Arkansas
- Married: 01 Jan. 1937 — Place: Hatfield, Arkansas
- Occupation: Farmer
- Church Affil.:
- Died: — Place:
- Buried: — Place:
- Other wives:
- Father: Louis Franklin MARTIN
- Mother (maiden name): Clara WEATHERBY

WIFE Ruby Cleo ALMONRODE
- Born: 28 Sept. 1916 — Place: Hatfield, Arkansas
- Church Affil.: Methodist — Occupation: Teacher
- Died: — Place:
- Buried: — Place:
- Other husbands:
- Father: Sherrod Wesley ALMONRODE (1886)
- Mother (maiden name): Nannie Bell WARD (1894)

NAME & ADDRESS OF PERSON FILLING OUT THIS SHEET: Joyce (Henson) TYSSEDAL

Sex M/F	CHILDREN	BORN DATE & PLACE	MARRIED TO WHOM DATE & PLACE	DIED DATE & PLACE
1	Rex Lee MARTIN	30 Aug. 1939 Hatfield, Arkansas	Caroleta Page 29 May 1961 Mena, Ark.	
2	Roy Glenn MARTIN	28 Dec. 1941 Mena, Arkansas	Glenda L. Fruen 14 Feb. 1970 Mena, Ark.	
3	Orvis Lamar MARTIN	15 Aug. 1950 Mena, Arkansas	Linda S. Denton 29 May 1970	

Ruby Cleo

BLUE

A BRIEF HISTORY of RUBY C. ALMONRODE

Born: September 28, 1916, at Munday, Knox County, Texas
Married: Orvis Elmo Martin, at Hatfield, Polk County, Arkansas - Jan. 1, 1937.
Education: Hatfield High School - Arkansas State Teacher's College and Henderson State University

When Ruby was just a small child, she and her parents left Munday, Texas, and came to Mena, Arkansas, where Ruby's maternal grandparents, John William and Docia (Hewitt) Ward had moved to from Texas. After visiting awhile with the Wards, they went to Tennessee to see grandparents, William Winston and Ella (Murdock) Almonrode, and thought that they might settle in Livingston, which was the birthplace of Ruby's father, Sherrod Almonrode. Ruby was four years old when they decided to move to Hatfield, Polk County, Arkansas, where the Wards were living by that time.

Ruby attended Hatfield Elementary and Hatfield High School, graduating with the class of 1935. She taught first grade at Potter, Arkansas, for one year and taught first grade at Hatfield for several years. She also worked at Cowden's Manufacturing Company at Mena for a few years, but later returned to work on a part time basis in the Hatfield School System as a substitute teacher - teacher's aid - school secretary, etc. She also helped with an adult reading program.

Ruby and Orvis live on a farm about seven miles west of Hatfield by Mountain Fork River. They have three sons, Rex Lee, Roy Glenn and Orvis Lamar. At the present time (1988) they have six grandchildren.

The children of Orvis Martin and Ruby (Almonrode) Martin

1. **REX LEE MARTIN** was born at the family home on August 30, 1939. At that time, his parents were renting a small farm about a quarter of a mile from the Ward farm southeast of Hatfield, Polk County, Arkansas. Living at the Ward farm was Rex's great grandfather, John William Ward, and his grandparents, Sherrod and Nannie Almonrode and their family.

   Rex graduated from Hatfield High School in 1957. He attended college at Texarkana, Arkansas, then went to a railroad school in Pueblo, Colorado. On May 29, 1961, he married Caroleta Page, daughter of State Criminal Investigator Carroll Page and Juanita (Blair) Page. Rex was working as an agent and telegraph operator for the Milwaukee Railroad Co., in Elgin, Illinois, when their daughter, Gina Lynn, was born.

   On August 4, 1964, Rex joined the Arkansas State Police. His first duty station was Mountain View, Arkansas, where he stayed for about a year. He was transferred to Murfreesboro, Arkansas, where he worked for twenty-one years, before returning to his home county of Polk in the spring of 1987. He is now stationed at Mena, where he and Caroleta have bought a home.

2. **ROY GLENN MARTIN** was born at Mena, Arkansas, on December 28, 1941. He graduated from Hatfield School and also graduated with honors from Draughons School of Drafting and Design in Oklahoma City, Oklahoma, where he majored in Tool and Die Design. He later served in the U.S. Marines and the Marine Reserves. Roy worked in Dallas for awhile, but missed the hills of Arkansas, so he returned to Hatfield and went into business for himself as a brick and rock mason. He does beautiful work and many homes and businesses in this area have been bricked by him.

   On February 14, 1970, Roy married Glenda Lea Fruen of Hatfield, daughter of Ellis and Evelyn (Pepper) Fruen. Shortly after their marriage, they built a new home on the Martin family farm west of Hatfield. Roy and Glenda have one daughter, Christina Dianne (Chrissy) and one son, Mitchell Roy (Mitch).

3. **ORVIS LAMAR MARTIN** was born on August 15, 1950 at Mena, Arkansas. He is a graduate of Hatfield High School, served in the Arkansas National Guards, and has been working for Weyerhauser for a number of years.

   Lamar married Linda Susan Denton at the Hatfield United Methodist Church on the 29th of May, 1970. For awhile they lived at Wickes, Arkansas, but moved back to Hatfield and built a new home on the Martin farm. Lamar and Linda have three children: Scottie Lamar, Wendy Lynn and Sondra Lea.

FAMILY GROUP RECORD

HUSBAND Rex Lee MARTIN
- Born: 30 Aug. 1939 Place: Hatfield, Arkansas
- Married: 29 May 1961 Place: Mena, Arkansas
- Occupation:
- Church Affil.: Methodist
- Died: ___ Place: ___
- Buried: ___ Place: ___
- Other wives:
- Father: Orvis Elmo MARTIN (1913-)
- Mother (maiden name): Ruby Cleo ALMONRODE (1916-)

WIFE Caroleta, PAGE
- Born: 16 November, 1942 Place: San Angelo, Tom Green Co., Texas
- Church Affil.: Methodist Occupation: Office work
- Died: ___ Place: ___
- Buried: ___ Place: ___
- Other husbands:
- Father: Carroll Page
- Mother (maiden name): Helen Juanita Blair

Sex M/F	CHILDREN	BORN DATE & PLACE	MARRIED TO WHOM DATE & PLACE	DIED DATE & PLACE
F 1	Gina Lynn Martin	05 Sept. 1963 Elgin, Kane Co. Illinois	Robert H. Briley, Jr. Little Rock, 06 June 1987 Pulaski Co., Arkansas	

The Ward Family History

Page 10—The Mena Star, Mena, Ark., Wednesday, April 15, 1987

Martin-Briley

Mr. and Mrs. Rex L. Martin of Mena announce the engagement of their daughter, Gina Lynn, to Robert Briley, Jr., son of Mr. and Mrs. Robert H. Briley, Sr., of Little Rock.

The bride-elect is the granddaughter of Mr. and Mrs. C.J. Page of Mena and Mr. and Mrs. O.E. Martin of Hatfield.

She graduated from the University of Arkansas at Fayetteville with a bachelor's degree in accounting and data processing and is presently employed with Frost and Company as a certified public accountant in Little Rock.

The groom-elect holds a master's degree in criminal justice from the University of Arkansas at Little Rock and a law degree from the University of Arkansas at Fayetteville. He is employed with the Veterans Administration Regional Office in Little Rock.

The couple will wed June 6 at the Otter Creek First Baptist Church in Little Rock.

Page 4-B • NASHVILLE NEWS • Thursday, October 8, 1987

PROMOTED
.... Gina Martin Briley, 1984 honors graduate of the University of Arkansas at Fayetteville and former resident of this area, has been promoted to senior accountant in the audit department at Frost & Company. Briley joined the Little Rock-based certified public accounting firm in 1984. She is a member of the Arkansas Society of CPAs and the American Institute of CPAs.

1988
Gina Lynn (Martin) Briley

Local

Gina M. Briley

Murfreesboro native is appointed controller for Richland Companies

Pate Pearson, president of the Richland Companies, today announced the appointment of Gina M. Briley, C.P.A., as controller.

Briley will be responsible for all financial affairs, accounting operations and tax management in the group's five subsidiaries.

Richland's operations include Richland Chrysler-Plymouth at North Little Rock, Richland Dodge at Jonesboro, Richland Leasing (Thrifty Car Rental) at Memphis, GSR Enterprise at Little Rock, and the group's newest acquisition, Richland Subaru-Volkswagen in North Little Rock.

Briley was formerly a senior auditor with Frost and Co. She is a summa cum laude graduate in accounding and data processing at the University of Arkansas.

Briley, daughter of Rex and Caroleta Martin, is a native of Murfreesboro.

FAMILY GROUP RECORD

HUSBAND Roy Glenn MARTIN
Born 28 Dec. 1941 Place Mena, Arkansas
Married 14 Feb. 1970 Place Mena, Arkansas
Occupation ___
Church Affil. ___
Died ___ Place ___
Buried ___ Place ___
Other wives ___
Father Orvis Elmo MARTIN (1913-)
Mother (maiden name) Ruby Cleo ALMONRODE (1916-)

WIFE Glenda Lea FRUEN
Born 28 December, 1952 Place Bates, Scott Co., Arkansas
Church Affil. ___ Occupation Homemaker
Died ___ Place ___
Buried ___ Place ___
Other husbands ___
Father Ellis L. C. Fruen
Mother (maiden name) Ola Evelyn Pepper

Sex M F	CHILDREN	BORN DATE & PLACE	MARRIED TO WHOM DATE & PLACE	DIED DATE & PLACE
F 1	Christina Dianne Martin	25 Dec. 1971 Mena, Polk Co. Arkansas		
M 2	Mitchell Roy Martin	27 Apr. 1974 Mena, Polk Co. Arkansas		
3				
4				
5				
6				
7				
8				
9				
10				
11				
12				

FAMILY GROUP RECORD

HUSBAND Orvis Lamar MARTIN
Born: 15 Aug. 1950 Place: Mena, Arkansas
Married: 29 May 1970 Place:
Occupation: Timber
Church Affil.:
Died: Place:
Buried: Place:
Other wives:
Father: Orvis Elmo MARTIN (1913-)
Mother (maiden name): Ruby Cleo ALMONRODE (1916-)

WIFE Linda Susan DENTON
Born: 30 October, 1951 Place: Mena, Polk County, Arkansas
Church Affil.: Baptist Occupation:
Died: Place:
Buried: Place:
Other husbands:
Father: Alfred Denton
Mother (maiden name): Anna Marie Wilson

Sex M/F	CHILDREN	BORN DATE & PLACE	MARRIED TO WHOM DATE & PLACE	DIED DATE & PLACE
M 1	Scottie Lamar Martin	11 May 1974 DeQueen, Sevier Co., Arkansas		
F 2	Wendy Lynn Martin	09 May, 1976 DeQueen Sevier Co., Ar.		
F 3	Sondra Lea Martin	18 Dec. 1980 DeQueen Sevier Co. Ar.		

HOLLIS K. ALMONRODE

Hollis was born at the home of his grandparents, Vinston and Ella Almonrode, Rt. 3, Livingston, Tennessee, on July 27, 1920. When he was just a few months old, his family moved to Hatfield, Arkansas. Hollis was a loving and obedient son, and a loving and very protective brother, who with patience and good humor, let his little sisters 'tag along' almost everywhere he went.

After graduating from Hatfield High School, he joined the CCC's, a Civilian Conservation Corp started by President Franklin Delano Roosevelt. He attended college at Jonesboro, Arkansas, Monticello A. & M. at Monticello, Arkansas, and Sam Houston State Teacher's College at Huntsville, Texas.

An aviation enthusiast, Hollis secured his private pilot's license and had been flying for some months before volunteering for the Army Air Corp during World War II. He returned to Hatfield to be with his family while waiting for his call. During the months that he was home, he was Youth Leader at the Hatfield Methodist Church, and taught History at Hatfield High School. Among his students were his sister Jo, and Jo's future husband, Eugene Foley.

During his last leave at home, Hollis gave his Mother a copy of a poem which he said expressed exactly how he felt about flying. It is entitled "High Flight" and was written by a young American who had enlisted in the Royal Canadian Air Force during World War II.

> "Oh, I have slipped the surly bonds of earth
> And danced the skies on laughter-silvered wings;
> Sunward I've climbed and joined the tumbling mirth
> of sun-split clouds - and done a hundred things
> You have not dreamed of - wheeled and soared and swung
> High in the sunlit silence.
> Hovering there,
> I've chased the shouting wind along and flung
> My eager craft through footless halls of air.
> Up, up the long delirious burning blue
> I've topped the wind-swept heights with easy grace,
> Where never lark, or even eagle, flew;
> And, while with silent lifting mind I've trod
> The high untrespassed sanctity of space,
> Put out my hand, and touched the face of God."

Lt. Almonrode served as a pilot with the Tenth Air Force in the China-Burma-India theatre of war under the command of General Joseph W. (Vinegar Joe) Stilwell. In addition to his regular missions, he flew over the famed Himmalayan Hump, delivering high octane gas to General Claire L. Chennault's "Flying Tigers."

Hollis was killed in action, November 5, 1944. He was 24 years old.

FAMILY GROUP NO.

Full Name: Hollis K. Almonrode

This Information Obtained From:
Hollis had no middle name - just the initial "K" after his great-grandfather, Ivin K. Murdock.

	Day Month Year	City, Town or Place	County or Province, etc.	State or Country
Birth	27 July 1920	Livingston,	Overton County,	Tennessee
Chr'nd				
Mar.				
Death	05 Nov. 1944	Udala		India
Burial				

Places of Residence: Tennessee-Arkansas (Stationed -Tx-Ariz.-N.Mex.-Ca & Colo.
Occupation: Pilot **Church Affiliation:** Methodist **Military Rec.** Army Air Corp. WWII
Other wives: never married
His Father: Sherrod Wesley Almonrode **Mother's Maiden Name:** Nannie Bell Ward

---

APRIL 11, 1945.

Receives Decoration After Death In India.

LT. HOLLIS K. ALMONRODE.

Mena, April 10 (Spl).—Second Lt. Hollis K. Almonrode, son of Mr. and Mrs. S. W. Almonrode of Hatfield, Polk county, has received the Purple Heart and Air Medal posthumously for service in India and China. He was killed while on a search mission in India November 5.

He was pilot of a B-24 Liberator bomber. He received the Air Medal for more than 100 hours' flying over enemy territory, including flights over the Hump. He was commissioned at Fort Sumner, N. M. in May.

He formerly attended Sam Houston State Teachers College, Huntsville. Surviving also are three sisters, Jo and Mrs. Ruby Martin of Hatfield, and Helen of Hot Springs.

Award of the Air Medal "for meritorious achievement in aerial flight" to Second Lieutenant Hollis K. Almonrode, son of Mr. and Mrs. S. W. Almonrode, Hatfield, has been announced by Headquarters, Tenth Air force in Burma. A B-24 pilot for the famous Seventh Bombardment group of the Tenth Air force that operates against the Japs throughout the India-Burma theatre, Lieutenant Almonrode has been a member of the armed forces for 25 months, five of which he has spent in India.

POSTHUMOUS AWARD

At a ceremony held at 3:30 o'clock, Tuesday afternoon, Sept. 4, 1945, Colonel John P. Wheeler, commanding officer of the Army Ground and Service Forces Redistribution Station, Hot Springs, Ark., presented the Oak Leaf Cluster to the Air Medal, posthumously awarded to 2nd Lt. Hollis K. Almonrode, son of Mr. and Mrs. Sherrod W. Almonrode, Hatfield, Ark., to the officer's sister, Miss Helen Almonrode of Hot Springs. The presentation was made in the office of Colonel Wheeler at the Redistribution Station.

The citation accompanying the Oak Leaf Cluster, awarded in lieu of a second Air Medal, was read by Capt. Robert A. Barr, Station Adjutant, and stated in part: "For meritorious achievement as a pilot from July 23, 1944 to Oct. 29, 1944 by participation in heavy bombardment missions and allied operational flights totaling more than 200 hours during which exposure to enemy fire was probable and expected. These flights flown from bases in India over Burma, Thailand, China and the Andaman Islands, have been eminently successful. The devotion to duty exhibited in the execution of these assignments and the cooperation displayed therein, as essential and vital parts of a combat team, contributed to the success of these missions."

AMERICAN LEGION POST 323 HOLLIS-ROSE HATFIELD, ARK.

Post 323 was named in honor of Hollis, who was killed during World War II, and for Hollis' cousin, Fred Rose, Jr. who was killed in Korea.

Second child and only son of Sherrod Vesley Almonrode and Nannie (Ward) Almonrode

Born: July 27, 1920   LT. HOLLIS K. ALMONRODE   Died: Nov. 5, 1944

HELEN (ALMONRODE) CRAFTON and JAMES BLAIR CRAFTON

Helen and Jim - December 24, 1952

FAMILY GROUP NO. _____   **Husband's Full Name** James Blair CRAFTON

This Information Obtained From:

- Birth: 23 Oct. 1924, Kansas City, Jackson Co., Missouri
- Mar: 24 Dec. 1952, Hazel, First Methodist Church, Vera, Ark.
- Occupation: retired teacher & Football coach   Military Rec.: Army Infantry
- His Father: Harry Edward CRAFTON   Mother's Maiden Name: Mabel BLAIR

Wife's Full Maiden Name Helen Penn ALMONRODE

- Birth: 15 Oct. 1923, Hatfield, Polk Co., Arkansas
- Places of Residence: Arkansas – Missouri & Illinois (and attended college in Louisiana)
- Occupation: Teacher and co-owner of two restaurants   Church Affiliation: Methodist
- Her Father: Sherrod Wesley Almonrode   Mother's Maiden Name: Nannie Bell WARD

Sex	Children's Names	Data	Day Month Year	City, Town or Place	County or Province	State or Country	Add. info
F	1. Carol Ann Crafton	Birth	09 Oct. 1953	Conway	Faulkner Co.	Arkansas	
F	2. Sharon Lee Crafton	Birth	28 Sept. 1956	St. Louis		Missouri	
F	3. Nancy Kay Crafton	Birth	20 Oct. 1959	St. Louis		Missouri	Nancy is in a home for disabled

Jim was about five years old when his family moved from Missouri to Little Rock, Ar. They lived there two years, then moved to Lake Village, Dermott and McGee, but moved back to Little Rock in 1935. He graduated from Little Rock Senior High School (now named L.R. Central H.S.) and enrolled at Louisiana State University at Baton Rouge, where he lettered in football and track.

From December, 1942, until July, 1946, he served in the U.S. Army Infantry and was in "The Battle of the Bulge", "Remagen Bridge," etc. He was awarded the Combat Infantry Badge, 3 Battle Stars and the Bronze Star. He received a Battlefield Commission to 2nd. Lieutenant and was a First Lt. when he was discharged.

In the fall of 1946, he enrolled at the University of Arkansas and played on the Arkansas Razorback Team. He had football scholarships at both L.S.U. and the U. of A. He graduated from the U. of A. in 1949 and received his Masters Degree in 1950.

He coached at Harrison High School in Harrison, Arkansas, from 1949 through 1951, and at Arkansas State Teachers College at Conway from 1952 through 1954. From 1955 through 1957 he coached at Principia High School in St. Louis, Missouri, and from 1958 until he retired in 1981, he was Head Coach and Director of Athletics at Principia College at Elsah, Illinois.

James Blair Crafton

A BRIEF HISTORY
of
HELEN ALMONRODE

Helen was born at Hatfield, Arkansas, on October 15, 1923. She was the daughter of Sherrod Wesley and Nannie (Ward) Almonrode. After graduating from Hatfield High School as Valedictorian of the class of 1940, she attended, and graduated from, Arkansas Teacher's College at Conway, Arkansas, which is now named The University of Central Arkansas. While there, she was elected to "Who's Who in American Colleges and Universities". She is also a graduate of Louisiana State University at Baton Rouge, Louisiana. She taught Physical Education at Hot Springs Junior High School in Hot Springs, Arkansas, then returned to Arkansas State Teacher's College as Professor of Health and Education.

On December 24, 1952, Helen and James Blair Crafton were married at the Chapel of the First Methodist Church in Mena. At that time, James was Football Coach at Arkansas State Teacher's College.

Helen and Jim have three daughters. Carol Ann was born at Conway and Sharon Lee and Nancy Kay were born after they moved to St. Louis, Missouri. They later moved to Elsah, Illinois, where Jim was Head Coach and Director of Athletics at Principia College.

Since 1975, Helen and Dorothy Lindgren, who had been an education and drama teacher on the college level, have owned the Elsah Landing Restuarant. Although the restaurant is small, they have gained national acclaim. All of the food is homemade and cooked or baked on the premises, including the bread for the sandwiches. In the early days of the restaurant, Helen baked all of the bread and pies and Dorothy made the soups and all other desserts. Now they are both primarily involved in administrative duties and have teams of bakers and cooks. They have been named to the "Best St. Louis Restaurants" list for several years, were listed in both editions of "Where to Eat in America", and some of their recipes were selected for inclusion in the Benson and Hedges "Recipes From Great American Inns." They were also featured in the September/October 1984 issue of Better Homes and Gardens "Country Home" magazine.

In 1981, Helen and Dorothy had a cookbook published - "The Elsah Landing Restaurant Cookbook" and shortly afterwards they opened another restaurant in fashionable Plaza Frontenac in St. Louis. In October, 1984, their second cookbook "Elsah Landing Heartland Cooking" was published and in 1986 they opened "The Elsah Landing Tea Room".

Helen and Jim now live in Godfrey, Illinois, just a few miles from Elsah on the banks of the Mississippi River.

Happy landing in Elsah

By KAREN K. MARSHALL
Globe-Democrat Food Editor

Elsah, Ill. — Helen Crafton planned on a teaching career as a teen-ager and really couldn't see the need for the four years of high school home economics she was required to take.

"But I guess I learned something," she said last week with a wry smile.

Whether she really learned to cook in those home ec classes might be up for discussion, but nobody will debate that she learned to cook somewhere.

So did her partner, Dorothy Lindgren.

Three and a half years ago, those two women and Al and Eric Mack took a collective deep breath, pooled their ideas and their elbow grease and opened The Elsah Landing Restaurant in this tiny river town 12 miles north of Alton.

They leased the old Singletary-Lazenby Building, once a drugstore and grocery, from the Elsah Historic Foundation and set to work.

The two-story, frame building with country-store bay windows had already been slightly renovated, one side into an ice cream parlor and the other into a gift shop. But no one had touched the cellar, where many years ago ice from the Mississippi had been stored and "where people had thrown junk for a hundred years." They cleared away "three feet of cobwebs and sand" to turn the area into a kitchen where they bake bread and pies daily. The homemade soups and sandwiches are made upstairs in another kitchen.

THE MACKS BROUGHT a collection of antique tools to the restaurant to use as decoration. A ceiling fan came from a cabin at the nearby Chautauqua. An old framed shock of wheat, a couple of counters and an aged chopping block came with the building.

They borrowed murals of early Elsah scenes from Glenn Felch, who teaches at Principia College on the bluffs above the town, to use as wall decorations.

The decor was purposely kept simple. The floors are shiny wood. The chairs are polished old desks, minus the arms. The wood tables have no cloths. The simple dishes are plain white. Even the little bouquets of fresh flowers on each table are simple, usually picked from the owners' gardens.

The menu is simple, too. Homemade pies made from fresh ingredients. Homemade cakes and cheesecakes. Homemade bread and sweet rolls. Crisp salads. Grinder sandwiches. And homemade soups to fit the seasons. Basic soups, such as Navy Bean and Ham, and exotic soups, such as Cream of Lettuce.

Homemade is the key, as you may have guessed.

"I was convinced if we could maintain food from scratch", we could make the restaurant work, said Mrs. Lindgren. "Scratch food is almost unavailable. I think people will come from a long distance to get it."

Most of the recipes, some of them quite unusual, have come from Mrs. Lindgren's and Mrs. Crafton's files. They still look through old cookbooks for more when they get a chance. And faithful customers often arrive with recipes or samples of pies and other dishes they think the women might be interested in trying. The Black Bottom Pie, which is often on the menu, is a variation of a customer's recipe.

PORTIONS ARE LARGE — ("The whole grinder's so large most people don't want that much unless they're at starvation's door," Mrs. Crafton warned a customer who was wavering between a whole grinder and a half.) — and the variety is great each day, although the menu changes with the seasons, with the ingredients available, with the cooks' moods.

Some people insist the soups are the best they've tasted. Others, who swear by the breads, keep the basement bakers busy, providing not only enough bread for sale in the restaurant, but special take-home orders, including stollens at Christmastime, as well.

But maybe it is the pies that are most popular of all. One day last week, customers could choose from Williamsbury Caramel Pie, Black Bottom Pie, Egg Custard or Fresh Purple Plum Pie, Mystery Pecan Pie, California Peach Pie, and Scintillating Lemon Pie, a not-too-tart, not-too-sweet two-crust creation with bits of lemon and shreds of coconut in a creamy filling.

Mrs. Crafton used to bake all of the pies, but now she only helps a full-time pie baker. They sometimes turn out 30 pies in a morning, moving into the basement kitchen when the two bread bakers finish. Those two bakers begin work between 2 and 3 a.m., turning out close to 100 small loaves of breads (some 15 varieties, including cornbread, potato bread, Swedish limpia, and pumpernickle), 50 grinder loaves and about 50 rye buns for the roast beef sandwiches.

Mrs. Crafton and Mrs. Lindgren make the soups themselves. Their senses of taste match beautifully, they say, and if one of them says the soup is right, it is.

They try not to have anything left over at the end of the day, except for some bread, such as the potato, which cuts better for sandwiches the second day. The other leftover bread is used for croutons, which show up in salads — and in bags for over-the-counter sale when there is enough.

The restaurant is open from 11:30 a.m. to 8 p.m. every day but Monday. Mrs. Crafton usually opens the restaurant and Mrs. Lindgren closes it, after she finishes teaching classes at Principia, where both the women's husbands teach.

NEITHER WOMAN had really thought much about having a restaurant before they had one, although Al Mack had always wanted to have a grinder shop. In fact, neither woman had thought much about going to Elsah before they got there — Mrs. Crafton nearly 20 years ago, Mrs. Lindgren seven years ago.

Mrs. Crafton at least was used to life in small towns, although when she first arrived in Elsah, the River Road was not finished and the town was somewhat isolated.

Mrs. Lindgren arrived in Elsah from Ohio, by way of New York, Tokyo and San Francisco. "The moving men couldn't believe I'd ever found the place," she remembers with a laugh.

The women, who are in the process of buying out the Macks, have big plans. They want to enlarge the bakery portion of the business. And they hope someday soon to publish a cookbook with their recipes. For that reason, they share only a few of those recipes now.

"It's sort of hard not to give them," Mrs. Crafton said. "I always thought it was sort of flattering when people asked."

But not everyone would be willing to duplicate their efforts even if the recipes were available, Mrs. Lindgren said. She remembered one case when a woman had asked for a recipe and was offered the card to write it down. "She took one look at it, said it was far too complicated to make and even too complicated to write down," Mrs. Lindgren said, chuckling.

The Lemon Pie is one recipe that the women won't share and, since it is a favorite among the customers, people are always trying to figure it out.

Customers try to get one ingredient each out of various employes in the hopes of getting enough of the recipe to work on it at home, Mrs. Crafton said. Sometimes they call newspaper food editors to see if they can supply the recipe.

Once in a while, a customer does unravel the mystery. That's how The Globe-Democrat first got the recipe for Mystery Pecan Pie nearly a year ago.

SOME DISHES ARE mysteries even to Mrs. Crafton and Mrs. Lindgren. There was the time, for example, when the carrot cake flopped three days in a row. It tasted just fine, but fell once out of the oven. The cook didn't have any idea what she was doing wrong. The women couldn't afford to simply throw away four to five cakes each day, so they put them on the menu. Topped with a lemon sauce, they became Harvest Pudding and were a big hit with the customers.

"I was passing by a table when I heard one woman say to another, 'I haven't had this dish since Grandmother made it,'" Mrs. Crafton said. "We were hysterical in the kitchen."

While Elsah residents do visit the Landing, the town is too small to support a restaurant alone. No problem. Customers come regularly from St. Louis, Belleville, Edwardsville and other nearby Illinois communities. They sometimes come from much farther away, as well, judging from the mail.

"I don't think we ever make anything twice the same way, especially the soups," said Mrs. Crafton.

The above article was in The St. Louis Globe Democrat -- Sept. 6, 1978

Helen (Almonrode) Crafton

4D St. Louis Globe-Democrat   Fri. Feb. 29, 1980
Dining out

Old fashioned country cuisine is the fare at Elsah Landing

By JOHN GARGANIGO
Special to Globe-Democrat

Periodic visits to Elsah, Ill., and Pere Marquette State Park near Grafton have highlighted many a St. Louisan's Sunday drive. The mighty river rolling by with its many barges, and the lofty bluffs along the Great River Road, provide some of the most beautiful scenery in the area. When my children were younger, spotting a soaring eagle circling overhead earned them a nickel prize. With inflation the stakes have increased to a quarter, but the trip — including a stop at Elsah Landing Restaurant — is still a bargain.

The town of Elsah, founded just before the Civil War, is nestled in a valley about 18 miles north of Alton. Many of the buildings have been tastefully restored to maintain the charm and simplicity of a bygone era.

WHEN YOU ENTER the restaurant at 18 La Salle St., you have the feeling that you've been transported back in time to a turn-of-the-century country store, complete with simple wooden shelves and just enough tables to accommodate about 30 customers. There is nothing presumptuous about the tiny two-room establishment that over the last six years has attracted a clientele from miles around, to say nothing of its loyal local customers. The atmosphere resembles that of the Spanish "ventas" or French inns that are within easy driving distance of many of those countries' major cities. The food there is always simple but wonderfully prepared, and a comfortable mealtime can be spent in attractive surroundings.

Often the simplest things are those that provide the greatest pleasures. The menu at Elsah Landing is the height of simplicity; it satisfies without being pretentious. On the day we visited, Vegetable Beef and Barley Soup and Chicken Noodle Soup were featured. (More than 30 soups have made their way onto the menu, each with the finest, freshest ingredients.)

A selection of sandwiches and the homemade breads and desserts that have made the restaurant famous complete the menu, which is written on a blackboard along with the admonition that no smoking was the wish of the establishment. Grinders, Hoagies, Poor Boys — whatever you want to call them — are available in a number of combinations: Ham ($2.80); Roast Beef ($2.50); and Salami and Cheese ($2.40). That, plus a number of salads topped with homemade croutons, is enough to satisfy anyone's appetite. Most sandwiches also are offered in half portions. The desserts, all homemade, vary. The day we visited the choices were Dutch Apple Pie, Williamsburg Caramel Pie, Blackbottom Pie, Landing Fruit Cake (all moderately priced at $1.25) and a gigantic Linzer Cookie (55 cents). Liquor is not served, but a variety of beverages including coffee and spiced teas are fine complements to the meal.

THE VEGETABLE BEEF Barley Soup could be a meal in itself if ordered with a choice of homemade Italian Bread, Pumpernickel or Potato Bread. The soup was prepared with fresh carrots, celery, onions, tomatoes and a generous supply of beef and barley, all simmered in a beef stock with a hint of spices to produce a most pleasing effect.

If my eyes were not bigger than my stomach, I would have been happy with that. I had to sample my daughter's order of Chicken Noodle Soup and it, too, was a delight. It was obvious that it had been cooked slowly over a long period of time without any outside food enhancers. The broth was clear, its taste subtle with plenty of fresh chicken pieces and a sufficient supply of homemade noodles.

An order of Roast Beef sandwich (a half portion would have sufficed) came with a creamy horseradish sauce that was just right. The same could be said for the Ham and Cheese sandwich, sliced before your eyes with an ample supply of smoky provolone cheese to provide the right bite. A fresh green salad with tomatoes, radishes and fresh buttery croutons, and just the right amount of oil and vinegar dressing, was superb.

The moment of truth arrived with the selection of desserts. While apple pie is as "American" as, well, apple pie, the Pennsylvania Dutch did something to it. I can't remember a place where this dessert, with its crispy freshness, flaky crust and simply delicious filling, was any better than at Elsah Landing. The flavor and texture of the apples was not spoiled by overcooking or too much sugar. The Linzer Cookie — a butter sugar cookie with a dollop of jam in the middle — would have made the Cookie Monster's mouth water. It disappeared before I could steal a second bite. Cakes, breads, croutons and an unusual selection of imported jellies, preserves and teas may be purchased for home consumption.

IF YOU VISIT Elsah before springtime, chances are you won't have to wait long before being served. On the other hand, if queues are too long, a visit to the spacious grounds of Principia College, high above the bluffs, is recommended. When the river is not frozen or flooded, we often return by way of the Grafton Ferry and enjoy the sunset along with the rolling hills of Calhoun County (between the Illinois and Missouri rivers) before embarking on the Golden Eagle Ferry to St. Charles County. In the summer a visit to one of the many orchards that sell peaches, especially the white variety not usually found in the markets, makes the entire trip extremely worthwhile.

The food at the Elsah Landing Restaurant smells, looks and tastes great

By PATTY COOPER
Staff Writer

Since it's very humble beginnings in 1975, the Elsah Landing Restaurant has grown and grown in popularity.

It is known far and wide for its consistently excellent, homemade cuisine.

Many of the customers come regularly from Springfield, Belleville, Quincy, Edwardsville, St. Louis and Waterloo.

The owners of the Elsah Landing Restaurants, one in Elsah and the other at Plaza Frontenac, are Helen Crafton and Dorothy Lindgren, both excellent cooks in their own right.

From their previous careers, a successful restaurant would seem a bit unusual.

Crafton is originally from Arkansas. At one time she taught physical education on the junior high and college levels, and teacher training at a college.

Lindgren hails from Ohio. Also a teacher, she taught education and drama on the college level.

Their husbands took jobs in this area, which transplanted them here. And the rest is all history.

Although they were complete strangers when Crafton became a partner in the business, they have since become fast friends.

The operation of two successful business and the upcoming promotion of their best-selling cookbook, Lindgren said, "we don't a great deal of time for anything else."

Both women attribute at least part of their success to their families, "both have been very supportive," Crafton said.

During the early days of the restaurant, Crafton would take care of the pies and the breads and Lindgren, the soups and the desserts. But success has a way of changing things. Now both women are primarily involved in administration, but still get to cook occasionally "in a pinch."

"It has been a lot of hard work and taken a lot of time," they agree, "but it was fun. We appreciate everything everyone has done for us."

"We have been fortunate to have good, loyal, dependable, friendly people to work for us."

And the customers, they said, "are really great! They are almost like family."

They agreed to share a few of the recipes that appear in their new cookbook, "The Elsah Landing Restaurant Cookbook."

at home cooking...

Helen (Almonrode) Crafton - Dorothy Lindgren

June 30, 1982 — CITIZEN AMERICAN JOURNAL

The children of Helen (Almonrode) Crafton and James Blair Crafton

1. CAROL ANN was born at Conway, Arkansas, on October 9, 1953. When she was about two years old, the family moved to St. Louis, Missouri, and in 1958 they moved to Elsah, Illinois. She attended elementary school at Elsah, and graduated from Jerseyville Community High School in Jerseyville, Illinois in 1971. She went to Trinity University at San Antonio, Texas, for two years, then went to the University of Arkansas at Fayetteville. She finished school during the summer of 1976 but received her diploma with the spring graduating class of 1977. She graduated from the University School of Law in 1979, and received her license in September of 1979. From July, 1979 - January 1, 1981, she worked in Little Rock, Arkansas for Judge Marian F. Penis on the Arkansas Court of Appeals. Judge Penix was appointed by Governor Bill Clinton. From Jan. 9, 1981 - June 24, 1984 she worked for Federal Law Judge Oren Harris in El Dorado, Arkansas. She later joined the law firm of Compton, Prewett, Thomas and Hickey in El Dorado.

On May 18, 1985, Carol Ann married Aubra H. Anthony, Jr. Aubra graduated from Tulane University and received his law degree from the University of Virginia at Charlottsville. He practiced law in Washington D. C. for about 8 years, then returned to his home town of El Dorado to work in the family businesses. He is now president of Anthony International Corporation.

On May 11, 1987, Carol Ann, at the age of 33, was sworn in as a Federal Judge, which makes her the second female Federal Judge in our state's history.

Carol and Aubra have two sons, Aubra Hayes III, and James Hunter.

2. SHARON LEE was born at St. Louis, Missouri on September 28, 1956. The family moved to Elsah, Illinois, when she was two years old. She attended grade school at Elsah and graduated from Jerseyville High School in 1974. She attended Centenary College at Shreveport, Louisiana and the University of Arkansas. While she was at Centenary, she was a member of the Centenary College Choir and one year they went to Europe and sang at various places in France, Germany, Holland, Austria and Switzerland. While they were in Paris, they sang at Notre Dame Cathedral.

Sharon works for a Travel Agency in Richardson, Texas, at the present time (1989), but has also worked for International Tours of Garland, Texas and for Park Central Travel Agency in Dallas. One of the things she enjoys about her job is the trips she gets to take. In addition to the many trips wihtin the U.S. including New York City, and California, she has vacationed in London, England, and Hawaii and has gone on Mexican and Caribbean cruises. Sharon owns a home in Garland, Texas, and is active in the First Methodist Church of Garland, where she sings in the choir, etc.

3. NANCY KAY was born Oct. 20, 1959 at St. Louis, Missouri. According to the doctor, she seemed normal at birth, but she took some childhood diseases from her sisters when she was a small baby and she has been totally handicapped since that time. Helen cared for her at home for years - as long as she possibly could - but finally had to put her in a home for the handicapped.

FAMILY GROUP NO.

Husband's Full Name Aubra Hayes Anthony II

	Day Month Year	City, Town or Place	County or Province, etc.	State or Country
Birth	09 Nov. 1946	Little Rock	Pulaski Co.,	Arkansas
Chr'nd				
Marr.	18 May 1985	El Dorado	Union Co.,	Arkansas
Death				
Burial				

Places of Residence: Arkansas, Louisiana, Virginia, Washington D. C.
Occupation:
Church Affiliation:
Other wives: (1) Audrey Sheppard
His Father: Aubra Hayes Anthony Mother's Maiden Name: Marion Anna Williams

Wife's Full Maiden Name Carol Ann Crafton

	Day Month Year	City, Town or Place	County or Province, etc.	State or Country
Birth	09 Oct. 1953	Conway	Faulkner	Arkansas
Chr'nd				
Death				
Burial				

Places of Residence: Arkansas-Missouri-Illinois (atteneed college in Texas)
Occupation: Atty/Fed. Judge Church Affiliation: Methodist
Her Father: James Blair Crafton Mother's Maiden Name: Helen Penn Atmonrode

Children

Sex	Name		Day Month Year	City, Town or Place	County	State
M	1. Aubra Hayes Anthony III	Birth	25 May 1986	El Dorado	Union	Arkansas
M	2. James Hunter Anthony	Birth	22 Feb. 1988	El Dorado	Union	Arkansas

The Ward Family History
Page 254

CAROL ANN (CRAFTON) ANTHONY

The first child of Helen (Almonrode) Crafton and James Blair Crafton

El Dorado NEWS-TIMES

Sunday, May 19, 1985 – Page 9

Historic house is site of reception

Carol Ann Crafton became the bride of Aubra H. Anthony Jr. at [8] m. May 18 at the First United Methodist Church in El Dorado with the Honorable Oren Harris officiating.

Parents of the couple are Mr. and Mrs. James B. Crafton of [Ge]ffrey, Ill. and Mr. and Mrs. [Au]bra H. Anthony Sr. of El Dorado.

[Music] was provided by Dr. [...] Farmer, organist, and [Ma]ry Pat Cook, soloist.

Given in marriage by her [fath]er, the bride wore a two [pie]ce gown of candlelight lace with cap sleeves over a canlight satin sheath. The tea[len]gth lace dress was edged with scallops and worn with a [sat]in cummerbund. An off-the[fac]e veil was attached to a garland with a gardenia and candlelight ribbon. The bride carried a bouquet of stephanotis, baby's breath, white roses and a gardenia.

Sharon Crafton served her sister as maid of honor and wore a pale pink satin sheath dress with a pink lace overlay. The mid-calf length dress was also edged with scallops. She carried a bouquet of mixed spring flowers.

Russ Anthony served his brother as best man. Ushers were the Honorable Beryl Anthony Jr. and Don Williams of El Dorado, Mark Anthony of Atlanta, Texas, Robert Howell of Nashville, Tenn., James Fuller III of Washington, D.C., and Hirschel Abbott of New Orleans, La.

A reception was held at the historic Rainey-Newton House in El Dorado which was decorated with magnolia blossoms, English ivy, ferns, pink bows, baby's breath and candles. The bride's table was covered with lace and held the four-tiered cake which featured five satellite cakes with fresh flowers amid votive candles.

The groom's table was decorated with brass and held a carrot cake and coffee service. Servers at the reception were Dr. Edwina F. Hunter, Maxine Canterberry, Memorie Hunter, Rita Taunton, Linda Gillaspie, Lillie Faye Oldham, Janice Beard, Janet Pulliam and Judi Kjeldgaard.

Following a wedding trip to New York City and Nantucket Island, Mass., the couple will reside in El Dorado and Washington, D.C. The bride is an attorney associated with Compton, Prewett, Thomas and Hickey and the groom is president of Anthony International Corporation.

Mrs. Aubra H. Anthony Jr.

El Dorado NEWS-TIMES
Local
Tuesday, May 12, 1987 – Page 2

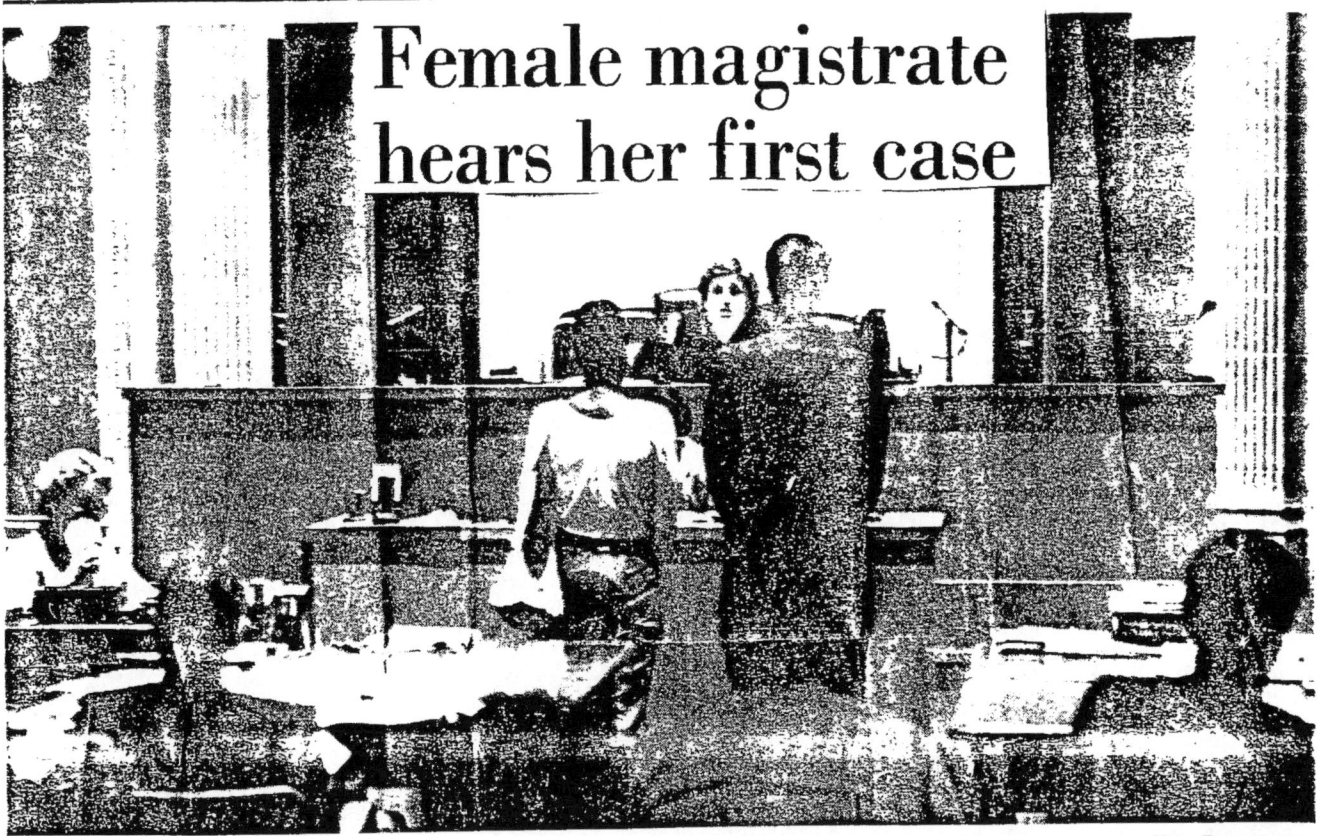

Female magistrate hears her first case

News-Times/Jim Len

New Judge

Carol Crafton Anthony tries a case in Federal Court in the El Dorado Post Office Building after being sworn-in as district magistrate Monday afternoon.

By GERALD HAMBLETON
Staff Writer

Arkansas now has its second female federal magistrate in the state's history – Carol Crafton Anthony of El Dorado.

Mrs. Anthony was sworn in at :30 p.m. Monday in the U.S. District Courtroom on the second floor of the Federal Building in El Dorado by U.S. District Judge Oren Harris.

Mrs. Anthony will be headquartered in El Dorado and serve the El Dorado Division of the Western District of Arkansas. The other magistrate is headquartered in Jonesboro, which is in the state's Eastern District.

The El Dorado Division has been without a magistrate for five months since J.S. Brooks resigned after serving several years in the post, Harris said.

Federal magistrates issue warrants on request from federal agents, set initial bonds for suspects arrested by federal agents and preside over misdemeanor cases. They also handle more serious cases on special assignment from district judges.

Immediately after administering the oath and permitting her husband, Aubra Anthony Jr., to help her don her new black robe, Judge Harris relinquished the bench to her for her first case.

She heard Jessie B. Thrower, 27, and Ella Mae Benton, 42, both of El Dorado, plead guilty to charges of stealing and cashing of a $744.13 federal check.

Each one pleaded guilty to one count of separate three-count indictments. The government dropped the other two counts of each indictment in exchange for the guilty pleas.

She said she would recommend that Judge Harris accept the pleas. He then returned to the bench, accepted the pleas and pronounced sentence.

Thrower was sentenced to 18 months in federal prison, and Benton was given a two-year suspended sentence.

Carol Ann is the daughter of Helen (Almonrode) Crafton and James Blair Crafton.

FAMILY GROUP NO.

Husband's Full Name: Elbert Eugene Foley

	Day Month Year	City, Town or Place	County or Province etc.	State or Country	Add. Info on Husband
Birth	01 Oct. 1928	Norman	Montgomery Co.	Arkansas	
Chr'nd					
Mar	20 Dec. 1951	Mena - Chapel First Methodist Church - Polk Co. Ark.			
Death					
Burial					

Places of Residence: Ark-Okla-Va-Tex-Wyo-England-Ca-Miss-Ala-So. Car.-Alaska
Occupation: USAF & Store Owner **Church Affiliation:** Methodist **Military Rec:** U.S. Air Force
Other wives, if any. No...: Retired

His Father: Elbert Dennis Foley **Mother's Maiden Name:** Mary Evelyn Benson

Wife's Full Maiden Name: Dorothy Jo Almonrode

	Day Month Year	City, Town or Place	County or Province etc.	State or Country	Add. Info on Wife
Birth	07 June 1927	Hatfield	Polk Co.	Arkansas	
Chr'nd					
Death					
Burial					

Places of Residence: Ark-England-Calif-Miss-Alabama & So. Carolina
Occupation if other than housewife:
Her Father: Sherrod Vesley Almonrode **Mother's Maiden Name:** Nannie Bell Ward

Children

1. M — Gene Keith Foley
Full Name of Spouse: Wanda Louise Rhodes
- Birth: 17 Apr. 1954, South Ruislip - Middlesex Co., England
- Mar: 20 Sep. 1974, Hatfield Methodist Church, Hatfield, Arkansas

Jo and Gene - Dec. 20, 1951

A BRIEF HISTORY of DOROTHY JO ALMONRODE

Jo, the youngest child of Sherrod and Nannie Almonrode, was born at Hatfield, Arkansas on June 7, 1927. She graduated from Hatfield High School -(Valedictorian, class of 1945) and from St. Joseph's Business School. Her first job was with the Civilian Personnel at Las Vegas Army Air Field, later named Nellis Air Force Base, at Las Vegas, Nevada. After returning to Arkansas, she worked for the Polk County Extension Service for a year, then as legal secretary for the law firm of Shaw and Spencer. She also did secretarial work for Attorney and Congressman Boyd Tackett, and for Attorney Hal Norwood, who had served a total of five terms as Attorney General for the State of Arkansas.

At the time of her marriage to Elbert Eugene 'Gene' Foley, she was working in a newspaper office, The Mena Star Company. Jo and Gene were married on Dec. 20, 1951, at the Chapel of the First Methodist Church at Mena. Two weeks after the wedding, Gene was sent to Camp Kilmer, New Jersey, for reassignment to England, and arrived at Southampton on February 6, 1952, the day that King George VI died. Jo arrived by plane at Burtonwood near Liverpool on May 25th. Their first winter in England was quite an initiation to what English weather can be. The fog and smog lasted for days, with visibility practically zero. Thousands of elderly people died that winter from respiratory trouble caused by the weather. It was England's worst fog in over 70 years.

Jo and Gene were in London the day of Queen Mary's funeral. She died on March 24, 1953. They were standing on the sidewalk near Marlborough House when the funeral procession came through the gates of the courtyard surrounding the house. The four Royal Dukes walked behind the carriage containing her casket. They were: The Duke of Edinburgh (Prince Phillip), the Duke of Kent, and Queen Mary's two surviving sons, the Duke of Gloucester and the Duke of Windsor, formerly King Edward VIII. They walked all of the way from Marlborough House to Westminister Abbey......The Foley's were living in England during another historic occasion: The coronation of Queen Elizabeth II on June 2, 1953.

On April 17, 1954, their son, Gene Keith, was born and in October they returned to America and were stationed at Castle Air Force Base, California. From there they went to Biloxi, Mississippi, then Eufaula, Alabama. Gene spent 13 months at a remote radar site in Alaska and was there during the bad earthquake on Good Friday in 1964. Jo and Keith lived in Hatfield during that time. They went back to Biloxi for two years, then were sent to Myrtle Beach, So. Carolina. They returned to Hatfield in October, 1968, and for 9½ years they owned and operated Foley's Grocery & Market. Because Gene's health continued to get worse, they leased their store and are now at home where they enjoy their grandsons, Rodney and Wesley, and their hobby of raising African Violets.

Merced, California - May, 1955

THE FOLEY FAMILY

Gene   Keith - age 13 Mo.)   Jo

THE MENA EVENING STAR
Mena, Ark., Mon., Oct. 28, 1968
PAGE 3

LIFE SCOUT KEITH FOLEY with his parents, T/Sgt. and Mrs. Eugene Foley and Capt. (Chap.) William M. Stricklin.

EARNS SCOUTING'S MOST DIFFICULT AWARD

Keith, a member of Scout Troop 861, received his God and Country Award at Myrtle Beach Air Force Chapel, S. C., on Oct. 6. The award was presented by his father who had encouraged him through the year long program which led to the winning of scouting's most difficult award. Eight scouts began working on the program a year ago, but only two completed the course.

Capt. (Chap.) William M. Stricklin guided the boys during their work for the award. Much memorization of Bible information was done and each phase of current church work was learned according to the Scout's denominational preference.

Many hours of manual labor was required during the program. This took the form of Chapel lawn care, helping in administrative tasks and interior clean up work.

Sgt. Foley retired from the Air Force on October 22nd, and they are now living in Hatfield with Mrs. Foley's mother, Mrs. S. W. Almonrode. Keith is a freshman at Hatfield High School.

September 20, 1974

MRS. GENE FOLEY

Polk County Couple Is Wed At Hatfield

Miss Wanda Louise Rhodes and Gene Keith Foley exchanged wedding vows at the Hatfield Methodist Church on Sept. 20

The bride is the daughter of Mr. and Mrs. Virgil Rhodes of Cove. She is a 1974 graduate of Van-Cove High School.

The groom is the son of Mr. and Mrs. E. Eugene (Gene) Foley of Hatfield. He a 1972 graduate of Hatfield High School and attended Southern State College at Magnolia.

The Rev. Bun Gantz, pastor, officiated at the double-ring ceremony before an archway entwined with ivy and carnations. Flanking the archway were baskets filled with greenery and orchid and white carnations and decorated with white satin bows. The altar was lighted by white cathedral tapers in seven branched candelabra.

A program of nupital music, including wedding marches as the processional and recessional was played by Miss Tammy Taylor. She also sang, "Day by Day" and "We've Only Just Begun."

The bride was escorted down the aisle by her brother, Ernest Rhodes, who gave her in marriage. She wore a floor length A-line gown of scalloped lace over bridal satin, with long, full sleeves of embroidered lace. She carried a bouquet of orchid and white carnations with white satin streamers. Her shoulder-length veil was attached to a floral headband.

Miss Gail Shephard, maid-of-honor, wore an orchid formal-length gown, fashioned similar to the brides, with white Lily-of-the-Valley trim on the bodice. She carried a long-stemmed orchid carnation with white satin bow and streamers.

Garry Stricklin served as best man. Larmar Martin of Wickes and Roy Martin of Hatfield, cousins of the groom, served as candle-lighters and ushers.

Miss Vicki Holder, cousin of the groom, served as flower girl. She wore a formal-length gown of orchid dotted swiss trimmed with white lace. She carried a basket of carnations. Master Douglas Rhodes, brother of the bride, was ring bearer.

For her daughter's wedding, Mrs. Rhodes chose a dress of orchid double-knit with white trim and wore a white carnation corsage. The groom's mother also was attired in orchid and wore a corsage of white carnations.

Following the ceremony, a reception was held in the church fellowship hall. The large three-tiered wedding cake featured grecian column dividers. Frosted in white, it was decorated with orchid roping and edged with orchid flowers and green leaves. It was topped with a miniature bride and groom.

Assisting in serving were Ruby Martin, Glenda and Linda Martin and Cathy Taylor.

After a short wedding trip, the couple now resides in Hatfield.

The Ward Family History

FAMILY GROUP NO. _____

Husband's Full Name Gene Keith Foley

	Day Month Year	City, Town or Place	County or Province etc.	State or Country
Birth	17 Apr. 1954	South Ruislip,	Middlesex Co.	England
Chr'nd				
Mar.	20 Sept. 1974	Methodist Church,	Hatfield, Polk Co.,	Arkansas
Death				
Burial				

Places of Residence: England, Calif-Miss-Alabama-So. Carolina & Arkansas
Occupation: Str. Mgr. & Const. Church Affiliation: Methodist Military Rec: None

His Father: Elbert Eugene Foley   Mother's Maiden Name: Dorothy Jo Almonrode

Wife's Full Maiden Name Wanda Louise Rhodes

	Day Month Year	City, Town or Place	County or Province etc.	State or Country
Birth	24 June 1956	Coos Bay	Coos Co.	Oregon
Chr'nd				
Death				
Burial				

Places of Residence: Oregon & Arkansas
Church Affiliation: Hatfield Methodist

Her Father: Virgil Andrew Rhodes   Mother's Maiden Name: Louise Lois Crozier

Sex	Children's Name in Full		Day Month Year	City, Town or Place	County or Province	State or Country
M	1. Rodney Keith Foley	Birth	17 Sept. 1977	Mena	Polk Co.	Arkansas
M	2. Wesley Clayton Foley	Birth	04 Oct. 1982	Mena	Polk Co.	Arkansas

Oct. 8, 1982. Wesley was 4 days old.

A BRIEF HISTORY of GENE KEITH FOLEY

Gene Keith was born on April 17, 1954, at the Air Force Hospital at Ruislip Air Force Base (3rd. A.F. Headquarters) in Middlesex County, England. He is the only child of Elbert Eugene Foley and Dorothy Jo (Almonrode) Foley. At that time his parents were living at "San Michele", Felden Lane in the little village of Boxmoor - Hemel Hempstead in Hertfordshire County.

In October of 1954, Keith and his parents left Southampton aboard the U.S. Naval ship "The Maurice Rose" to come to the United States. The trip took a little longer than usual because of trying to detour around the worst of "Hurrican Hazel". They arrived at New York, dressed in their warm English clothes, to find that N.Y. was experiencing one of the worst October heat waves in a number of years. There was also a dock strike! While driving down the east coast, Hurrican Hazel caught up with them again, but they arrived at Hatfield, Arkansas, at the home of his grandparents, Sherrod and Nannie Almonrode, the day he was six months old.

They lived in Merced and Atwater, California until the fall of 1959, where Keith's father was stationed at Castle Air Force Base with the Strategic Air Command. They moved to Biloxi, Mississippi for about a year. Keith started 1st. grade at Hatfield, but a few weeks later the family moved to Eufaula, Alabama, where he attended Western Heights Elementary until he completed the 3rd. grade. He went to 4th. grade at Hatfield while his dad was stationed at a remote radar site in Alaska. He attended 5th. grade at Northeastern Elementary at Gulfport, Mississippi, 6th. grade at Passroad Elementary at Gulfport and 7th and 8th grades at Woodland Park School at Myrtle Beach Air Force Base, South Carolina. He had just started his freshman year at Socastee High School in Socastee, So. Carolina, when his dad got a medical discharge from the Air Force and the family moved back to Hatfield. Keith graduated from Hatfield High School in 1972 with many of the same students that had been in his first grade class. In the fall of 1972 he enrolled at Southern State University at Magnolia, Arkansas.

On September 20, 1974, he married Wanda Louise Rhodes at Hatfield United Methodist Church. Wanda was born at Coos Bay, Oregon, but for several years she and her family had lived at Cove, Arkansas, just a few miles south of Hatfield.

Keith worked for several years in the family store at Hatfield, but is now (1987) Assistant Manager of Mena Hardware Company at Mena, Arkansas. Keith and Wanda live on Rt. 4, Mena, just down the hill from his parents' home. They have two sons: Rodney Keith and Wesley Clayton.

MARY A. (GRIFFITH) WARD and ELMER WARD

Elmer was the 5th child of John William Ward and Docia (Hewitt) Ward

"Annie" Elmer

FAMILY GROUP RECORD

HUSBAND   Elmer WARD
Born 16 April 1897   Place
Married 24 June, 1917   Place Brownfield Texas
Occupation Packing Plant Worker
Church Affil. Baptist
Died 4 September, 1957   Place Sweetwater, Texas
Buried Sweetwater cemetary   Place Sweetwater, Texas
Other wives
Father John William WARD
Mother (maiden name) Docia HEWITT

WIFE   Mary Ann Griffith
Born 7 May, 1899   Place
Church Affil. Baptist   Occupation Homemaker
Died 02 March 1985   Place Sweetwater, Texas
Buried   Place Sweetwater Cemetery
Other husbands
Father L. Griffith
Mother (maiden name) Mary Ann ~~GRIFFITH~~

NAME & ADDRESS OF PERSON FILLING OUT THIS SHEET

Joyce Henson TYSSEDAL

Relationship of above to Husband

Relationship of above to Wife

NAMES OF HUSBAND AND WIFE ON THIS CHART ARE THE SAME PERSONS AS NOS. ___ & ___ ON LINEAGE CHART NO ___

Sex M/F	CHILDREN	BORN DATE & PLACE	MARRIED TO WHOM DATE & PLACE	DIED DATE & PLACE
1	Delbert WARD	13 April, 1920	Ruthelma Smythe Dec. 1945	1970
F 2	Geraldine WARD	11 Jan, 1928	George Mosley 21 April, 1946	
F 3	Wanda Jo WARD		Bob Samble 1951 W.A. Miles 1954 George Owen 1967 (Divorced)	13 Jan. 1989 Arkansas
4				
5				
6				
7				
8				
9				
10				
11				

Delbert Ward -- Son of Elmer WARD and Mary Ann GRIFFITH

Delbert Ward 1920-1970

FAMILY GROUP RECORD

HUSBAND Delbert Leon WARD
Born 13 April 1920 Place Scurry Co. Texas
Married 31 Dec. 1945 Place Miami, Florida
Occupation Accountant...Store Owner (Needlework)
Church Affil. Disciples of Christ...(Convert) Presbyterian
Died 01 Jan. 1978 Place Winter Haven, Florida
Buried Cremated... Place Ashes scattered, Florida
Other wives
Father Elmer WARD (1897)
Mother (maiden name) Mary Annie GRIFFITH (1899)

WIFE Ruthelma STEVENS (Foster name-Smyth)
Born 21 Jan 1927 Place Miami, Florida
Church Affil. Presbyterian Occupation Needlework (Own-Business)
Died Place
Buried Place
Other husbands
Father Willard N. Stevens
Mother (maiden name) Marjorie Sulzner

NAME & ADDRESS OF PERSON FILLING OUT THIS SHEET

Joyce (Henson) TYSSEDAL

Sex M F	CHILDREN	BORN DATE & PLACE	MARRIED TO WHOM DATE & PLACE	DIED DATE & PLACE
1	James Christian WARD	26 Dec. 1946 Miami, Florida	Terry O'Reilly 10 April 1981 Houston, Texas	
2	Carol WARD	24 Jul. 1948 Miami, Florida	Michael Denmark 06 April 1968	
3	Mary Margaret WARD	12 Apr. 1950 Miami, Florida	William R. Monty 03 March 1978	
4				
5				
6				
7				
8				
9	NOTE: Delbert left his body to the living bank... He died from a Heart attack			
10	(Body used at the Univ. of Florida Gainesville Research Center)			
11			Ruthelma Ward 1506 Meadow View N.E. Winter Haven, Florida	33881
12				

FORM NO. FGR-8   PRINTED IN U.S.A.   **BLUE**   © GENEALOGY SYSTEMS OF AMERICA 1978

FAMILY GROUP RECORD

HUSBAND George MOSLEY
- Born: 22 FEB 1922 — Place: Halton, TEXAS
- Married: 21 APR 1946 — Place: Sweetwater, TEXAS
- Occupation: Cabinet Shop Owner
- Church Affil.: Baptist
- Died: — Place:
- Buried: — Place:
- Other wives:
- Father: Charlie MOSLEY
- Mother (maiden name): Nora SMITH

WIFE Jeraldine WARD
- Born: 11 JAN 1928 — Place: Sweetwater, TEXAS
- Church Affil.: Baptist — Occupation: Secretary
- Died: — Place:
- Buried: — Place:
- Other husbands:
- Father: Elmer WARD (1897)
- Mother (maiden name): Mary Annie GRIFFITH (1899)

Name & Address of Person Filling Out This Sheet: Joyce (HENSON) TYSSEDAL

Sex M/F	Children	Born Date & Place	Married to Whom Date & Place	Died Date & Place
1	Ronnie L. MOSLEY	12 DEC 1946	Trudy GRACEY 14 AUG 1946 Brownfield, TEXAS	
2	Reggie D. MOSLEY	09 NOV 1952	Nancy HAZARD 27 DEC 1973	
3	Rickie G. MOSLEY	27 MAY 1961		11 DEC 1973 Dallas, TEX (Leukemia)

JERRY MOSLEY
RT. 3 BOX 86 A
SWEETWATER, TEX 79556

BLUE

Sweetwater, Texas

Sweetwater Reporter, Thursday December 11, 1973

Rickie Mosley Dies After Long Illness

Rickie Glenn Mosley, 12-year old son of Mr. and Mrs. George Mosley, a leukemia patient for about a year, died at 9:30 p.m. Tuesday in the Wadley Blood Research Center in Dallas where he had been treated as an in and out patient.

Funeral services were at 4 p.m. Thursday at Cate-Spencer Chapel. The Rev. Orvel Brantley, pastor of the Lamar Street Baptist Church and the Rev. Charles Reece, pastor of the First Christian Church, officiated.

Burial was in the Garden of Memories.

Rickie a sixth grade student was born May 27, 1961 in Sweetwater.

Survivors are his parents; two brothers, Ronnie of Dallas and Reggie of Sweetwater; the maternal grandmother, Mrs. Elmer Ward and the paternal grandparents, Mr. and Mrs. V. D. Harris.

Pallbearers were Corkey Frazier, Jack Hendley, J. W. Bradbury, Jimmy Whitworth, Wayne Wilson and J. O. Steele.

RICKIE MOSLEY

FAMILY GROUP RECORD   Prepared By: Billie Ward Creech
                                Last Update: 1 March 1988
HUSBAND.William (Willy, Bill) Byron WARD
Born.18 August 1900..................Place.Hodges, TX Jones Co.
Married.9 January 1926...............Place.Guthrie, OK Logan Co.
Occupation.Machinist
Church Affil.Born Again Christian
Died.4 September 1983................Place.Okla.City, OK.
Buried.6 September 1983..............Place.Chapel Hill Cem.,OKC OK.
Places of res.Hodges,Jones Co.TEXAS Munday,Knox Co.TEXAS Brownsfield,Terry
  Co.TEXAS Hatfield & Mena Polk Co. ARK OKC OK Co. OK.
Other Wives.None.
Father.John William WARD.
Mother(maiden name) Docia HEWITT.

WIFE.Julia Josephine TAYLOR.
Born..2 July 1904....................Place.Ft Smith, Arkansas.
Church Affil..None..................Occupation Homemaker.
Died..2 January 1987.................Place..Okla. City, OK.
Buried..4 January 1987...............Place Chapel Hill OKC OK.
Places of res.Ft.Smith Crawford Co. ARK Mena,Polk Co ARK Guthrie, OK OKC
  OK.
Other husbands.None.
Father.Thomas Edward TAYLOR.
Mother(maiden name).Susie Elizabeth FRAZIER.

Sex	CHILDREN	BORN	MARRIED TO WHOM	DIED
M.F		Date/Place	Date/Place	Date/Place
F 1	Billie Mae WARD	6 Feb. 1927 Muskogee, OK. Muskogee Co.	Ronnie J. CREECH 1 August 1959 Wichita, Kansas Sedwick Co.	
M 2	Jack Wilburn WARD	28 March 1929 Okla.City, OK Okla. Co	Jeannie Newland 1954 ? OKC OK	
3				
4				
5				
6				
7				
8				
9				

FAMILY GROUP RECORD Prepared By: Billie Ward Creech
Last Update: 11 November 1987

HUSBAND. Ronald James CREECH
Born. 15 May 1932 .... Place. Mercy Hospital, Okla. City, OK.
Married. 1 August 1959 .... Place. Wichita, Kansas, Sedgwick Co..
Occupation. Computer specialist, Federal Aviation Adm. MMAC, Okla. City, OK..
Church Affil. Methodist-Baptist.............
Died.. Place.........
Buried.. Place.........
Places of res.. OKC OK - Lawton OK Wichita KAN OKC OK.....
Other Wives. None.................
Father. CREECH, Raymond James..........
Mother(maiden name). WHITE, Nellie Mae.....

WIFE. Billie Mae WARD
Born. 6 February 1927 .... Place. Muskogee, OK - At Home.......
Church Affil. Baptist- Putnam City Bapt. Occupation. Med. Sec. X-ray tech.*1..
Died.. Place.........
Buried.. Place.........
Places of res. OKC OK Wichita, KANSAS OKC OK........
Other husbands.. None..................
Father. WARD, Willie Byron or Wm or Bill............
Mother(maiden name). TAYLOR, Julia Josephine........

Sex:	CHILDREN	BORN Date/Place	MARRIED TO WHOM Date/Place	DIED Date/Place
F 1:	Ronna Kylene CREECH	21 March 1960 OKC, OK Okla. Co.	PERKINS, Mark Russell 23 August 1980 OKC, OK Okla. Co.	
F 2:	Lori Ellen CREECH	16 June 1961 OKC, OK Okla. Co.	Buthion, Alain Jean-Pierre 26 Sept. 1987 OKC, OK. OKLA. Co.	
F 3:	Terri Ann CREECH	2 April 1966 OKC, OK Okla. Co.		
F 4:	Linda Kay CREECH	6 Sept. 1967 OKC, OK Okla. Co.		
5:				
6:				
7:				
8:				

*1 X-ray tech. & Med. Sec. 1948 to 1959 -
   Homemaker 1959 to present

FAMILY GROUP RECORD

HUSBAND William Byron WARD
Born 18 April 1900   Place Hodges Texas
Married 9 JAN, 1926   Place Guthrie OKLA
Occupation Machinist
Church Affil. Protestant
Died 4 SEPT, 1983   Place OKLA City OKLA
Buried Chappel Hill   Place OKLA City OKLA
Other wives
Father John William WARD
Mother (maiden name) Docia HEWITT

WIFE Julia Josephine TAYLOR
Born 2 July 1904   Place Ft. Smith ARK
Church Affil. None   Occupation Homemaker
Died   Place
Buried   Place
Other husbands
Father Thomas Edward TAYLOR
Mother (maiden name) Susie Eliz FRAZIER

Sex M F	CHILDREN	BORN DATE & PLACE	MARRIED TO WHOM DATE & PLACE	DIED DATE & PLACE
1	Billie Mae WARD	6 FEB, 1927 Moskogee OKLA,	Ron CREECH 1 Aug, 1959 Wichita, Kansas	
2	Jack Wilburn WARD	28, March 1929 OKLA, City OKLA	Jeannie NEWLAND	
3				
4				
5				
6				
7				
8				
9				
10				
11				

NAME & ADDRESS OF PERSON FILLING OUT THIS SHEET

Relationship of above to Husband
Relationship of above to Wife
NAMES OF HUSBAND AND WIFE ON THIS CHART ARE THE SAME PERSONS AS NOS.   &
ON LINEAGE CHART NO.

FAMILY GROUP RECORD

HUSBAND Ron J. CREECH
Born: 15 MAY 1932   Place: Okla. City, OKLA
Married: 01 AUG 1959   Place: Wichita, KANSAS
Occupation: Computer Science F.A.A.
Church Affil.:
Died: Place:
Buried: Place:
Other wives: None
Father: Raymond CREECH
Mother (maiden name): Nellie WHITE

WIFE Billie Mae WARD
Born: 06 FEB 1927   Place: Muskogee, OKLA
Church Affil.: Baptist   Occupation: Medical Tech.
Died: Place:
Buried: Place:
Other husbands: None
Father: William Byron WARD
Mother (maiden name): Julia TAYLOR

NAME & ADDRESS OF PERSON FILLING OUT THIS SHEET

Joyce (HENSON) TYSSEDAL

Sex M/F	CHILDREN	BORN DATE & PLACE	MARRIED TO WHOM DATE & PLACE	DIED DATE & PLACE
1	Ronna K. CREECH	21 MAR 1960 Okla City, OKLA	Mark PERKINS 23 AUG 1980 Okla City, OKLA	
2	Lori E. CREECH	16 JUN 1961 Okla City, OKLA		
3	Terri A. CREECH	02 APR 1966 Okla City, OKLA		
4	Linda K. CREECH	06 SEP 1967 Okla City, OKLA		

Billie Ward Creech
5800 N. W. 45
Okla. City, Okla.
73122

FAMILY GROUP RECORD

1st Marriage

HUSBAND Jack Wilburn WARD
- Born: 28 MAR 1929 Place: Okla. City, OKLA
- Married: 1953 Place: Okla. City, OKLA
- Occupation: _____
- Church Affil.: None
- Died: _____ Place: _____
- Buried: _____ Place: _____
- Other wives: #2 _____ #3 _____
- Father: William B. WARD (1900)
- Mother (maiden name): Julia J. TAYLOR (1904)

WIFE Jeannie NEWLAND
- Born: _____ Place: Okla. City, OKLA
- Church Affil.: _____ Occupation: _____
- Died: _____ Place: _____
- Buried: _____ Place: _____
- Other husbands: _____
- Father: _____
- Mother (maiden name): _____

NAME & ADDRESS OF PERSON FILLING OUT THIS SHEET
Joyce (HENSON) TYSSEDAL

Sex M F	CHILDREN	BORN DATE & PLACE	MARRIED TO WHOM DATE & PLACE	DIED DATE & PLACE
1	Jackie Rene WARD	16 AUG 1958 Okla. City, OKLA	Joe RIGGALL Okla City, OKLA	
2				
3				
4				
5				
6				
7				
8				
9				
10				
11				
12				

FORM NO. FGR-8   PRINTED IN U.S.A.   **BLUE**   © GENEALOGY SYSTEMS OF AMERICA 1978

7th child of J.W. Ward

FAMILY GROUP NO. _____

Husband's Full Name: Dewey Ward

Husband's Data	Day Month Year	City, Town or Place	County or Province, etc.	State or Country	Add. Info. on Husband
Birth	24 June 1903	Knox City	Knox	Texas	
Chr'nd					
Marr.					
Death	14 Mar. 1974	Mena	Polk	Arkansas	
Burial		Mena RFD.	(Rocky Cemetery)		

Places of Residence: Texas-Arkansas-California
Military Rec.: Army WWII
His Father: John William Ward
Mother's Maiden Name: Docia Hewitt

Wife's Full Maiden Name

DEWEY WARD 1974

Funeral service for Dewey Ward, 70-year-old resident of Mena, was held Saturday afternoon in the Rocky Methodist Church with Rev. Clermon Rogers officiating.

Interment was in the Rocky Cemetery under the direction of the Geyer-Quillin Funeral Home. Pallbearers were Jim Terrell, Thomas Thacker, Logan McLelland, Herbert Lance, Gerald Johnson and Joe Lance.

Ward was born June 24, 1903, at Knox City, Texas, and died March 14, at Mena. He attended school in Knox City and moved to Polk County in 1958. He spent the remainder of his life here. He was a member of the Methodist Church and a Veteran of World War II.

Survivors include six brothers, M. M. Ward of Anaheim, Calif., Oscar S. Ward of Mena, Fred S. Ward of Brea, Calif., W. B. Ward of Okla. City, Okla., Dale A. Ward of Fayetteville and Olie Ward of Hatfield, and one sister, Mrs. Nannie Almonrode of Hatfield.

KATIE ELIZABETH (STOCKTON) WARD and FRED STANLEY WARD

Fred was the 8th child of John William and Docia Ward

Katie
(1908-1986)

Fred
(1906-1984)

FAMILY GROUP NO.

Husband's Full Name: Fred Stanley Ward

Husband's Data	Day Month Year	City, Town or Place	County or Province, etc.	State or Country	Add. Info. on Husband
Birth	04 Mar. 1906	Knox City	Knox	Texas	
Chr'nd					
Marr.					
Death	12 Mar. 1984			California	
Burial		Brea (Memory Garden Mem. Park) Ca.			

Places of Residence: Texas - Arkansas - California
Occupation: Hunt's Packing Co.
Other wives: None
His Father: John William Ward
Mother's Maiden Name: Docia Hewitt

Wife's Full Maiden Name: Katie Elizabeth Stockton

Wife's Data	Day Month Year	City, Town or Place	County or Province, etc.	State or Country	Add. Info. on Wife
Birth	01 June 1908	Hatfield	Polk	Arkansas	
Chr'nd					
Death	02 Jan. 1986	Whittier	Los Angeles Co.	Ca.	
Burial	04 Jan. 1986	Brea (Memory Garden Memorial Park)		Ca.	

Places of Residence: Arkansas - California
Other husbands: None
Her Father: Lenox L. Stockton
Mother's Maiden Name: Virgie Mangus

Children

Sex	Children's Names in Full	Data	Day Month Year	City, Town or Place	County or Province, etc.	State or Country	Add. info. on Children
F	1. Jacqueline Ward	Birth	17 May 1926	Hatfield	Polk	Arkansas	
	Full Name of Spouse:	Marr.					
		Death	09 Sep. 1927	Fort Smith	Sebastian Co.	Arkansas	
		Burial		Cove	Polk	Arkansas	(Shady Grove emetery)
F	2. Barbara Faye Ward	Birth	04 Sep. 1932	Hatfield	Polk (Old Cove Community)		(cemetery)
	Full Name of Spouse: Calvin Longstaff	Marr.					
		Death					
		Burial					
M	3. Fred Lee Ward	Birth	23 Mar. 1940	Fullerton	Orange Co.	California	
	Full Name of Spouse: Dana White	Marr.					
		Death					
		Burial					

* For additional children use Everton Publishers' Children Continuation Sheet, Form A11

Barbara Faye WARD — Daughter of Fred Stanley WARD and Katie STOCKTON

FAMILY GROUP RECORD

HUSBAND Calvin LONGSTAFF
- Born _____ Place _____
- Married _____ Place _____
- Occupation _____
- Church Affil. _____
- Died _____ Place _____
- Buried _____ Place _____
- Other wives _____
- Father _____
- Mother (maiden name) _____

WIFE Barbara Faye WARD
- Born 04 September, 1932 Place Old Cove, Polk Co., Arkansas
- Church Affil. Lutheran Occupation _____
- Died _____ Place _____
- Buried _____ Place _____
- Other husbands _____
- Father Fred Stanley WARD (1906-1984)
- Mother (maiden name) Katie STOCKTON

NAME & ADDRESS OF PERSON FILLING OUT THIS SHEET
Joyce (Henson) TYSSEDAL

Sex M F	CHILDREN	BORN DATE & PLACE	MARRIED TO WHOM DATE & PLACE	DIED DATE & PLACE
F 1	Carol Ann Longstaff		02 May 1960 John Riggins	
2				
3				
4				
5				
6				
7				
8				
9				
10				
11				
12				

FAMILY GROUP NO.

Husband's Full Name: John Riggins

Husband's Data	Day Month Year	City, Town or Place	County or Province, etc.	State or Country	Add. Info. on Husband
Birth					John and Carol are divorced
Chr'nd					
Marr.					
Death					
Burial					

Places of Residence: Arkansas
Occupation: **Church Affiliation:**   **Military Rec.:**
His Father: **Mother's Maiden Name:**

Wife's Full Maiden Name: Carol Ann Longstaff

Wife's Data	Day Month Year	City, Town or Place	County or Province, etc.	State or Country	Add. Info. on Wife
Birth	02 May 1960	Fayetteville	Washington Co.	Arkansas	
Chr'nd					
Death					
Burial					

Places of Residence: Arkansas
Occupation: **Church Affiliation:**   **Military Rec.:**
Her Father: **Mother's Maiden Name:**

Children

Sex	Children's Names in Full	Data	Day Month Year	City, Town or Place	County or Province, etc.	State or Country
F	1. Kimberly Diane Riggins	Birth	02 May 1981	Fayetteville	Washington Co.	Ar.

FAMILY GROUP RECORD

HUSBAND Fred Lee WARD
Born: 23 March, 1940   Place: Fullerton, Orange Co. California
Married: _____ Place: _____
Occupation: _____
Church Affil.: _____
Died: _____ Place: _____
Buried: _____ Place: _____
Other wives: _____
Father: Fred Stanley WARD (1906-1984)
Mother (maiden name): Katie STOCKTON (   )

WIFE Dana White
Born: _____ Place: _____
Church Affil.: _____ Occupation: _____
Died: _____ Place: _____
Buried: _____ Place: _____
Other husbands: _____
Father: _____
Mother (maiden name): _____

NAME & ADDRESS OF PERSON FILLING OUT THIS SHEET

Joyce (Henson)
TYSSEDAL

Sex M/F	CHILDREN	BORN DATE & PLACE	MARRIED TO WHOM DATE & PLACE	DIED DATE & PLACE
1				
2				
3				
4				
5				
6				
7				
8				
9				
10				
11				
12				

BLUE

FAMILY GROUP NO.

Husband's Full Name: Dale Arlington Ward

Husband's Data	Day Month Year	City, Town or Place	County or Province, etc.	State or Country	Add. Info. on Husband
Birth	23 June 1908	Knox City	Knox County,	Texas	
Chr'nd					
Mar.					
Death					
Burial					

Places of Residence: Texas - Arkansas - California - Oklahoma (now Arkansas)
Occupation:
Church Affiliation:
Military Rec.:
Other wives, if any No. (1) (2) etc: No. 1. Mildred Gaddis
His Father: John William Ward
Mother's Maiden Name: Docia Hewitt

Wife's Full Maiden Name: Fay Athena Henson

Wife's Data	Day Month Year	City, Town or Place	County or Province, etc.	State or Country	Add. Info. on Wife
Birth	07 July 1923	Webbers Falls,	Muskogee Co.,	Oklahoma	
Chr'nd					
Death					
Burial					

Places of Residence: Oklahoma - California - Arkansas

Children

Sex	Children's Name in Full	Event	Day Month Year	City, Town or Place	County or Province, etc.	State or Country
F	Karen Sue Ward / Spouse: Charles Neff	Birth	05 Oct. 1947			California
M	Stephen Dale Ward	Birth	20 Oct. 1952			California

Caption: Karen Sue   Dale   Stephen & Fay

The Ward Family History
Page 282

FAMILY GROUP RECORD

HUSBAND Charles Neff
Born 15 Oct. 1943 Place Springdale, Arkansas
Married ___ Place ___
Occupation ___
Church Affil. ___
Died ___ Place ___
Buried ___ Place ___
Other wives ___
Father Don S. Neff
Mother (maiden name) Dorothy Johnson

WIFE Karen Sue WARD
Born 05 Oct. 1947 Place California
Church Affil. ___ Occupation ___
Died ___ Place ___
Buried ___ Place ___
Other husbands ___
Father Dale Arlington WARD (1908-)
Mother (maiden name) Fay Athena HENSON (1923-)

NAME & ADDRESS OF PERSON FILLING OUT THIS SHEET

Joyce (Henson)

TYSSEDAL

Relationship of above to Husband ___

Relationship of above to Wife: ___

NAMES OF HUSBAND AND WIFE ON THIS CHART ARE THE SAME PERSONS AS NOS. ___ & ___ ON LINEAGE CHART NO. ___

Sex M/F	CHILDREN	BORN DATE & PLACE	MARRIED TO WHOM DATE & PLACE	DIED DATE & PLACE
M 1	Kevin Charles Neff	28 Oct. 1980 Fayetteville Arkansas		
2				
3				
4				
5				
6				
7				
8				
9				
10				
11				
12				

BLUE

FAMILY GROUP RECORD

FIRST MARRIAGE....

HUSBAND Olie WARD
Born 21 March 1911 Place Knox City, Texas (Knox Co)
Married ___ Place ___
Occupation Long Shoreman and Carpenter
Church Affil. ___
Died ___ Place ___
Buried ___ Place ___
Other wives #2- Opal Martin
Father John William WARD (1864)
Mother (maiden name) Docia HEWITT (1868)

WIFE Ethel REED
Born ___ Place ___
Church Affil. ___ Occupation ___
Died ___ Place ___
Buried ___ Place ___
Other husbands ___
Father Andy REED
Mother (maiden name) ___

NAME & ADDRESS OF PERSON FILLING OUT THIS SHEET

Joyce (Henson) TYSSEDAL

Sex M F	CHILDREN	BORN DATE & PLACE	MARRIED TO WHOM DATE & PLACE	DIED DATE & PLACE
1	Bobbie Jean WARD	21 Oct. 1935 Hatfield, Arkansas	James Nickles #-1 Golden Moore #-2	
2	Jerry Leo WARD	23 Dec. 1936 Las Nietos, California	Pat	

Jerry, Olie and Bobby

The Ward Family History
Page 284

FAMILY GROUP NO.

Husband's Full Name: James Nickles (Golden)

This Information Obtained From:

James did not know that his real name was Golden instead of Nickles until after he was married and his children were born.

Husband's Data	Day Month Year	City, Town or Place	County or Province, etc.	State or Country	Add. Info. on Husband
Birth					
Chr'nd					
Mar.					
Death					
Burial					

Places of Residence:

Occupation: Church Affiliation: Military Rec.:

His Father: Mother's Maiden Name:

Wife's Full Maiden Name: Bobby Jean Ward

Wife's Data	Day Month Year	City, Town or Place	County or Province, etc.	State or Country	Add. Info. on Wife
Birth	21 Oct. 1935	Hatfield	Polk Co.	Arkansas	
Chr'nd					
Death					
Burial					

Places of Residence: Arkansas - California - Texas (now Calif.)

Her Father: Olie Ward   Mother's Maiden Name: Ethel Reed

Sex	Children's Name in Full	Children's Data	Day Month Year	City, Town or Place	County or Province, etc.	State or Country	Add. Info. on Children
F	1. Jeri Lynn Nickles — Spouse: Gerold Croteau	Birth	24 Dec. 1955			California	
M	2. James Perry Nickles	Birth / Death	18 Jan. 1957 / 07 Sep. 1977			"	
F	3. Jeanne Rene Nickles — Spouse: Danny Boyd Moore	Birth	19 Feb. 1959			"	
F	4. Joanna Lea Nickles — Spouse: Fred Faulk	Birth	20 June 1960			"	
M	5. Jon Patrick Nickles (Golden)	Birth	09 May 1962			"	

FAMILY GROUP NO.

Husband's Full Name: Gerold Croteau

	Day Month Year	City, Town or Place	County or Province, etc.	State or Country
Birth	09 May 1952	Rialto		California
Chr'nd				
Mar.				
Death				
Burial				

Places of Residence:
Occupation: Church Affiliation: Military Rec.:
His Father: Mother's Maiden Name:

Wife's Full Maiden Name: Jeri Lynn Nickles

	Day Month Year	City, Town or Place	County or Province, etc.	State or Country
Birth	24 Dec. 1955			California
Chr'nd				
Death				
Burial				

Places of Residence:
Occupation if other than housewife: Church Affiliation:
Her Father: James Nickles (Golden) Mother's Maiden Name: Bobby Jean Ward

Children

Sex	Name	Event	Day Month Year
M	1. Gerold Scott Croteau	Birth	16 Jan. 1972
M	2. Jeremy Michael Croteau	Birth	06 Nov. 1975

The Ward Family History, Page 286

FAMILY GROUP NO. _____

This Information Obtained From:
Danny is the son of one of Bobby Jean's husbands.

Husband's Full Name: Danny Boyd Moore

Husband's Data	Day Month Year	City, Town or Place	County or Province, etc.	State or Country	Add. Info. on Husband
Birth	08 Dec. 1955				
Chr'nd					
Mar.					
Death					
Burial					

Places of Residence:
Occupation: Church Affiliation: Military Rec.:
Other wives, if any. No. (1) (2) etc. Make separate sheet for each mar.
His Father: Mother's Maiden Name:

Wife's Full Maiden Name: Jeanne Rene Nickles

Wife's Data	Day Month Year	City, Town or Place	County or Province, etc.	State or Country	Add. Info. on Wife
Birth	19 Feb. 1959			California	
Chr'nd					
Death					
Burial					

Places of Residence:
Occupation if other than housewife: Church Affiliation:
Other husbands, if any. No. (1) (2) etc. Make separate sheet for each mar.
Her Father: James Nickles (Golden)   Mother's Maiden Name: Bobby Jean Ward

Sex	Children's Name in Full	Children's Data	Day Month Year	City, Town or Place	County or Province, etc.	State or Country	Add. Info. on Children
M	1 Danny Boyd Moore Jr.	Birth	01 Dec. 1976				
		Mar.					
	Full Name of Spouse*	Death					
		Burial					
F	2 Jamie René Moore	Birth	12 Dec. 1980				
		Mar.					
	Full Name of Spouse*	Death					
		Burial					

*If married more than once No. each mar. (1) (2) etc. and list in "Add. info. on children" column. Use reverse side for additional children, other notes, references or information.

The Ward Family History
Page 288

FAMILY GROUP NO. _____

Husband's Full Name Jerry Leo Ward — **FIRST MARRIAGE**

This Information Obtained From:

Husband's Data	Day Month Year	City, Town or Place	County or Province, etc.	State or Country	Add. Info. on Husband
Birth	23 Dec. 1936	Los Nietos		California	
Chr'nd					
Mar.					
Death					
Burial					

Places of Residence: California - Texas
Occupation: | Church Affiliation: | Military Rec.:
Other wives, if any. No. (1) (2) etc. Make separate sheet for each mar.

His Father: Olie Ward | Mother's Maiden Name: Ethel Reed

Wife's Full Maiden Name _____

Wife's Data	Day Month Year	City, Town or Place	County or Province, etc.	State or Country	Add. Info. on Wife
Birth					
Chr'nd					
Death					
Burial					

Compiler: | Places of Residence:
Address: | Occupation if other than housewife: | Church Affiliation:
City, State: | Other husbands, if any. No. (1) (2) etc.
Date: | Her Father: | Mother's Maiden Name:

Sex	Children's Name in Full (Arrange in order of birth)	Children's Data	Day Month Year	City, Town or Place	County or Province, etc.	State or Country	Add. Info. on Children
F	1. Toni Ruth Ward Spouse: Jeff Dean Croteau	Birth Mar. Death Burial	05 Sept. 1956			California	
	2.						
	3.						
	4.						
	5.						
	6.						
	7.						
	8.						
	9.						
	10.						

FAMILY GROUP NO.

This Information Obtained From: Jeff Dean Croteau is Gerold Croteau's brother

Husband's Full Name: Jeff Dean Croteau

Husband's Data	Day Month Year	City, Town or Place	County or Province, etc.	State or Country	Add. Info. on Husband
Birth	20 June 1954				
Chr'nd					
Mar.					
Death					
Burial					

Places of Residence:

Occupation: Church Affiliation: Military Rec.:

Other wives, if any. No. (1) (2) etc. Make separate sheet for each mar.

His Father: Mother's Maiden Name:

Wife's Full Maiden Name: Toni Ruth Ward

Wife's Data	Day Month Year	City, Town or Place	County or Province, etc.	State or Country	Add. Info. on Wife
Birth	05 Sept. 1956			California	
Chr'nd					
Death					
Burial					

Places of Residence:

Occupation if other than housewife: Church Affiliation:

Other husbands, if any. No. (1) (2) etc. Make separate sheet for each mar.

Her Father: Jerry Leo Ward   Mother's Maiden Name:

Sex	Children's Name in Full	Children's Data	Day Month Year	City, Town or Place	County or Province, etc.	State or Country	Add. Info. on Children
F	1. Courtney Taylor Croteau	Birth	21 May 1983				
		Mar.					
	Full Name of Spouse	Death					
		Burial					
	2.	Birth					
	3.	Birth					
	4.	Birth					
	5.	Birth					
	6.	Birth					
	7.	Birth					
	8.	Birth					
	9.	Birth					
	10.	Birth					

*If married more than once No. each mar. (1) (2) etc. and list in "Add. info. on children" column. Use reverse side for additional children, other notes, references or information.

FAMILY GROUP NO. ___

Husband's Full Name Jerry Leo Ward — SECOND MARRIAGE

Husband's Data	Day Month Year	City, Town or Place	County or Province, etc.	State or Country	Add. Info. on Husband
Birth	23 Dec. 1936	Los Nietos	Los Angeles Co.	California	
Chr'nd					
Mar.					
Death					
Burial					

Places of Residence: California - Texas
Occupation: Mobil Home Repair   Church Affiliation: Military Rec. Marine Corp. 1954-55
Other wives: Pat Ingram
His Father: Olie Ward   Mother's Maiden Name: Ethel Reed

Wife's Full Maiden Name Shirley Pruitt

Wife's Data	Day Month Year	City, Town or Place	County or Province, etc.	State or Country	Add. Info. on Wife
Birth					
Chr'nd					
Death					
Burial					

Her Father: Mother's Maiden Name:

Sex	Children's Name in Full	Data	Day Month Year	City, Town or Place	County or Province, etc.	State or Country
F	Bobbie Jean Ward	Birth	09 Sept. 1962	San Bernadino	San Bernadino Co.	Calif.
F	Shauna Lynn Ward	Birth	Sept. 1963	"	"	"

FAMILY GROUP RECORD

SECOND MARRIAGE....

HUSBAND Olie WARD
- Born: 21 March 1911 Place: Munday, Texas
- Married: _____ Place: _____
- Occupation: _____
- Church Affil.: _____
- Died: _____ Place: _____
- Buried: _____ Place: _____
- Other wives: #1- Ethel Reed... (Divorced)
- Father: John William WARD (1864)
- Mother (maiden name): Docia HEWITT (1868)

WIFE Opal Irene MARTIN
- Born: _____ Place: _____
- Church Affil.: _____ Occupation: Bookkeeper
- Died: _____ Place: _____
- Buried: _____ Place: _____
- Other husbands: _____
- Father: _____
- Mother (maiden name): _____

NAME & ADDRESS OF PERSON FILLING OUT THIS SHEET
Joyce (Henson)
TYSSEDAL

Sex M F	CHILDREN	BORN DATE & PLACE	MARRIED TO WHOM DATE & PLACE	DIED DATE & PLACE
1	James Clinton WARD	23 Apr. 1947 Houston, Texas		
2				
3				
4				
5				
6				
7				
8				
9				
10				
11			Olie Ward Rt. 1 Box 202 A.A. Mena, Arkansas 71953	
12				

BLUE

JAMES CLINTON (JIM) WARD

The son of Olie Ward and Opal Irene (Martin) Ward

TWO-TIME WINNER

Little Jim Ward, 8-year-old son of Mr. and Mrs. O. Ward, 9826 Branum St., is shown with two first-prize cups he won in consecutive annual piano contests sponsored by the Houston Music Teachers Assn. A piano student for two years, Jim won in a field of 40 contestants this year. He is a third grade student at John R. Harris Elementary School, Broadway and Manchester.

The Ward Family History

FAMILY GROUP NO. _____

Husband's Full Name James Clinton Ward

	Husband's Data	Day Month Year	City, Town or Place	County or Province, etc.	State or Country	Add. Info. on Husband
	Birth	23 Apr. 1947	Houston	Harris	Texas	
	Chr'nd					
	Marr.					
	Death					
	Burial					

Places of Residence: Texas – Arkansas – Kansas
Occupation: _____ Church Affiliation: _____ Military Rec.: Viet Nam
Other wives, if any. No. (1) (2) etc. Make separate sheet for each marr.
His Father: _____ Mother's Maiden Name: _____

Wife's Full Maiden Name Elizabeth (Liz) Pipkin

	Wife's Data	Day Month Year	City, Town or Place	County or Province, etc.	State or Country	Add. Info. on Wife
	Birth					
	Chr'nd					
	Death					
	Burial					

Places of Residence: _____
Occupation: _____ Church Affiliation: _____ Military Rec.: _____
Other husbands, if any. No. (1) (2) etc. Make separate sheet for each marr.
Her Father: _____ Mother's Maiden Name: _____

Sex	Children's Names in Full	Children's Data	Day Month Year	City, Town or Place	County or Province, etc.	State or Country
M	1. Oly Thomas Ward	Birth	27 June 1987	Wichita		Kansas
M	2. Robert Leo Ward	Birth	Dec. 1988	Mena	Polk	Arkansas

James Clinton (Jim) Ward

Jim was in the Green Berets and served two tours of duty in Viet Nam.

JIM WARD of Board Camp, stands beside the cage of one of his "patients" a big Red Shouldered Hawk, whose wing was injured by a .22 bullet. Ward has earned the unofficial title of Polk County Bird Doctor for his care of injured wild birds.

Board Camp resident is county 'bird doctor'

By TROY WILLIAMS
NEWS EDITOR

Most counties have a veterinarian, usually more than one, but few counties can boast of a bird doctor, someone who can heal and care for injured wild birds.

Such a person must not only have an interest in birds but love the feathered creatures enough to exercise an infinite patience in first, learning how to care for their injuries, and then feeding and caring for them until they can again fend for themselves.

Out in the Board Camp community, what began years ago as a hobby has earned for James Ward the unofficial title of bird doctor for Polk County.

In his spare time from his profession as piano tuner, Ward ministers to a variety of injured wild birds, most of them brought to him by officers of the Game and Fish Commission.

Most of them are designated by state and federal law as "birds of prey" such as hawks, owls and eagles.

Although a few of his patients are hit by cars or injured in similar accidents, most of them have been shot by thoughtless hunters, usually young boys with their first .22 rifles.

"What they don't realize is how beneficial these larger birds, such as hawks and owls, are to us," Ward said. "Their diet consists almost entirely of rodents--snakes and rats and mice. They help maintain an important ecological balance."

Warming to his subject, he continued, "Besides being beneficial, they are beautiful and fascinating creatures. Take the time to watch them in flight sometime. It's absolutely criminal to shoot one."

Ward has always been interested in birds, and a few years ago while living in Dallas, he had an opportunity to learn how to care for their injuries.

Ward has always kept cockatoos. In Dallas, he took his birds to Dr. B.J. Lilly for their treatment and care. Lilly, a veterinarian who specializes in treatment of birds, formerly was curator of birds at the Dallas Zoo. From Lilly and by studying on his own, he learned how to splint broken legs and wings and doctor various injuries, even to administering anesthesia and performing operations, which he did recently on a large, Red-Shouldered Hawk whose wing was broken by a gunshot from a .22.

Experience as a para-medic with the army in Vietnam gave Ward a good background in medicines and treating injuries, but he credits Lilly with his specialized knowledge in treating birds.

"I still call him for advice when I get a real difficult case," he said. "Sometimes over the phone, he will talk me through a difficult procedure."

The Red-Shouldered Hawk is a good example of the knowledge Ward has acquired. Brought in with a wing broken by a gunshot wound, the big predator was near death. Ward administered anesthesia, operated to repair the broken bone, and then applied a splint. Now, in a special cage, the hawk glares at his benefactor with yellow eyes, eats well and waits for his wing to heal.

Ward has cared for a variety of hawks and owls--including one Great Horned Owl--since moving to Polk County. Although he treated one eagle while still living in Texas, he has yet to have one brought to him here.

At present he has only two patients, the big Red-Shouldered Hawk and a screech owl, a fist-sized ball of fluff with enormous eyes that he nicknamed Screechy. Screechy was hurt when he flew in front of a car.

Important in the care of wild birds is their routine treatment while recovering. "I don't try to make pets of them," Ward said. "I don't even pamper them at feeding time." Bits of raw meat are placed in the cage so the wounded birds can grasp it with their claws and tear out bites as they do in the wild."

"The more you pamper them, the harder it will be for them to readjust to their old life when you turn them loose," he explained.

Ward houses his patients in cages he makes himself. He receives nothing for his work. His pay is the healthy bird he turns back to the wild.

According to Wildlife Officer Robert Davis, Ward's help is a boon to his department in this area. "We had no place to take them before James came along," Davis said. "About the only thing we could do was destroy them to keep them from suffering."

Davis also cautioned area residents who find injured birds against trying to keep them. "You have to have a permit to keep birds of prey, such as hawks, owls and eagles; even buzzards are on the list."

Davis continued, "If someone does find an injured bird, if he will call a wildlife officer, we will pick it up and take it to James."

The son of Mariah A. Ward Holmes and Walter Holmes

OLIVER WENDELL HOLMES

FAMILY GROUP No. ___

Husband's Full Name: EMMY WALTON HOLMES

This Information Obtained From: the HOLMES family Bible and JOHN KELLER HOLMES who was 90 years the day I saw him in the hospital in Floydada. Also from the 1900 and the 1910 Census of Johnson and Knox Countys of TEX.

WITH SPECIAL THANKS TO John Kellers Daughter Joyace Holmes 313A West 11Th Street Amarillo, Tex. 79101

Husband's Data	Day Month Year	City, Town or Place	County or Province, etc.	State or Country	Add. Info. on Husband
Birth	15 NOV 1860			TEX.	
Chr'nd					
Mar.	08 JUL 1880		JOHNSON	TEX.	
Death	29 OCT 1929	LUBBOCK	LUBBOCK	TEX.	
Burial		FLOYDADA	FLOYD	TEX.	

Places of Residence: PARKER, KNOX CITY, FLOYDADA
Occupation: FARMER Church Affiliation: METHODIST Military Rec.
Other wives, if any. No. (1) (2) etc.: (2) THETUS T. SMITH
His Father: ___ Mother's Maiden Name: ___

Wife's Full Maiden Name: MARIAH ALMETTIE WARD

Wife's Data	Day Month Year	City, Town or Place	County or Province, etc.	State or Country	Add. Info. on Wife
Birth	19 NOV 1867	RIO VISTA	JOHNSON	TEX.	
Chr'nd					
Death	08 APR 1891		JOHNSON	TEX.	
Burial			JOHNSON	TEX.	

Places of Residence: ___
Occupation if other than Housewife: ___ Church Affiliation: METHODIST
Her Father: MARVIN FULLER WARD Mother's Maiden Name: ELIZABETH JANE ROSE

Compiler: ALVIN L. Ward
Address: P.O. Box 1756
City, State: Denver City Tex.
Date: 02 Feb. 1989

Sex	Children's Names in Full (Arrange in order of birth)	Children's Data	Day Month Year	City, Town or Place	County or Province, etc.	State or Country	Add. Info. on Children
M	1. OLIVER WINDELL HOLMES Full Name of Spouse:	Birth Mar. Death Burial	22 MAY 1887		JOHNSON	TEX.	
M	2. MARVIN CLAUDIUS HOLMES Full Name of Spouse:	Birth Mar. Death Burial	07 SEP 1889 / 23 Mar 1891		JOHNSON / JOHNSON	TEX. / TEX.	
F	3. MATTIE MAY HOLMES Full Name of Spouse: FRED TAYLOR	Birth Mar. Death Burial	02 FEB 1891	KNOX CITY	JOHNSON / KNOX	TEX. / TEX.	
	4.						
	5.						
	6.						
	7.						
	8.						
	9.						
	10.						

The Ward Family History
Page 297

Family Group

Husband's Full Name: EMMY WALTON HOLMES

Husband's Data	Day Month Year	City, Town or Place	County or Province, etc.	State or Country	Add. Info. on Husband
Birth	15 NOV 1860			LA.	
Chr'nd					
Mar.	12 MAR 1893		JOHNSON	TEX.	
Death	29 OCT 1929	LUBBOCK	LUBBOCK	TEX.	
Burial		FLOYDADA	FLOYD	TEX.	

Places of Residence:
Occupation: FARMER **Church Affiliation:** METHODIST **Military Rec.:**
Other wives: (1) MARIAH AIMETTE WARD
His Father: **Mother's Maiden Name:**

Wife's Full Maiden Name: THETUS T. SMITH

Wife's Data	Day Month Year	City, Town or Place	County or Province, etc.	State or Country	Add. Info. on Wife
Birth	09 NOV 1869			MISS.	
Chr'nd					
Death	01 OCT 1955	FLOYDADA	FLOYD	TEX.	
Burial		FLOYDADA	FLOYD	TEX.	

Places of Residence:
Occupation if other than Housewife: **Church Affiliation:** METHODIST
Other husbands:
Her Father: **Mother's Maiden Name:**

Children

Sex	Children's Names in Full	Data	Day Month Year	City, Town or Place	County or Province, etc.	State or Country
M	1. LACY RAYMOND	Birth	03 AUG 1894		JOHNSON	TEX.
		Mar.				
		Death	23 JUN 1900		JOHNSON	TEX.
		Burial			JOHNSON	TEX.
M	2. SAMUELL LUTHER	Birth	11 SEP 1896		JOHNSON	TEX.
		Mar.				
		Death				
		Burial				
M	3. JOHN KELLER — MABEL FAYNE OLIVER	Birth	19 MAY 1898		JOHNSON	TEX.
		Mar.				
		Death				
		Burial				
M	4. ELBERT WALTON	Birth	12 SEP 1901	KNOX CITY	KNOX	TEX.
		Mar.				
		Death	06 MAY 1936			
		Burial				
M	5. ROY ALONZO	Birth	23 JUN 1905	KNOX CITY	KNOX	TEX.
		Mar.				
		Death				
		Burial				

July 7 —

My dear I — I have
received your letter
was glad you found our
but did find your
address —
Thought you might
like to have account
of (my niece's) wedding
Pat (my niece's) wedding
& Lubbock —
So many things have
happened but did
happen their information
copy their Bible &
will pass it on
to you —

Marvin and I have (Ella?)
Frances — but I don't think
that was their daughter
I think Marvin was the
youngest — Dent Smith & Mollie
Plum Smith were married Feb. 14th. She
He was 27 & she
1889 — was 19 in Johnson County
was 19 in Johnson County
Rio Vista I think at home
at 8 o'clock before the
fireplace in living room
by two large house. Rev.
Patton — Methodist minister
performed the ceremony
Sam started teaching
school in a few days

3

Grandpa Ward was born
& reared in Louisiana
(Marvin Ward Feb 26, 1836
Grandmother Ward was
born in Louisiana in
1835. She was of French
descent and Grandpa more
was scotch Irish. more
Irish than scotch Irish
Mother's name was
Elizabeth Jane Rose. I
think they called her
Betty. Their Children
were Lacy, Mittie, Creasy
John, Milam, Mollie, (Mary Jane

Dad said there were
no Road beggers or jail
breakers in this Sunah.
My Dad told me this
one day while he was
living. about 1945
He died in 1947. He had
a very vivid memory &
the past the last few
years.
I'm in a rush
but wanted to get this
letter off to you —
Thanks for writing
Love
Delta Hamilton

Mrs. S. F. Smith Died Here Today

23 Nov 1934

Mrs. Mollie Jane Smith, 65, wife of S. F. Smith, 1314 Kokomo street, died at the family residence this morning following a prolonged illness.

Funeral arrangements had not been completed this afternoon, pending the arrival of children living at a distance.

The body is being prepared for burial by Lindsey Funeral Home.

She had been a resident of Plainview for the past three years, having moved here with her family from Floydada, where they had lived since 1921.

Her maiden name was Mollie Jane Ward and she was born September 1, 1869, in Johnson County, Texas.

She is survived by her husband, three sons and five daughters. The sons are Alva and Collier of Lubbock and Otto of Stamford. The daughters are Mesdames A. C. Hatchell of Longview, E. T. Reese of Abilene, Ura Hendrix of Munday and Harold Hamilton of Plainview and Miss Opal Smith of Plainview.

Members of the N. O. N. Club have been named as flower bearers at the funeral, other arrangements for which are incomplete.

Last Rites For Mrs. S. F. Smith Held Saturday

25 Nov 1934

Funeral services were held Saturday afternoon at the First Methodist Church for Mrs. S. F. Smith, 65, who died at her home in Plainview Friday morning. Rev. C. R. Hooton delivered the funeral address. Mrs. Smith had been in ill health for several months.

She is survived by her husband and five daughters, Mrs. E. P. Reese, Abilene; Mrs. Frank Hendrix, Munday; Mrs. Austin Hatchel, Longview; Mrs. Harold Hamilton and Miss Opal Smith, both of Plainview; three sons, Otto of Stamford, Collier and Alva of Lubbock; two brothers, Marvin Ward, Wilson, Oklahoma; and J. W. Ward, Hatfield, Arkansas.

Pallbearers were: Bob Hurlbut, Vivian Graham, John Lowdon, Lee Bedford, L. W. Kiker, Boyce Ginn, ... Ballenger and Roy C. ...

..., Margaret Kenady, Juanity Largent, Rebecca Meyers, Adelaide Slaton, Jackie Rogers, Mattie Siler, Mavis Smith, Teresa Stockton, Ethel Linville, Eloise Willis and Ada Clare Bain.

Interment was in the Plainview cemetery. The W. H. Lindsey Funeral Home was in charge of arrangements.

Mrs. Smith had been a member of the Methodist church since she was eleven years old. She had resided in Plainview the past three years and had lived a few miles southwest of Lockney for 11 years prior to the family's moving to Plainview.

Services Today For S. F. Smith

19 Dec 1947
21 Dec 1947

The funeral of Samuel Frederick Smith, 86, of Plainview will be conducted this morning at 10 o'clock at the M. W. Lemons funeral chapel. Smith, a resident of Plainview for the past fifteen years, died at his home at 1314 Kokomo street Friday night.

Rev. W. E. Peterson, pastor of the First Methodist Church of which Smith was a member, will officiate. Interment will be in the Plainview cemetery beside the grave of his wife who died in 1934.

A retired farmer, Smith moved to Plainview in 1932 from Floyd County where he had lived for twelve years. He was a native of Mississippi and moved to Hill County, Texas, in 1880. He and the late Mrs. Smith, nee Mary Jane Ward, were married in 1889, in Johnson County. He was a Mason.

Survivors include eight children, Mrs. E. R. Reese, El Paso; Mrs. Frank Hendrix, Munday; Mrs. Austin Hatchell, Longview; Mrs. Harold Hamilton and Miss Opal Smith, both of Plainview; S. O. Smith, Stamford; C. F. Smith and Alva Smith, both of Lubbock. Nine grandchildren survive.

SAM SMITH - MARY JANE (MOLLIE) WARD SMITH

Sam Smith and Mollie J. (Ward) Smith.

Mollie J. was the daughter of Marvin Fuller Ward and Elizabeth Jane (Rose) Ward, and a sister to John William Ward.

The Sam Smith family

Sam and Mollie (Ward) Smith, with children Alma, Ura, Otto, Collier and Vera. They later had another daughter.

Otto, Una and Alma Smith —children of Sam F. Smith and Mary Jane (Mollie) Ward Smith.

The Ward Family History
Page 304

FAMILY GROUP No. _____ **Husband's Full Name** SAMUEL FREDRICK SMITH

This Information Obtained From:
MARY JANE KING
1407 WEST 7th STREET
PLAINVIEW, TEX
Who is the Daughter of SELETA.

Husband's Data	Day Month Year	City, Town or Place	County or Province, etc.	State or Country	Add. Info. on Husband
Birth	1862			MISS.	WAS ALSO TEACHER
Chr'nd					
Mar.	14 FEB 1889		JOHNSON	TEX.	
Death	19 DEC 1947	PLAINVIEW	HALE	TEX.	
Burial		PLAINVIEW CEMETARY			

Places of Residence BLUM, KNOX CITY, FLOYDADA, & PLAINVIEW
Occupation FARMER   Church Affiliation METHODIST   Military Rec.
Other wives, if any. No. (1) (2) etc.
His Father _____   Mother's Maiden Name _____

Wife's Full Maiden Name MARY JANE (MOLLY) WARD

Wife's Data	Day Month Year	City, Town or Place	County or Province, etc.	State or Country	Add. Info. on Wife
Birth	01 SEP 1869		JOHNSON	TEX.	
Chr'nd					
Death	23 NOV 1934	PLAIN VIEW	HALE	TEX.	
Burial		PLAINVIEW CEMETARY			

Compiler ALVIN L. WARD
Address P.O. BOX 1756
City, State DENVER CITY, TEX
Date _____

Places of Residence _____
Occupation if other than Housewife _____   Church Affiliation METHODIST
Other husbands, if any. No. (1) (2) etc.
Her Father MARVIN FULLER WARD   Mother's Maiden Name ELIZABETH JANE ROSE

Sex	Children's Names in Full (Arrange in order of birth)	Children's Data	Day Month Year	City, Town or Place	County or Province, etc.	State or Country	Add. Info. on Children
M	1 OTTO SAMUEL / Spouse: ADDIS	Birth Mar. Death Burial	1892				
F	2 URA E / Spouse: FRANK HINDRIX	Birth Mar. Death Burial	1894				
M	3 COLLIER / Spouse: EVALEE	Birth Mar. Death Burial	1897	LUBBOCK	LUBBOCK	TEX.	
F	4 VERA T. (BEE) / Spouse: AUSTIN HATCHELL	Birth Mar. Death Burial	1899				
F	5 MARY SELETA / Spouse: HAROLD HAMILTON	Birth Mar. Death Burial	23 JUN 1901				
M	6 ALVA WARD SMITH / Spouse: FLOY M.	Birth Mar. Death Burial	1905	LUBBOCK	LUBBOCK	TEX.	
F	7 OPAL CANZY	Birth Mar. Death Burial	12 OCT 1908				
F	8 ALMA / Spouse: E. PRICE REESE	Birth Mar. Death Burial					
	9	Birth Mar. Death Burial					
	10	Birth Mar. Death Burial					

Marvin N. Ward and wife Lydia

Marvin was the youngest son of Marvin Fuller Ward and Elizabeth Jane (Rose) Ward and the youngest brother of John William Ward.

"Is" (Rose) Bolin. On the back of the picture is written "Aunt Is Bolin, sister of Elizabeth Jane (Rose) Ward.

The John Bell & Lula Thomas Moore Family
L to R: Back row: James, Ruby, Willard, Beatrice, Charles, Eva, Rupert
L to R second row: Wayne, Kenneth, Howard, John Bell, Emma Jean, Lyla and Arol Moore

Friday, March 16, 1945.

J. B. Moore Dies At O'Donnell Home

J. B. Moore, 73, died at his farm home one and a half miles northeast of O'Donnell Monday night while Mrs. Moore was in town attending revival services. A heart attack is believed to have brought about his death.

Mr. Moore had not been feeling well, and his youngest son, Kenneth, stayed at home with him.

Funeral services were conducted at 3:00 p. m. Thursday in the O'Donnell Methodist Church by the pastor, Rev. Crandall, and Rev. R. L. Flowers, who is in the revival there, and burial followed in the O'Donnell cemetery.

Mr. Moore came to the T-Bar Kuykendall farm for 13 years, and community in 1923. He lived on the moved to his farm at O'Donnell in 1940. Mr. Moore was a good man, and will be missed by a host of friends.

He is survived by the wife, four daughters, Mrs. Bertrice Ward, Lamesa, and Mrs. Ruby Billing, Eva Dorman, and Emma Jean Todd, all of this county; and seven sons, Raye, Kenneth and Howard of O'Donnell, Ben of Brownfield, Oral the Armed forces stationed in ...a, and Wayne, who is in the ... in the Pacific.

Lula Moore

O'DONNELL (Special) — Services for Lula Estell Moore, 98, of Tahoka will be at 10 a.m. Tuesday in First United Methodist Church with the Rev. Norman Patton, pastor, officiating.

Burial will be in Tahoka Cemetery under direction of White Funeral Home in Tahoka.

Mrs. Moore died about 11 a.m. Sunday in Lynn County Memorial Nursing Home in Tahoka of an illness.

She was born in Dennis and attended schools at Brock. She married John Bell Moore in Brock on Nov. 11, 1903. They moved to Lynn County in 1923 from Parker County and lived in O'Donnell. He died in 1945. She was a Methodist.

Survivors include three daughters, Bertrice Ward of Seagraves, Eva Dorman of Tahoka and Ruby Prestidge of Wolfforth; six sons, Ray of O'Donnell, Rupert of Millsap, Howard of Tahoka, Arol of O'Donnell, Wayne of Seattle, Wash., and Kenneth of Seagraves; 27 grandchildren; 63 great-grandchildren; and 22 great-great-grandchildren.

Grandsons will serve as pallbearers.

Sept 28, 1980

John & Lula Thomas Moore Wedding Picture

11 Nov. 1903 - Brock, Parker Co., Texas

Burnard Ward Services Today

Last rites for James Burnard Ward, 21, killed in combat in Korea on July 16, 1950, will be held at 3:00 p. m. today, Friday, at the Methodist Church here, and burial will follow in Tahoka Cemetery.

Rev. Jim Sharp, pastor of the local church, assisted by Rev. Aubrey Haymes of Seagraves, will officiate. Tahoka VFW post will furnish the honor guard, and interment will be under direction of Stanley-Jones Funeral Home.

The body arrived in Lubbock at 6:40 p. m. Wednesday from Oakland, California, and was accompanied here by Sgt. Albert S Roth.

Burnard was born in Lynn county on March 5, 1929, the son of Mr. and Mrs. Jim Ward, who moved from Tahoka to Seagraves about two years ago. He spent most of his life here, and attended Tahoka High School.

He went into the U. S. Army in August, 1949, and after brief training, he was sent overseas to Japan. He was sent to Korea, and shortly after going up to the firing lines, was killed while fighting the Communists along the Kum River on July 16, 1950.

Survivors include the parents, Mr. and Mrs. Jim Ward of Seagraves; three brothers, Alvin of Fort Worth, Donald and Charles of Seagraves; and two grand parents, Mrs. Lula Moore of O'Donnell and Mrs. Viola Ward of La Pryor.

JAMES BURNARD WARD
TEXAS
PFC 19 INF 24 INF DIV
KOREA PH
MARCH 5 1929   JULY 16 1950

Pfc. James Ward Killed In Korea

Pfc. James B. Ward, 21, of Tahoka, was killed in action in Korea on July 16, 1950, his parents were officially notified by telegram from the War Department last Friday. He had previously been reported missing in action.

The parents, Mr. and Mrs. Jim Ward, who moved to a farm near Seagraves a few weeks ago, were here Tuesday and revealed to local friends the sad news. They were informed that further details on their son would follow in a letter.

James was born at T-Bar, Lynn county, March 5, 1929. The family lived at O'Donnell and later at Tahoka. While a Senior in Tahoka High School in 1948, he enlisted in the Army.

Following about four months training, he was sent to Japan and he served in that country about two years with the First Cavalry. He was transferred to the 19th Infantry, 24th Division, and sent into action in Korea, where he met death at the of the enemy.

Printed in Great Britain
by Amazon